Reading Ephesians and Colossians after Supersessionism

Series Preface

The **New Testament after Supersessionism** (NTAS) is a series that presents post-supersessionist interpretations of the New Testament. By post-supersessionism, we mean "a family of theological perspectives that *affirms God's irrevocable covenant with the Jewish people as a central and coherent part of ecclesial teaching.* It rejects understandings of the new covenant that entail the abrogation or obsolescence of God's covenant with the Jewish people, of the Torah as a demarcator of Jewish communal identity, or of the Jewish people themselves" (spostst.org). Although the field of New Testament studies has made significant strides in this direction in recent years, the volumes in this series, written by Jewish and gentile believers in Jesus, seek to advance the conversation by offering post-supersessionist readings of the New Testament that address the question of ongoing Jewish particularity, and the relationship of interdependence and mutual blessing between Jew and gentile in Messiah.

SERIES EDITORS

J. Brian Tucker
Moody Theological Seminary, Plymouth, MI

David Rudolph
The King's University, Southlake, TX

Justin Hardin
Palm Beach Atlantic University, West Palm Beach, FL

PROJECTED VOLUMES

New Testament after Supersessionism, Introductory Volume
—Justin K. Hardin, David J. Rudolph, and J. Brian Tucker

Reading Matthew after Supersessionism
—Anders Runesson

Reading Mark after Supersessionism
—Vered Hillel

Reading Luke-Acts after Supersessionism
—Mark S. Kinzer and David J. Rudolph

Reading John after Supersessionism —tbc

Reading Romans after Supersessionism
—J. Brian Tucker

Reading 1 Corinthians after Supersessionism
—Kar Yong Lim

Reading 2 Corinthians after Supersessionism
—James A. Waddell

Reading Galatians after Supersessionism
—Justin K. Hardin

Reading Philippians after Supersessionism
—Christopher Zoccali

Reading Hebrews after Supersessionism
—David M. Moffitt

Reading 1 Peter after Supersessionism
—Kelly D. Liebengood

Reading Revelation after Supersessionism
—Ralph Korner

New Testament after Supersessionism, Supplementary Volume
—edited by Justin K. Hardin, David J. Rudolph, and J. Brian Tucker

Reading Ephesians and Colossians after Supersessionism

CHRIST'S MISSION THROUGH
ISRAEL TO THE NATIONS

Lionel J. Windsor

 CASCADE *Books* · Eugene, Oregon

READING EPHESIANS AND COLOSSIANS AFTER SUPERSESSIONISM
Christ's Mission through Israel to the Nations

Copyright © 2017 Lionel J. Windsor. All rights reserved. Except for brief quotations in critical publications or reviews, no part of this book may be reproduced in any manner without prior written permission from the publisher. Write: Permissions, Wipf and Stock Publishers, 199 W. 8th Ave., Suite 3, Eugene, OR 97401.

Cascade Books
An Imprint of Wipf and Stock Publishers
199 W. 8th Ave., Suite 3
Eugene, OR 97401

www.wipfandstock.com

PAPERBACK ISBN: 978-1-4982-1906-8
HARDCOVER ISBN: 978-1-4982-1908-2
EBOOK ISBN: 978-1-4982-1907-5

Cataloguing-in-Publication data:

Names: Windsor, Lionel J., 1974–

Title: Reading Ephesians and Colossians after supersessionism : Christ's mission through Israel to the nations / Lionel J. Windsor.

Description: Eugene, OR: Cascade Books, 2017 | Series: New Testament after Supersessionism | Includes bibliographical references and index.

Identifiers: ISBN 978-1-4982-1906-8 (paperback) | ISBN 978-1-4982-1908-2 (hardcover) | ISBN 978-1-4982-1907-5 (ebook)

Subjects: LCSH: Bible. Ephesians—Criticism, interpretation, etc. | Bible. Colossians—Criticism, interpretations, etc. | Jews in the New Testament | Gentiles in the New Testament | Jews—Election, Doctrine of | Paul, the Apostle, Saint

Classification: BS2695.52 W452 2017 (print) | BS2695.52 (ebook)

Manufactured in the U.S.A.   OCTOBER 26, 2017

Unless otherwise indicated, all extended Scripture quotations are from the ESV® Bible (The Holy Bible, English Standard Version®), copyright © 2001 by Crossway, a publishing ministry of Good News Publishers. Used by permission. All rights reserved.

For Bronwyn, Adelaide, Harry, and Eleanor

"And Christ came and preached the gospel: peace to you who were far away, and peace to those who were near—because through him, both of us have access by one Spirit to the Father." (Eph 2:17–18, my translation)

Table of Contents

Acknowledgements

THIS BOOK IS, IN several ways, a product of Moore Theological College in Sydney. In my teenage and university years, I was taught to know and love the Bible by many able Moore graduates. I studied for my Bachelor of Divinity at Moore, and now have the great privilege of working as a member of the faculty team here. Moore is the home of a biblical-theological ethos that has become known throughout the world. It sees the Bible as a living account of God's purposes being worked out through the ages, in wonderfully diverse ways, yet united by a single goal: the gospel of Jesus Christ. In this book, I am seeking to read two New Testament letters in a way that is sensitive to one facet of this dynamic, biblical-theological unity-in-diversity.

There are many individuals at Moore and elsewhere who have made significant contributions to this biblical-theological ethos, clarifying it through publications, and teaching it to generations of students. In the chapters that follow, I will acknowledge my indebtedness to the works of Donald Robinson and Graeme Goldsworthy. Here, I also wish to acknowledge Peter O'Brien, former Vice Principal at Moore College. Peter is a pastor, teacher, and writer whom I deeply admire. Peter's faith in the Lord Jesus Christ and his love for all the saints is a source of great thanksgiving; his warmth and humility are clear to all who known him; and his rare combination of pastoral depth and theological clarity shine through in all his writings. While a recent publisher's decision has made it problematic for me to cite his Ephesians commentary, he has always been for me a model of gospel-driven, pastorally-motivated scholarship, and remains so to this day. Of course, not all proponents of the biblical-theological ethos to which I am indebted agree in every detail, and I acknowledge there are some differences between my perspective and theirs. Any infelicities or unconvincing arguments that may appear in the book, therefore, remain my own responsibility.

I also owe a debt of love and gratitude to my family: my dear wife Bronwyn, and my precious children Adelaide, Harry, and Eleanor. I have appreciated their patience and cheerful attitude as they have lived through the book-writing process with its various distractions on top of my busy teaching schedule. I have been blessed by many discussions around the dinner table about the significance of individual verses in Ephesians. I am especially grateful to Bronwyn, who carefully read through earlier drafts of the book to pick up errors and inconsistencies. Working on the book side-by-side with Bronwyn has made the whole process far more enjoyable.

This book would not have been possible without the initiative, encouragement, and oversight of the series editors. I am particularly grateful to Brian Tucker, with whom I have had many fruitful conversations. While it is not always on the surface in the book, Brian's insights into social identity theory and its application to New Testament studies have informed my work at many points. Robin Parry and the team at Wipf & Stock have been incredibly efficient and professional; they have been an absolute pleasure to work with. I am also profoundly grateful for my colleagues here at Moore College who have provided resources, encouraged me, and allowed me great flexibility in finishing the book. I would particularly like to thank the Principal, Mark Thompson, and my New Testament Department colleagues Peter Bolt (now at Sydney College of Divinity), Philip Kern, Peter Orr, and Will Timmins. I would also like to acknowledge yet again those who, through prayer and financial support, enabled me to complete my PhD studies, in which I examined Paul's Jewish identity and its relationship to his apostolic ministry in Romans. This study of Ephesians and Colossians picks up many similar themes, albeit in a different key.

> Now to him who is able to do far more abundantly than all that we ask or think, according to the power at work within us, to him be glory in the church and in Christ Jesus throughout all generations, forever and ever. Amen. (Eph 3:20–21)

List of Abbreviations

BDAG   Walter Bauer, Frederick W. Danker, W. F. Arndt, and F. W. Gingrich, *Greek-English Lexicon of the New Testament and Other Early Christian Literature*. 3rd ed. Chicago: University of Chicago Press, 2000.

CD   Karl Barth, *Church Dogmatics*. Translated by G. T. Thomson et al. Edinburgh: T. & T. Clark, 1936–77.

TDNT   *Theological Dictionary of the New Testament.* 10 vols. Edited by Gerhard Kittel and Gerhard Friedrich. Translated by Geoffrey W. Bromiley. Grand Rapids: Eerdmans, 1964–76.

All abbreviations of ancient texts follow Collins, Billie Jean, project director. *The SBL Handbook of Style: For Biblical Studies and Related Disciplines.* 2nd ed. Atlanta: SBL, 2014.

1

Introduction

Ephesians, Colossians, and the Apostolic Mission

To all appearances, Ephesians and Colossians are situated within the apostle Paul's ongoing mission. Both letters begin: "Paul, an apostle of Christ Jesus by the will of God" (Eph 1:1; Col 1:1). According to the viewpoint expressed in these letters, Paul's world has been turned upside down by his encounter with the risen Christ Jesus. He has received a divine mandate to proclaim the "gospel" concerning Christ to "the gentiles" (Eph 3:1–13; 6:19; Col 1:24–29). This Pauline mission is, we read, a work still in progress. The apostle is striving and suffering in prison (Eph 3:1; 4:1; 6:20; Col 1:29; 2:1; 4:3, 18). The gospel of Christ, and the "church" or "body" of Christ to which it gives rise, is expanding, with the prospect of continued future growth and increasing unity (Eph 2:21–22; 4:14–16; Col 1:6, 10; 2:19). Furthermore, the apostle wishes to catch his readers up in this gospel momentum (Eph 6:10–20; Col 4:2–6). Ephesians and Colossians, in other words, explicitly locate themselves and their readers within the ongoing dynamic of Paul's divinely appointed apostolic mission to preach Christ to "the gentiles."

Yet modern readers of Ephesians and Colossians often approach the letters as documents situated outside, not within, Paul's historical mission. On the one hand, many of those who reject the historical Pauline authorship of Ephesians do so in part because they regard the viewpoint of its author as somewhat detached from the realities of this mission. Ephesians, it is argued, seems to be written later, at a time when

1

the "apostles" were no longer active figures in the early Christ-believing community, but rather were revered heroes of a former generation (Eph 2:20; 3:5; 4:11). The initial ferment and conflict associated with Paul's mission, with its explosive expansion from a Jewish sect to a worldwide movement, has cooled off. In Ephesians, so it is argued, the mission is portrayed as a *fait accompli* to be theologized about, rather than a task to be striven for.[1] Even some who argue that the historical Paul is the author of both letters still have a tendency to approach them as if they are primarily theological tracts. The struggles of Paul's gentile mission as he preached Christ from Israel to the nations (cf. Rom 1:1–5; 9–11; 15:14–33),[2] and the concomitant dynamics of interaction between Jews and gentiles, while acknowledged as a historical reality, too infrequently play a significant role in the interpretation of the letters.[3]

This is in some ways understandable, given our own position as twenty-first-century readers. Since we ourselves are located outside, rather than within, the Jew-gentile dynamics of the first-century apostolic mission, our default assumption is that the author(s) and original readers of Ephesians and Colossians are in the same position. Yet something important is lost when we make this assumption. Granted, our overall understanding of these letters' statements about the crucified and risen Christ, along with the resulting soteriological benefits and ethical imperatives, are not shattered by re-imagining their location with respect to the Pauline mission. Nevertheless, Paul's mission forms the explicit context and provides the contours in which the letters' Christology, soteriology, and ethics are expressed. If we ignore the significance of Paul's mission for the interpretation of the letters, we risk missing the details, and so misunderstanding the nuances, of these key themes. Furthermore, to understand the missiological and ecclesiological themes of the letters, we do need to come to grips with how the letters describe the dynamics of the mission and the consequent gathering of believers. There is great value, therefore, in reading Ephesians and Colossians in a

---

1. See e.g., Lincoln, *Ephesians*, 134; Lincoln, "Church and Israel," 619–20; Best, *Ephesians*, 269; cf. Käsemann, "Ephesians and Acts," 288.

2. For a summary see Schnabel, *Early Christian Mission*, 923–1030.

3. See, for example, Hoehner's purpose statement for Ephesians: "The purpose of Ephesians is to promote a love for one another that has the love of God and Christ as its basis" (*Ephesians*, 106). Cf. Percy, *Die Probleme*, 284–86. A notable exception is Roels, *God's Mission*.

way that is sensitive to the specific dynamics that arise from the apostolic mission in which they are framed.

A key dynamic of the apostolic mission involves the relationship between Israel and the nations. Paul's mission is, as noted above, a mission to proclaim Christ to "the gentiles." This expression "the gentiles" (or "the nations," τὰ ἔθνη: Eph 2:11; 3:1, 6, 8; 4:17; Col 1:27) arises from an Israel-centered worldview—a view that assumes a bipartite distinction within humanity between Israel and all the other nations.[4] By using this term "gentiles"/"nations," Ephesians and Colossians assume this traditional distinction, even as they seek to reinterpret the nature of the distinction in light of the gospel of Christ. Hence, to take the dynamics of Paul's mission seriously in these letters, one must take into account the distinction between Jew and gentile which the letters presuppose.

This book aims to present an *evangelical post-supersessionist reading of Ephesians and Colossians*.

By using the term *evangelical*, I am not simply stating my confessional convictions and my position as an author who believes in the gospel of Jesus Christ. I am indicating that the dynamic of gospel proclamation (i.e., "evangelism") will inform my reading of these New Testament letters. I will read Ephesians and Colossians as gospel-driven documents—that is, as documents at least ostensibly situated within and arising from the early apostolic mission to proclaim the gospel of Christ to the nations. This is a mission in which the apostle Paul plays a key role (Eph 1:1; Col 1:1), yet it is also part of a broader missionary endeavor founded on a wider group of "apostles" and those associated with them (Eph 2:20; 3:5; 4:11; cf. Col 1:6). Thus, I will pay special attention to themes within the letters such as mission, commission, proclamation, evangelism, ministry, and vocation.

By using the term *post-supersessionist*, I am referring to a hermeneutical stance capable of yielding much exegetical fruit in this endeavor. *Post-supersessionism* refers to a constellation of differing—and often mutually contradictory—perspectives, with a common thread. This common thread is that "supersessionism" (i.e., the idea that the Christian church has superseded Israel without remainder) should be regarded as a flawed and even harmful viewpoint that has had its day.[5] Advocates

4. Barclay, *Mediterranean Diaspora*, 387–89; Frey, "Jewish Identity," 299–300; Johnson Hodge, *If Sons, Then Heirs*, 43–66; Dahl, "Gentiles, Christians, and Israelites," 31–33.

5. Cf. Soulen, "Post-Supersessionism."

for post-supersessionist interpretation tend to argue for the significance of a special place or calling for Israel, even in relation to Christ and his people, within the texts they are reading. They refuse to concede that unity in Christ necessarily destroys the positive value of all distinctions between Jews and gentiles. My own post-supersessionist stance is, as I have indicated, an evangelical one. I am seeking to read Ephesians and Colossians in a way that is sensitive to the position and role of Israel in relation to the proclamation of the gospel of Christ to the nations, in this case within the horizon of the apostolic mission.

I am not in this book advocating a wholesale reconfiguration of our understanding of every theme in Ephesians and Colossians. For example, I agree with Hoehner that Ephesians' understanding of God is essentially "Trinitarian," that its teaching concerning salvation by grace is consistent with the teaching about justification in the other letters in the Pauline corpus, and that it has a grand vision of Christ-centered reconciliation grounded in God's eternal purposes.[6] I also agree with O'Brien that while Colossians emphasizes the cosmic dimensions of ecclesiology and Christology, and the realized dimensions of eschatology, it does not deny the existence of other dimensions.[7] I am not seeking to negate the central significance of these theological themes. Nevertheless, I am seeking to demonstrate that a greater emphasis on the apostolic mission and its associated Jew-gentile dynamic will enable us fruitfully to reconceive some of the contours in which these theological themes are expressed. While I cannot fully resolve every exegetical issue that arises, I do hope to provide a coherent reading of these letters that may in turn stimulate further investigation. In this way, I hope that modern readers will be assisted to understand the multifaceted theological dimensions of these two rich New Testament documents more deeply (cf. Eph 3:14–19; Col 1:9–12).

A post-supersessionist reading of these letters does not rob them of their contemporary applicability to modern believers in Christ. Some might be concerned that if Ephesians and Colossians are seen to occupy a location different to that of modern believers—that is, a location within the historical apostolic mission through Israel to the nations—then they cannot speak to modern believers at all. Such a concern, however, would be unfounded. Of course, such a result does imply that we cannot thoughtlessly assume that every individual statement in the letters

6. Hoehner, *Ephesians*, 106–14.

7. O'Brien, *Colossians, Philemon*, xlv–xlvii.

automatically provides us with a "timeless truth" for today. However, there are many other ways in which the letters may speak to us. Firstly, and most obviously, there is still a fundamental common ground between the original readers of the letters and modern believers: faith in the crucified and risen Christ. In this respect, as I have already noted, being more sensitive to the specific contours of the letters will simply enable modern believers to gain a more precise appreciation of the Christological, soteriological, and ethical teachings that are expressed by them. Secondly, however, even the "distance" between our own situation and the situation of the letters is of great benefit. As believers read about the unfolding of the apostolic mission from a certain historical distance, they can gain a wider view of the scope and significance of God's plan, which he enacted through Israel to the nations. This can and should lead not only to praise of God (cf. Eph 1:3–14 with Rom 11:33–36) but also to deeper insights into contemporary issues.

There are several specific implications that will arise from this evangelical post-supersessionist reading of Ephesians and Colossians. Most fundamentally, we will see that the overall dynamic portrayed in both letters involves a strong connection between *gospel proclamation* and *social transformation*. Not only is this vital for understanding the nature of the relationship between Jews and gentiles within the apostolic mission, it is also fundamental to understanding the other human relationships discussed in the letters. There will also be *missiological* implications. Ephesians and Colossians present us with an apostle who is proclaiming a message about the God and Messiah of Israel to many other "nations" who have their own gods and social worlds. Reading Ephesians and Colossians in a way that is sensitive to these dynamics should assist those engaged in Christian mission today to reflect on their own endeavors in speaking this gospel to new people groups. Connected to this, there will also be *ecclesiological* implications. My focus on the apostolic mission from Israel to the nations will enable us to understand the connection between the vision of the "church" as the body of the heavenly Christ (e.g., Eph 1:22; Col 1:18) and local, earthly gatherings of Christ-believers. Furthermore, there will also be *anthropological* implications. As we read these two letters in a way that is sensitive to human differences and distinctions, without automatically seeing such differences in a negative light, we should gain a more nuanced understanding of the nature of unity in Christ. Finally, I hope that my reading of Ephesians and Colossians will make a small contribution toward the discussion of the *authorship* of the letters. I am adopting a perspective on these letters that locates the implied author (Paul) within the historical apostolic mission, i.e., within the timeframe in which the gospel of Christ is going out through Israel to the nations. If my reading is judged to be coherent, this may provide one piece of evidence that the implied author and the real author are identical. Thus, while my reading does not ultimately depend on historical Pauline authorship, it may go a small way toward supporting it.

Currents in Post-supersessionist Interpretation

As noted above, the term *post-supersessionist* can be applied to a variety of perspectives. Post-supersessionist interpreters of the New Testament: (i) reject the view that the Christian church has superseded or replaced Israel without remainder, (ii) see a special place or calling for Israel within God's purposes through Christ, and therefore (iii) assign a positive value to Jewish distinctiveness. However, there is a wide variety of perspectives that exhibit these features, and which thus can be labelled "post-supersessionist." To gain a handle on these varying perspectives, it is useful to look at the differing contexts in which they have arisen. Although these varying contexts are not entirely separate (and sometimes overlap with one another), they are distinct enough that it is useful to discuss them one by one. In what follows I will demarcate and summarize these contexts and the kinds of conversations that occur within them. My aim is to help us both to understand some of the currents that flow in to my own evangelical post-supersessionist reading of Ephesians and Colossians, and also to understand where I differ from each of them.

Dispensationalism

The first context in which post-supersessionist interpretation has arisen is in debates between *dispensationalism* and *covenantalism*. These debates have been taking place for at least two centuries in the English-speaking world.

Reformed covenantalism derives from post-Reformation discussions concerning the nature of God's dealings with humanity. A central concept for reformed covenantalists is the "covenant of grace," which unites the elect of God through all ages. In its classical form, covenantalism tends to be supersessionist. Brand summarizes covenant theology this way:

> The covenant of grace subsumes within itself all of the biblical covenants that are enjoined in the postfallen condition of humanity (Noahic, Abrahamic, Mosaic, Davidic, and the new covenant). . . . [T]he church now has virtually replaced Israel in the economy of salvation, though some covenant theologians still hold out hope for a future ingathering of Jews into the church. In effect, in covenant theology, the new covenant is a *renewal* of the Abrahamic covenant rather than being something inherently *new*.[8]

Dispensationalism, on the other hand, is an alternative theological system that arose in the nineteenth century. It is especially indebted to the writings of J. N. Darby. Charles Ryrie, a key defender and promoter of dispensationalism, outlines its key principles: it involves a literalistic hermeneutic that posits various "dispensations" in God's dealings with humanity over the ages, it focuses on the glory of God, and most significantly, it has as its *"sine qua non"* that Israel and the church must be kept distinct. This distinction arises from "two purposes" of God for the two groups.[9] For dispensationalists:

> Use of the words *Israel* and *church* shows clearly that in the New Testament national Israel continues with her own promises and that the church is never equated with a so-called "new Israel" but is carefully and continually distinguished as a separate work of God in this age.[10]

For classical dispensationalists, the principal relevance of Israel's distinctiveness for the church is not for the present dispensation, but for the future millennial period.[11] In this age, Israel and the church are not only distinct; they are effectively separate. Thus, any given individual cannot both be a member of the church and a member of Israel. Indeed, any Jewish person who accepts Christ today belongs exclusively to the body of Christ, shares in a gentile destiny, and no longer inherits Israel's future blessings.[12]

8. Brand et al., *Perspectives*, 6–7.
9. Ryrie, *Dispensationalism*, 45–48.
10. Ibid., 150.
11. Ibid., 172.
12. Ibid., 153, 159.

The influence of dispensationalism has been enormous. Historically, in many circles, whether one was a "supersessionist" or a "non-supersessionist" tended simply to be a function of whether one identified with covenantalism or dispensationalism respectively.[13] However, more recently, the lines of demarcation between the two views on the question of supersessionism have become blurred. On the one hand, "progressive dispensationalists" allow for the existence of "Jewish Christians," who are members of the church, but who keep their connection with God's future promises to Israel.[14] On the other hand, there are modern covenantal theologians who, even while expressing a view that the church is the true Israel, seek to distance themselves from the charge of supersessionism.[15] There are also, as indicated above, premillennial covenantalists who see a future role for Israel within a covenantal framework.[16]

While this book is at times aligned with some of the tendencies of dispensationalist interpretation—e.g., its impulse to resist an overemphasis on unity that can obscure or eradicate different roles for different people within God's purposes[17]—I will not follow dispensationalism's demarcation of "dispensations" nor its eschatological schemas. Furthermore, I will not follow dispensationalism's effective separation between Israel and the church in the present age. This separation, I believe, obscures the dynamics of gospel-preaching through Israel to the gentiles within the apostolic mission, and is thus ultimately counterproductive to understanding Ephesians and Colossians.

---

13. Diprose, *Israel and the Church*, xii; Fritz, *To the Jew First?* 31–33; Vlach, *Has the Church Replaced Israel?* 72–73.

14. Bock and Blaising, *Progressive Dispensationalism*, 68; cf. Brand et al., *Perspectives*, 231–80.

15. E.g., Horton, while emphatic that the church is a "new commonwealth" (citing Eph 2:12) which is therefore the "true Israel," warns against a "supercessionism" [sic] or replacement theology which sees the church as the "new people of God" (*The Christian Faith*, 729–33); cf. Ridderbos, who advocates a replacement theology, yet concedes that in Paul this "does not exclude continuing concern with historical Israel," which "as the once chosen people of God remains involved in the fulfillment of his promises" (*Paul*, 333–41, quotation from 334).

16. E.g., Horner, *Future Israel*.

17. Ryrie maintains: "*Variety can be an essential part of unity*" (*Dispensationalism*, 38–39, emphasis original). Vlach maintains that "spiritual unity does not necessarily cancel ethnic and functional distinctions between groups" (*Has the Church Replaced Israel?*, 3).

Soulen's Economy of Consummation

Another key conversation directly relevant to post-supersessionist interpretation has arisen in the context of systematic theology. A leading voice
in this regard is R. Kendall Soulen, Professor of Systematic Theology at
Wesley Theological Seminary, Washington DC. Soulen's theological project is to reconceive the standard Christian "canonical narrative"—i.e., our
view of the Bible's overarching narrative framework—in such a way that
avoids supersessionism and consequently is more coherent.[18]

Soulen identifies three kinds of supersessionism: (1) economic
supersessionism, in which Israel's obsolescence after the coming of
Christ is a key element of the canonical narrative, (2) punitive supersessionism, in which God abrogates his covenant with Israel as a punishment for their rejection of Christ, and (3) structural supersessionism, in
which Israel's special identity as God's people is simply not an essential
element of the "foreground" structure of the canonical narrative itself.
Soulen sees structural supersessionism as the most problematic form of
supersessionism, because it is the most deep-rooted. He identifies structural supersessionism in the "standard model" of the canonical narrative,
which has held sway throughout much of the history of the Christian
church. This standard model is structured by four main movements:
creation, fall, Christ's incarnation and the church, and the final consummation. In this standard model, God's dealings with Israel are seen
merely as a prefiguration of his dealings with the world through Christ.
Thus, the Hebrew Scriptures are only confirmatory; they are not logically
necessary for the narrative.[19] The standard model leads to an interpretive method that involves "trying to appropriate the blessing of creation
while discounting the core of covenant history, that is, discounting the
open-ended economy of difference and mutual dependence that unfolds
among the Lord, Israel, and the nations."[20] This "renders God's identity as
the God of Israel and the center of the Hebrew Scriptures almost wholly
indecisive for grasping God's antecedent purpose for human creation."[21]

Soulen's basic thesis is that

---

18. Soulen, *God of Israel.*

19. Ibid., 28–33, 109.

20. Ibid., 154.

21. Ibid., 156.

Christians should acknowledge that God's history with Israel
and the nations is the permanent and enduring medium of God's
work as the Consummator of human creation, and therefore it
is also the permanent and enduring context of the gospel about
Jesus.[22]

Soulen advocates an "economy of consummation," in which God is
understood fundamentally as the "Consummator" *of* creation rather than
simply as the redeemer *from* creation. Significantly, this "economy of consummation is constituted as *an economy of mutual blessing* between those
who are and who remain different."[23] Thus, referring to the Scriptures:

> Jewish and gentile identity are not basically antithetical or even
> "separate but equal" ways of relating to God. They are, rather,
> two mutually dependent ways of participating in a single divine
> *oikonomia* of blessing oriented toward the final consummation
> of the whole human family in God's eschatological *shalom*.[24]

Soulen's economy of consummation requires a radical hermeneutical move. He argues that Christian theology must reject a "Christocentric" model that regards the incarnation of Christ as the sole center for
hermeneutics.[25] Rather, the "indispensable hermeneutical context" for
the gospel of Christ remains the eschatological reign of the God of Israel.[26]
For Soulen, then,

> *the gospel is good news about the God of Israel's coming reign,
> which proclaims in Jesus' life, death, and resurrection the victori-
> ous guarantee of God's fidelity to the work of consummation, that
> is, to fullness of mutual blessing as the outcome of God's economy
> with Israel, the nations, and all creation.*[27]

Soulen claims that this hermeneutical move will enable Christian
theology to affirm that "[t]he distinction between Jew and Gentile, being
intrinsic to God's work as the Consummator of creation, is not erased but
realized in a new way in the sphere of the church."[28] "What the church

---

22. Ibid., 110.

23. Ibid., 111, emphasis original.

24. Ibid., 134.

25. Ibid., 138. For the term "Christocentric" see e.g., pp. 89–93 where Soulen
discusses Karl Barth.

26. Ibid., 113.

27. Ibid., 157, emphasis original.

28. Ibid., 169.

rejects is not the difference of Jew and Gentile, male and female, but rather the idea that these differences essentially entail curse, opposition, and antithesis. . . . Reconciliation does not mean the imposition of sameness, but the unity of reciprocal blessing."[29]

Soulen's emphasis on consummation resonates in several ways with the subject matter of Ephesians and Colossians. Both letters strongly affirm that redemption occurs in the context of consummation (e.g., Eph 1:7–10; Col 1:15–20). However, Soulen's hermeneutical move has the unfortunate effect of reducing the significance of Christ, in a way that is antithetical to the thrust of Ephesians and Colossians. For these letters, *both* redemption *and* consummation are explicitly and emphatically Christocentric (e.g., Eph 1:7, 10; Col 1:14, 20). Soulen's insistence that Jesus' life, death, and resurrection is a "victorious guarantee"[30] of future eschatological blessing and the consummation of the relationship between Israel and the nations is too out of step with the language and concerns of Ephesians and Colossians, for which "Christ is all, and in all" (Col 3:11; cf. Eph 1:3).[31] For Soulen, "while everything about Jesus pertains to God's eschatological reign, Jesus himself is not that reign in its fullness. . . . God's victory presently appears among Christ's followers not in the form of 'fullness,' but in participation in Christ's sufferings."[32] However, for Ephesians and Colossians, "fullness" is precisely what Jesus is and brings (e.g., Eph 1:23; Col 1:19; 2:9–10).

In interpreting Ephesians and Colossians, then, it is difficult to follow every element of Soulen's post-supersessionist theological project. This does not mean, however, that we must abandon Ephesians and Colossians as irredeemably supersessionist. Neither does it mean that we must reject all of Soulen's theological insights. In the reading of Ephesians and Colossians in this book, I am indebted to Soulen's insistence that the unity of consummation does not necessarily entail the erasure of creational differences. However, I believe that this insight must be appropriated in a more Christ-focused way. This is because it is not Christocentrism *per se* that is the problem, but rather it is an insufficiently *biblical* Christocentrism. As we shall see in a moment, the biblical theology of Robinson and Goldsworthy, which is explicitly Christ-centered yet

29. Ibid., 170.

30. Ibid., 157.

31. Cf. Barth, *Israel and the Church*, 99, who speaks of the "Christocentric heart of Paul's argument" concerning Israel and the church.

32. Soulen, *God of Israel*, 165.

which is not guilty of the reductionism of the "standard model" described by Soulen, will be a useful guide for us in this regard.

Messianic Judaism

A third context in which post-supersessionist interpretation has arisen is Messianic Judaism. While Messianic Jewish theology itself involves a wide spectrum of opinions, a common conviction is that Messianic Judaism is in direct continuity with the earliest Christ-believing movement.[33] Post-supersessionist interpretation of the New Testament is consistent with many aspects of modern Messianic Judaism.[34] In fact, the core ecclesiological definition of the Union of Messianic Jewish Congregations uses language that alludes to Ephesians and interprets it in a post-supersessionist way:

> Together the Messianic Jewish community and the Christian Church constitute the ekklesia, the one Body of Messiah, a community of Jews and Gentiles who in their ongoing distinction and mutual blessing anticipate the shalom of the world to come.[35]

Mark Kinzer, President Emeritus of the Messianic Jewish Theological Institute in San Diego, California, has been a significant voice among Messianic Jewish theologians. In his book *Postmissionary Messianic Judaism*, Kinzer seeks to read the New Testament in a non-supersessionist manner, in order to provide theological foundations for Messianic Jewish congregational life and polity.[36] Kinzer argues that the historical situation in which the identity of Jewish and Christian communities "has been defined over against one another for at least 1700 years" has strongly affected academic discourse on the New Testament.[37] This has tended to place the burden of proof onto any modern interpreter who seeks to read

33. Yaakov, "A Different Kind of Dialogue?" 324.

34. Rudolph, "Introduction," 18. See especially the various essays in Part II of this volume. Cf. Hocken, *Challenges*, 106 cf. 105; Rudolph, *A Jew to the Jews*.

35. Cited in Rudolph, "Messianic Judaism in Antiquity," 33. See: the description of the "ekklesia" (ἐκκλησία) as the "body" (σῶμα) of the "Messiah" (Χρίστος) in Eph 1:20–23, the description of the unity of Jew and gentile "in one body" (ἐν ἑνὶ σώματι) in Eph 2:16, and the description of this state in terms of "peace" or "shalom" (εἰρήνη) in Eph 2:14, 15, 17.

36. Kinzer, *Postmissionary Messianic Judaism*.

37. Ibid., 32.

the New Testament as a collection of *Jewish* documents. Kinzer, however, seeks to shift this burden of proof in the opposite direction. He points to an important feature of the social context of the New Testament documents: many, if not all, of them are written at a time when the church had an obvious "Jewish nucleus." Kinzer argues that we need to be aware of this situation when interpreting the passages before us, especially in relation to the question of supersessionism:

> When the ekklesia contained a visible Jewish nucleus, its right to claim continuity with Israel was reasonable and not necessarily supersessionist. When that nucleus disappeared, the claim to direct continuity *with* Israel became spiritual and abstract, and easily morphed into a claim to be a replacement *for* Israel.[38]

Kinzer examines several New Testament passages often cited to support a supersessionist view of Jewish practice and asks whether they *necessarily* imply or teach that Christ-believing Jews should give up their distinctive Jewish observances. In each case, Kinzer finds plausible alternatives to a supersessionist interpretation.[39] He concludes that "[w]e have good grounds for upholding the view that the New Testament as a whole treats Jewish practice as obligatory for Jews."[40] He further argues that the New Testament, particularly Luke-Acts and Romans 9–11, describes an essential and positive role in the world for non-Christ-believing Jews.[41] "[T]he Jewish people are still Israel, a holy people, upon whom the redemption of the world ultimately hinges."[42]

On this basis, Kinzer argues that the New Testament supports a "Bilateral Ecclesiology in Solidarity with Israel."[43] In the New Testament period, and following from the teaching of the early Christian leaders:

> Only one structural arrangement would allow for distinctive Jewish communal life within the context of a transnational community of Jews and Gentiles: the one ekklesia must consist

38. Ibid., 43, emphasis original.

39. Ibid., 49–96. It is worth noting that Kinzer here does not examine Col 2:16–17, an omission noted as highly significant by Blomberg ("Non-Supersessionist Alternative," 46). My own conclusions about Col 2:16–17 (see chapter 7) are consistent with Kinzer's views.

40. Kinzer, *Postmissionary Messianic Judaism*, 96.

41. Ibid., 97–149.

42. Ibid., 149.

43. Ibid., 151–79, quotation taken from the title of the chapter.

of two corporate subcommunities, each with its own formal or informal governmental and communal structures. . . . [T]he ekklesia is bilateral—one reality subsisting in two forms. . . . [T]he Jewish branch of the twofold ekklesia must identify with the Jewish people as a whole and participate actively in its communal life.[44]

In this way, through the Jewish branch of the "ekklesia," the gentile branch can be brought into relationship with Israel and so experience the benefits of mutual blessing between Israel and the nations.[45]

Kinzer argues for a continuity between the Jewish religious practice of New Testament times and modern rabbinic Judaism.[46] He argues for a vision of "postmissionary Messianic Judaism," in which traditional concepts of mission to and conversion of Jews are replaced with the concept of "bear[ing] witness to Yeshua within the people of Israel."[47] This involves a modern form of "bilateral ecclesiology" in which Messianic Jews are connected with gentile Christians, but see their "home" within the Jewish community.[48] In his final chapter, Kinzer suggests ways in which this vision could be achieved.[49] This includes a "return to the assumptions prevailing at the Jerusalem Council of Acts 15," in which "the churches must . . . assert that Jewish Yeshua-believers are not only free to live as Jews, but obligated to do so."[50]

Craig Blomberg has offered a critique of and an alternative to Kinzer's approach.[51] Blomberg understands Kinzer to be claiming that "*all* Jewish believers *must* keep these laws [i.e., the Torah rituals apart from the temple worship] and do so in the specific forms mediated to the contemporary world through post-Christian rabbinic tradition."[52] Blomberg, by way of contrast, argues that in the New Testament, due to the advent of Christ, "participating in Israel's covenantal privileges does not *require* even Jewish believers to obey the ritual law, even though they

44. Ibid., 152.

45. Ibid.

46. Ibid., 235–62.

47. Ibid., 301. This vision is connected directly with the Union of Messianic Jewish Congregations.

48. Ibid., 263–302.

49. Ibid., 303–10.

50. Ibid., 308.

51. Blomberg, "Non-Supersessionist Alternative."

52. Ibid., 43, emphasis original.

certainly may *choose* to do so."[53] He critiques various exegetical moves Kinzer makes in support of his bilateral ecclesiology.[54] Blomberg's non-supersessionist alternative is a "heterogeneous" ecclesiology—a multicultural vision of "congregations where a rich variety of forms of worship and instruction, prayer and fellowship alternate or rotate so that everyone can have their preferred forms from time to time."[55]

Blomberg's critique at times seems to be speaking past Kinzer's position rather than directly to it. For Blomberg, terms such as "mandatory" or "obligatory" appear to mean "necessary for salvation." Thus, Blomberg begins by identifying Kinzer's work with the "two-covenants" perspective, which holds out salvation for Jews under the Mosaic covenant apart from Christ.[56] This identification, however, is problematic. Kinzer is primarily concerned with issues of practical observance and ecclesiology rather than with soteriology. Thus, Kinzer's description of Jewish "obligation" to obey the Torah is focused more on communal identity and vocation—i.e., as an obligation for Israel to be the people God has made Israel to be—rather than on salvation—i.e., as an obligation to keep the Torah as a means for achieving eternal life.

Nevertheless, Blomberg's critique does highlight an issue in Kinzer's work—an issue which we also saw above with respect to Soulen's views. Kinzer's post-supersessionist understanding, like Soulen's, is at times insufficiently Christological, especially when compared with the highly Christocentric letters of Ephesians and Colossians. Granted, Kinzer does argue that there is a hidden, obscure, invisible unity between Christ and the Jewish people: even in Israel's "no" to God's purposes and their ongoing suffering, they are acting Christologically (cf. Rom 11:12).[57] However, the Christological unity between Jews and gentiles that is promoted in Ephesians is more concrete, requiring expression in terms of faith in Christ (see e.g., Eph 4:3–6).[58]

53. Ibid., 44, emphasis original.

54. Ibid., 46–54.

55. Ibid., 55.

56. Ibid., 41–42. For advocates of this approach, also known as the *Sonderweg* interpretation, see Mussner, *Tractate*; Gaston, *Paul and the Torah*; Gager, *Origins of Anti-Semitism*.

57. Kinzer, *Postmissionary Messianic Judaism*, 213–33.

58. Markus Barth, for this reason, opposes the idea of separate church structures: "The enterprise of promoting, forming, and maintaining separate Judaeo-Christian theologies and congregations is excluded by the Christocentric heart of Paul's argument" (*Israel and the Church*, 99).

Regarding the contemporary application of the New Testament, Kinzer has helpfully and insightfully demonstrated that the New Testament witness is at least consistent with Messianic Jews maintaining a distinct Jewish identity, expressed in a form of *halakhah*.[59] Nevertheless, Kinzer's concentration on the "legitimacy, value, and importance" of *rabbinic* Judaism leaves little room for alternative contemporary expressions of Jewish identity. Kinzer argues that "[i]f rabbinic Judaism is not valid, then no Judaism is valid. It is the only Judaism available—at least for the overwhelming majority of Jews in the world."[60] However, the New Testament's perspectives on the matter of communal Jewish identity are far more complex than this. For example, I have argued that in Rom 2:17–29, Paul is claiming that distinct Jewish identity should be found elsewhere than in the (for him) mainstream Jewish community.[61] Indeed, Kinzer's own insightful discussion of the "fence" in Eph 2:14–15 implies that the *halakhah* of Jewish believers in Christ is not necessarily dependent on "Jewish communal authorities":

> The fence itself is an illustration of a legal decree (*dogma*) by Jewish communal authorities, an interpretive application of the Torah that sought to guard the holy things entrusted to Israel. Such interpretive decrees drew firm lines between the holy people and the nations, and (as an unintended consequence) provoked pride, envy, and mutual animosity. While these decrees may have been necessary before the coming of Israel's Messiah, the situation has now changed. The sacrificial work of the Messiah brings Jews and gentiles near to God in fellowship with one another—and new *halakhah* must reflect the transformed conditions.[62]

In other words, an appreciation of the value of distinct Jewish identity in the New Testament, such as has been insightfully demonstrated by Kinzer, need not imply that the particular expression of Jewish identity in view should be defined by the prevailing Jewish authorities. The Messiah brought a new *halakhah*. This last observation is, of course, consistent

59. The term refers to practical interpretation of the law for everyday communal Jewish life. Bockmuehl maintains that Pharisaic and Rabbinic *halakhah* was essentially "a way of giving increasingly definitive traditional shape to the practice of Judaism" by interpretation of the Torah for a new situation (*Jewish Law in Gentile Churches*, 4). For more details see chapter 6.

60. Kinzer, *Postmissionary Messianic Judaism*, 235–60, quotations from p. 260.

61. Windsor, *Vocation of Israel*, 140–94.

62. Kinzer, *Searching Her Own Mystery*, 77.

with the variety of expressions of tradition amongst Messianic Jewish communities today.[63]

The reading of Ephesians and Colossians in this book is indebted to Kinzer's approach in many ways. It affirms the value of distinct Jewish identity, and explores this identity in relation to the apostolic mission through Israel to the nations. However, it does not affirm every ecclesiological implication posited by Kinzer.

Of most interest to the present study is Kinzer's discussion of Ephesians.[64] In a work addressing Vatican II's "Declaration on the Relation of the Church to Non-Christian Religions" (*Nostra Aetate*), Kinzer explores the link between "Israel's priesthood and the Apostolic Office."[65] He argues that Eph 2:11–22 is a central passage within Ephesians, which provides a warrant to read the entire letter as a description of Israel's priestly ministry to the nations. In chapter 2, I will outline the details of Kinzer's exegesis of Ephesians.

"Paul within Judaism"

Post-supersessionist interpretation is also a key feature of a recent movement in Pauline scholarship dubbed the "Paul within Judaism" perspective.[66] This perspective has some resonances with the earlier *Sonderweg* interpretation, which claimed that Paul believed in a "special path" of salvation for Jewish people apart from faith in Christ.[67] However, the Paul-within-Judaism perspective is far more diverse, and not all proponents accept a soteriological *Sonderweg*. In the foreword to the 2015 multi-author volume *Paul within Judaism*, Mark Nanos writes about the contributors:

> While these scholars stand at the forefront of this new development, their views on particular details still represent

63. See Kinbar, "Messianic Jews."

64. Kinzer, *Postmissionary Messianic Judaism*, 165–71.

65. Kinzer, *Searching Her Own Mystery*, 65–82.

66. Proponents of this perspective include, among others, the various contributors to Nanos and Zetterholm, *Paul within Judaism*; Johnson Hodge, *If Sons, Then Heirs*; Eisenbaum, *Paul Was Not a Christian*; Rudolph, *A Jew to the Jews*.

67. The term *Sonderweg* or "special path" was coined by Roman Catholic theologian Franz Mussner, *Tractate*, 34. It has been further expounded by Gaston, *Paul and the Torah*, 135–50; Gager, *Reinventing Paul*, 128–43; cf. Stowers, *Rereading of Romans*, 189–91; Stendahl, *Paul among Jews and Gentiles*, 4. For a critique both of the *Sonderweg* view and of the replacement view see Longenecker, "Assessing Supersessionism."

considerable diversity. The conviction they share is that Paul should be interpreted *within* Judaism. The diverse expressions of their research have been variously described in recent years collectively as the "Radical New Perspective," "Beyond the New Perspective," and "Post-New Perspective." Yet these monikers do not fully communicate the major emphases of this research paradigm, since it is not primarily a new development either *within* the New Perspective paradigm or in reaction *against* it, as important as interaction with the New Perspective has been and continues to be. Instead, this research represents a radically different approach to conceptualizing both Judaism and Paul. The challenge these scholars have undertaken is to interpret Paul within his most probable first-century context, Judaism, before putting him into conversation with their own contexts or any of the discourses that have formed around the interpretation of Paul over subsequent centuries.[68]

An illuminating example of a post-supersessionist mode of interpretation from within this paradigm is found in the writings of Paula Fredriksen. Fredriksen seeks to understand Paul in the context of the Christian movement "in its earliest, most Jewish, most radioactively apocalyptic stage."[69] She posits that Paul's insistence that Christ-believing gentiles should not be circumcised arises from the inner logic of his Jewish apocalyptic vision. Paul believes that the gentile ingathering is happening and that he has an eschatological mission to proclaim the risen Christ to the nations. However, consistent with this Jewish eschatological vision, Paul never expected members of the nations to become Israelites.[70] For Fredriksen, Paul assumed both that Jewish believers in Christ would retain their distinctiveness and remain Torah-abiding, and also that gentile believers in Christ would remain distinctly gentile. Nevertheless, there was also a sense in which these gentiles must become radically "Jewish" in their way of life and thinking. This occurred, not through the gentiles becoming Jews, but through giving up their worship of other gods in favor of worshipping the God of Israel, and through living "holy" lives according to standards of community behavior found in the law of Moses.[71]

---

68. Nanos, "Introduction," 1–2.

69. Fredriksen, "Later Contexts," 17.

70. Ibid., 50–51.

71. Fredriksen, "'Law-Free' Apostle?"; cf. Fredriksen, "Judaizing."

Another example is the work of Caroline Johnson Hodge on Romans.[72] Johnson Hodge "argue[s] for a new way to read kinship and ethnic language in Paul that dismantles the contrast between a universal, 'non-ethnic' Christianity and an ethnic, particular Judaism."[73] She sees Paul creatively reworking the identities of his audience, through the use of kinship and ethnic language:

> Paul makes a place for the gentiles—the ethnic and religious "other" for the *Ioudaioi*—in the story of Israel, so that they may be made righteous before the God of Israel. Although *Ioudaioi* and gentiles now share a common ancestor, Paul does not collapse them into one group (of "Christians," for example). Gentiles-in-Christ and Jews are separate but related lineages of Abraham.[74]

For Johnson Hodge, the concept of "multiple identities" or "nested identities" is key to understanding the complexity of Paul's identity construction.[75]

The "Paul within Judaism" perspective is often critical of the "New Perspective on Paul."[76] Nanos argues that the "New Perspective" has built into it a kind of structural supersessionism.[77] While critiquing the "Old Perspective" for demonizing Jewish legalism, the "New Perspective" has

> gone on to replace the traditionally supposed "wrongs" of works-righteousness and legalism . . . with the supposed sin of ethnic particularism, variously described and named. On the premises of the New Perspective, this "wrong" is assumed to be the necessary sin involved in celebrating and guarding the boundaries of Jewish identity and behavior, as if claiming to be set apart for God was inherently arrogant, mistaken, and evidence of bigotry. It is this essentially Jewish sin to which the New Perspective says Paul objected.[78]

72. Johnson Hodge, *If Sons, Then Heirs*, 3–77.

73. Ibid., 4.

74. Ibid., 5.

75. Ibid., 117–35.

76. Interestingly, the dispute between the "Paul within Judaism" perspective and the "New Perspective" is analogous at several points to the earlier dispute between Dispensationalism and Covenantalism (see above).

77. Nanos himself does not use this term (which comes from our discussion of Soulen above), but it is a useful summary of Nanos' argument.

78. Nanos, "Introduction," 7.

Other authors level similar critiques against the "New Perspective." Neil Elliott writes:

> The only theological principle to be celebrated in the "new perspective" is a "universalism" that effectively excludes Torah-observant Jews (who are, by definition, "exclusivistic").[79]

Jae-won Lee also writes:

> The so-called "New Perspective on Paul" locates him [Paul] once again in a Jewish setting but only provisionally in that the notion prevails that Paul set the Jesus movement free from ethnic particularity and made the people of God universal. In both cases Jewish identity is set aside so that E. P. Sanders concludes that the only kind of Judaism that Paul advocated was a messianic Judaism that moved beyond living according to the Law.[80]

While proponents of the New Perspective often deny the charge of supersessionism, they still advocate positions that can be regarded as implicitly supersessionist, at least in some respects. N. T. Wright, for example, while rejecting the terminology of supersessionism as too ambiguous,[81] still argues that Paul saw all Christ-believers as "'the Jew,' 'the circumcision' and even 'Israel.'"[82] Terence Donaldson, too, on the one hand sees Paul as being committed to a principle of "an ethnically identified Israel, differentiated from the Gentiles,"[83] yet on the other hand sees this in inevitable conflict with another of Paul's principles: a "redefinition of Abraham's family (Israel) based instead on Christ."[84] Tet-Lim Yee, who as we will see in the next chapter advocates a "New Perspective on Ephesians," while resisting the idea that the "church" has become the "true Israel,"[85] nevertheless seeks to "redefine" Israel so that it is no longer understood in "ethnic" categories.[86] Thus, while the New Perspective on

---

79. Elliott, *Liberating Paul*, 70.

80. Lee, *Paul and the Politics of Difference*, 61.

81. Wright, "Romans 9–11," 403–4.

82. Wright, *Paul and the Faithfulness of God*, 538–39. I have critiqued this position in Windsor, *Vocation of Israel*, 45–67.

83. Donaldson, *Paul and the Gentiles*, 185.

84. Ibid., 246. Donaldson's position is highlighted and critiqued by Kinzer, *Post-missionary Messianic Judaism*, 161–63.

85. Yee, *Ethnic Reconciliation*, 187.

86. Ibid., 143.

Paul cannot be labelled "supersessionist" in the fullest sense, its tendency to interpret the disputes in Paul's letters in terms of a reaction to "ethnocentrism" can obscure Israel's distinct place and role with regard to the Pauline mission.

Several features from the "Paul within Judaism" perspective will inform my reading of Ephesians and Colossians. These features include: an emphasis on the positive value of Jewish distinctiveness and vocation in light of Israel's role in God's purposes, an emphasis on the positive value of difference in a way that promotes mutual interdependence, and the critique of the "New Perspective" for its overemphasis on the problem of "ethnocentrism." However, yet again, I regard many Paul-within-Judaism interpretations to be insufficiently Christological to provide an adequate reading of the highly Christological letters of Ephesians and Colossians. Often interpreters within this perspective place too little weight on the way faith in Christ transforms Jewish, as well as gentile, identity.[87] In Ephesians and Colossians, the Christological transformation of *both* gentile *and* Jewish identity cannot be ignored.

An Evangelical Post-supersessionist Reading

As I have noted, I will be drawing on many of the insights of the post-supersessionist interpreters surveyed above. However, my own post-supersessionist approach is most strongly indebted to the biblical theology advocated by Donald W. B. Robinson, Graeme Goldsworthy and others associated with them. Here I will briefly outline their views

---

87. See the critique of various proponents from the Paul-within-Judaism perspective in a series of footnotes in Barclay, *Paul and the Gift*, 359–60, 361, 372, 397–98, 551, nn. 26, 29, 54, 23, 75 respectively. Barclay's own reading of Paul is one in which Israel is paradoxically "simultaneously *special* and *not at all unique*" (418, emphasis original): "With regard to worth, salvation for Israel is as incongruous as for the whole of humanity: both Paul and his Gentile converts were 'called through grace' ([Rom] 1:6, 15). Yet is it possible that Israel has a special place in the story, a role hinted at by these references to 'we/us,' [in Galatians] but left tantalizingly unexplained?" (420). Barclay finds the specialness possibly emerging in Gal 6:16 in the phrase the "Israel of God," and certainly emerging in Romans, especially in Rom 9–11. Thus, Barclay's reading of Paul cannot be described as boldly "supersessionist" (421). Ultimately, his reading of Paul sees a special place for Jews, but he is insistent that "the demands of the good news surpass the authority of the Torah. Paul's paradigmatic 'death to the law' strips it of its ultimate authority, so that at moments critical for the enactment of the good news (such as common meals at Antioch), the Torah's rules may be suspended for the sake of Christ" (445).

in relation to the relationship between Jews and gentiles in the New Testament.

Donald Robinson was active as a teacher of New Testament at Moore Theological College in Sydney, Australia in the 1950s and 1960s. Prior to this, during three formative years at Queen's College, Cambridge, Robinson had developed a distinctive framework for biblical theology. He enthusiastically taught and advocated this biblical theological framework in subsequent decades.[88] A key feature of this framework involved the centrality of the relationship between Jews and gentiles for the interpretation of the New Testament. Robinson was dissatisfied with the notion of the "covenant" as the unifying element of the biblical narrative and firmly rejected supersessionism. However, he also explicitly rejected the dispensationalist schema because of its relegation of the promises to Israel to a time in the future, beyond the age of the church. Robinson's schema, by contrast, saw a key role for the distinction between Jew and gentile in terms of scriptural prophetic eschatological expectations. He argued:

> The significance of early Jewish Christianity is that it fulfilled the Old Testament promise of God to restore the tabernacle of David that had fallen and then to use the restored remnant of Israel as an instrument to save the Gentiles. The popular view that God rejected the Jews and that the gospel became a wholly Gentile matter is so far at variance with the New Testament as well as with the expectation of the Old Testament that a complete reappraisal of the New Testament is called for.[89]

Robinson emphasized the divine promises to Abraham in Gen 12:1–3, including the climactic promise that "in you all the families of the earth shall be blessed" (Gen 12:3). He understood this promise to be developed in the Old Testament prophetic expectations that the gentiles would flock to the new temple on the Day of the Lord and consequently experience blessing from God. However, as Robinson asserted at many points, *"they are not represented as becoming Israelites, or a new Israel."*[90] Rather, the prophets envisioned Israel acting as a priestly nation—a channel of blessing to gentiles. In the New Testament, this prophetic expectation is fulfilled through the coming of Christ, the preaching of the gospel, and the constitution of Jews and gentiles together through faith

88. Shiner, "Reading the New Testament," 185–90.

89. Robinson, *Faith's Framework*, 97.

90. Robinson, "Israel and the Gentiles," 18, emphasis original.

in Christ. It found expression both in the wider relationship between the Jerusalem church and the gentile churches, and also at the local level, within individual congregations.[91] Referring to Eph 2–3, Robinson writes:

> Each Gentile church had its nucleus of Jews, or at least it had its Jewish apostle and his colleagues through whom the word of God had been mediated to it. Such Jews did not become so absorbed into the local membership that they lost their distinctive character. They remained, especially the founding apostle, as representing the royal priesthood ministering salvation to the Gentiles. . . . The place of the Jews, though theologically significant and of great practical usefulness, must not in any wise depress the status and dignity of the Gentile believers themselves, for God had revealed to the apostles and prophets that the Gentiles were sharers on equal terms in the blessings of salvation. This mystery not previously revealed did not abolish the long-standing Old Testament picture of Israel's role in the salvation of the Gentiles, but it showed that the purpose behind it all was to create such an ultimate unity of Israel and the Gentiles that the resultant body would be nothing less than a new creation of mankind. This unity was in its full sense eschatological, but it was meant to find expression also here and now where Jew and Gentile met together with Christ in the midst.[92]

Robinson's overall vision for biblical theology has been developed further and disseminated widely in the works of one of his former students, Graeme Goldsworthy.[93] Goldsworthy sees the Scriptures and their description of the nation of Israel as essential to the structure of Christian theology. Nevertheless, Goldsworthy's biblical theology also has a strongly Christocentric character. He views the Scriptures as progressively revealing the "Kingdom of God" in three stages: firstly through the history of Israel, then through the eschatological vision of the prophets, and ultimately in Christ.[94] In Goldsworthy's earlier writings, he did not emphasize the distinction between Jews and gentiles in the New Testament. More recently, however, Goldsworthy has returned to a greater appreciation of Robinson's insights into this distinction:

91. Robinson, "Jew and Greek," 84. This is a reprint of Robinson's 1961 InterVarsity Fellowship Annual Lecture.

92. Ibid., 84–85.

93. See e.g., Goldsworthy, *Gospel-Centred Hermeneutics*; Goldsworthy, *Christ-Centred Biblical Theology*.

94. Goldsworthy, *Christ-Centred Biblical Theology*, 24–27.

I have been spurred on by the writings of Donald Robinson who has written a number of articles in which he cogently argues that the distinction between Jew and Gentile is not lost in the New Testament. That is, although Jew and Gentile believers are made into one new man in Christ (Eph. 2:15), this unity does not remove all distinctions until its final eschatological fulfilment . . . .[95]

Given the importance of the covenant promises to Abraham relating to the blessing to all the nations (Gen 12:3), and the perpetuation of this perspective in the Old Testament with regard to the salvation of the gentiles, it seems unlikely that such a significant distinction would simply disappear in the New Testament. Certainly the apostolic experience in Acts shows how vital it was for the early church to get the relationship of Jew and gentile right. They could not ignore the constant emphasis in the Old Testament that Israel was called as God's servant to be a light to the gentiles. While Israel was not given an active evangelistic task in Old Testament times, the prophetic picture was one of an eschatological event in which Israel's mission would flourish. The effect of the law of Sinai was to establish the exclusiveness of Israel in separation from the nations round about. This was a necessary move in view of the propensity of the people to absorb, and even convert to, the polytheism of the nations. It would require the ultimate saving act of God on the Day of the Lord for the great Jewish mission and the ingathering of the nations to take place.[96]

This vision for biblical theology is clearly not supersessionist. At the same time, it is not subject to those features of some other forms post-supersessionist interpretation identified in the previous section that are problematic for reading Ephesians and Colossians. The Robinson-Goldsworthy vision for biblical theology is *both* strongly Christological *and* structurally Israel-shaped. It sees Christological unity being achieved through Israel's particularity, in a dynamic way, focusing on Israel's divinely appointed mission with respect to the nations. Thus, it has great potential for understanding the nature of Israel's distinct role, even in these deeply Christological letters. While I will depart from Robinson on several points, I acknowledge a debt to his fundamental insights. Of

---

95. Ibid., 164.

96. Ibid., 165. See also Goldsworthy's discussion of "Israel and the church" (ibid., 201–6).

special note is his understanding of the way that the concept of gospel mission and ministry can shed light on the relationship between Israel and the nations in the New Testament, and *vice-versa*.[97]

Robinson's view of the distinction between Jew and gentile in the New Testament has given rise to questions about its modern applicability, particularly in the areas of missiology and ecclesiology. Some of these questions were discussed above. In the works of Robinson and Goldsworthy, these questions are still unresolved.[98] While I cannot hope to achieve a full resolution within the scope of this book, I hope that the reading of Ephesians and Colossians presented here will provide some pointers in this direction.

Methodology

My method in this book will be to examine key sections of the text of Ephesians and Colossians, interacting with the discussions surrounding supersessionism outlined above, with a special focus on Ephesians' and Colossians' portrayal of the progress of the apostolic mission.

The focus of this book has some connection with the focus of my earlier book, *Paul and the Vocation of Israel*, in which I argued that in Romans, "Paul, through preaching Christ to the Gentiles, was in fact fulfilling Israel's distinct divine vocation."[99] In the present book, I will be seeking to understand the connections that can be discerned in Ephesians and Colossians between 1) the apostolic mission and 2) the relationship between Israel and the nations. As we shall see, Ephesians has more material that touches explicitly on the relationship between Israel and the nations than does Colossians. Hence the bulk of the book will be devoted to Ephesians (chapters 3–6). Once the examination of Ephesians has been completed, the findings and insights gained from that letter will be brought to bear on the most relevant texts in Colossians, to see if they can yield any further insights (chapter 7).

While my reading interacts with questions surrounding supersessionism, I am not primarily aiming to provide an ecclesiological model,

---

97. I have already explored some of these themes in relation to Romans in Windsor, *Vocation of Israel*.

98. Robinson, "Jew and Greek," 109; Goldsworthy, *Christ-Centred Biblical Theology*, 201–6; cf. Shiner, "Reading the New Testament," 192–93.

99. Windsor, *Vocation of Israel*, 1.

nor to make definitive conclusions concerning modern Jewish identity in relation to Christian identity. My primary concern, rather, is to discern something of the dynamic nature of the proclamation of the gospel of Christ through Israel to the nations within the apostolic mission as portrayed in Ephesians and Colossians. The implied author of Ephesians and Colossians will be examined in relation to his role as the "apostle" (Eph 1:1; Col 1:1) to "the gentiles" (Eph 2:11, 3:1, 6, 8; Col 1:27), who is writing to believers who themselves are caught up in his apostolic mission. The distinction between Jews and gentiles, between Israel and the nations, will be explored primarily in relation to the progress and results of the apostolic mission.

Because my exploration is concerned with Jewish and gentile identity and its relationship to the apostolic mission, the concept of *social identity* will be relevant at several points.[100] In an earlier book, I discussed the value of social identity theory for understanding Paul's undisputed letters, especially Romans.[101] Relevant insights from the theory include 1) the idea that social identity is "continuously formed through ongoing constructive interaction";[102] 2) the idea that "Paul's Jewish identity . . . cannot be understood without reference to his even more fundamental Christ-identity";[103] and 3) the idea that "there is great value in describing positive aspects of intergroup relations: valued distinctions which allow for interdependence and complementarity between different groups."[104] However, I also noted that certain limitations arise when the object of study is an ancient document rather than a contemporary social group. These limitations make it advisable to "generally avoid pressing the theory for detailed models or theoretical categories,"[105] and rather to "provide a largely 'emic' account, favoring those terms and categories which arise from Paul's own self-description."[106] These observations are applicable, *mutatis mutandis*, to the present study of Ephesians and Colossians.

---

100. For descriptions of the theory, see Jenkins, *Social Identity*; Lawler, *Identity*; Esler, "An Outline of Social Identity Theory."

101. Windsor, *Vocation of Israel*, 6–8.

102. Ibid., 6.

103. Ibid., 7.

104. Ibid., 8.

105. Ibid.

106. Ibid., 9.

Outline of the Argument

In chapter 2, I will survey certain prior readings of Ephesians and Colossians that are significant for this study. Firstly, I will summarize common supersessionist readings of certain texts in Ephesians and Colossians. Then, I will provide an overview of some key prior post-supersessionist readings of Ephesians.[107] I will also discuss some important critical issues in the interpretation of Ephesians and Colossians which bear on this study.

In chapters 3–6, I will conduct a focused exegesis of Ephesians. I will demonstrate how a post-supersessionist perspective enables us to discern the dynamic of divine blessing "in Christ" proceeding through Israel to the nations by means of the apostolic mission. In chapter 3 (Eph 1), we will see how the apostolic mission was the means by which Christ's blessings have come through Israel to the nations. In chapter 4 (Eph 2), we will see how the apostolic mission plays a climactic role in Christ's work of reconciliation for Israel and the nations. In chapter 5 (Eph 3), we will see how the apostolic mission is continuing through Paul, even in his suffering, so that Christ's riches are being poured out through Paul's ministry to the nations. In chapter 6 (Eph 4–6), we will see how the gentile readers of the letter are urged to "walk" in a way that reflects and maintains what the apostolic mission through Israel to the nations has achieved in and through them.

In chapter 7, we will see how Colossians illustrates a local instance of the apostolic mission through Israel to the nations. While Colossians is aimed at countering a particular alternative religious philosophy (or philosophies) that includes Jewish elements, it never implies that Jewish identity itself is nullified or replaced.

I chapter 8, I will summarize my findings from this evangelical post-supersessionist reading of Ephesians and Colossians. I will also suggest some implications of these findings with regard to gospel proclamation, missiology, ecclesiology and anthropology.

---

107. There are, as far as I am aware, no detailed and sustained post-supersessionist treatments of Colossians.

2

Prior Readings of Ephesians and Colossians

IN THE PREVIOUS CHAPTER, I outlined the aim of this book: to present an *evangelical post-supersessionist reading of Ephesians and Colossians*. In this chapter, I will summarize some prior readings of these letters that are particularly relevant to the question of supersessionism. Firstly, I will provide an overview of the main supersessionist tendencies in prior readings of Ephesians and Colossians. Then, I will discuss some significant prior post-supersessionist readings of Ephesians.[1] Following this, I will summarize some of the relevant critical questions raised by scholars concerning the two letters. Finally, in light of these earlier readings and critical questions, I will outline the main features of my own evangelical post-supersessionist reading of Ephesians and Colossians.

Supersessionist Over-readings of Texts in Ephesians and Colossians

There are certain key texts in Ephesians and Colossians that have given rise to supersessionist interpretations. In this section, I will introduce these texts, and describe the main tendencies of such interpretations. It must be noted from the outset that most of the authors discussed in this section are not seeking to promote supersessionist views or a "replacement" theology directly. Their primary concerns usually lie elsewhere.

---

1. Because questions concerning Israel are not explicit in the text of Colossians, there are few, if any, significant post-supersessionist readings of this letter.

Nevertheless, in advocating for their particular concerns, they at times engage in supersessionist over-readings of certain key texts within these letters. That is, they extrapolate from the explicit statements found in the texts to make further conclusions about race, ethnicity, or Jewish practice—conclusions that are not necessary implications of the texts themselves.

Supersessionist over-readings of texts in Ephesians and Colossians fall into three general categories: (1) that Christ, by bringing a new spiritual reality, has rendered physical circumcision invalid for all (based on Eph 2:11–12; Col 2:11–13); (2) that Christ, through his crucifixion, has abolished the Jewish observance of the law of Moses (based on Eph 2:14–15a; Col 2:13–23); and (3) that Christ, by forming a new kind of humanity, has nullified all forms of Jewish distinctiveness (based on Eph 2:14–16; Col 3:11).

These over-readings are sometimes used to draw a contrast between the undisputed Pauline epistles on the one hand, and Ephesians and Colossians on the other. It is generally agreed that the undisputed Pauline epistles, especially Romans, exhibit a nuanced view of the relationship between Jews and gentiles. This nuance arises from the realities of Paul's mission and the dynamics of interaction between real Jews and real gentiles in Paul's experience. Ephesians and Colossians, it is sometimes claimed, are at odds with the undisputed Pauline epistles at this point. They show no such nuance, and are not concerned with the realities of Paul's mission nor with the dynamic of Jew-gentile interaction. These claims are often based on supersessionist over-readings of key passages.

We will now look at some examples of each of these supersessionist over-readings of Ephesians and Colossians. The following survey is not intended to be exhaustive.[2] Rather, the aim is to highlight representative instances of the key trends.

Physical Circumcision Rendered Invalid?
(Eph 2:11–12; Col 2:11–13)

The first category of supersessionist over-reading involves the claim that Christ, by bringing a new spiritual reality, has rendered physical circumcision invalid for all. This claim tends to arise from interpretations

---

2. For a comprehensive review of the literature on Eph 2:11–22 up to the mid-twentieth century, see Rader, *Racial Hostility*.

of Eph 2:11–12 and Col 2:11–13. Ephesians 2:11 reminds its readers of their previous status as those called the "uncircumcision" (ἀκροβυστία) by what is called the "circumcision, which is made in the flesh by hands" (περιτομῆς ἐν σαρκὶ χειροποιήτου). Colossians 2:11–13 contains a more extended discussion of circumcision and uncircumcision. The readers are described as those who were formerly in a state of "uncircumcision of the flesh" (τῇ ἀκροβυστίᾳ τῆς σαρκός; Col 2:13) but who have now been "circumcised with a circumcision made without hands" (περιετμήθητε περιτομῇ ἀχειροποιήτῳ; Col 2:11):

> In him [i.e. Christ] also you were circumcised with a circumci-
> sion made without hands, by putting off the body of the flesh,
> by the circumcision of Christ, having been buried with him in
> baptism, in which you were also raised with him through faith
> in the powerful working of God, who raised him from the dead.
> And you, who were dead in your trespasses and the uncircumci-
> sion of your flesh, God made alive together with him, having
> forgiven us all our trespasses, . . . (Col 2:11–13)

Several interpreters have understood these texts to be implying that Christ has rendered physical circumcision entirely invalid for all, even for Jewish people. As we will see, the clearest statements in this regard are found in comments on Colossians. Nevertheless, similar statements are at times also made about Ephesians. As we noted above, most of the interpreters in this category do not have Jewish identity directly in their sights. However, since physical circumcision was a key Jewish identity marker in the first century,[3] the claim that physical circumcision has been rendered invalid implies that ethnic Jewish distinctiveness has also been rendered invalid.

Circumcision Opposed to Christ

Most readings of Eph 2:11–12 and Col 2:11–13 take as their starting point the premise that Jewish circumcision was a physical sign designed to point to a greater spiritual reality (cf. Col 2:17). This premise by itself is relatively unremarkable. Indeed, it is a common theme in the Jewish Scriptures themselves (e.g., Deut 10:16; 30:6; Jer 4:4); it also appears in roughly contemporary Jewish writings (e.g., Philo, *Migration* 89–93; *Spec.*

---

3. For this association see e.g., Est 8:17 LXX; Philo, *Spec. Laws* 1.1–2; Josephus, *Ant.* 20.38, *War* 2.454; Rom 2:28—3:1.

Laws 1.6, 305; *QG* 3.46–47). However, some interpreters of Ephesians and Colossians take this premise a step further. They understand these texts in Ephesians and Colossians to be arguing that, now that the greater spiritual reality has arrived in Christ, the physical sign stands in direct *conflict* with the spiritual reality. Hence the physical sign of circumcision must be removed entirely, even for Jews.

The sixteenth-century Reformer John Calvin, for example, uses this line of reasoning when commenting on Col 2:11:

> From this it appears that he has a controversy with the false apostles, who mixed the law with the Gospel, and in that way constructed, so to say, a bi-form Christ. And he specifies one instance as an example. He proves that the Mosaic circumcision is not merely superfluous, but even alien to Christ, because it destroys the spiritual circumcision of Christ. For circumcision was given to the Fathers to be the figure of something absent. Those, therefore, who retain that figure after Christ's advent, deny the accomplishment of what it figures. Let us, therefore, bear in mind that outward circumcision is here compared with spiritual, just as a figure with the reality. The figure is of something absent; hence it destroys the presence of the reality. What Paul contends for is that, because what was shadowed forth by a circumcision made with hands has been fulfilled in Christ, it now has no fruit or practice. Hence he declares that the circumcision which is made in the heart is *the circumcision of Christ,* and that therefore what is outward is not now required; for where the reality exists, that shadowy sign vanishes, since it has no place except in the absence of the reality.[4]

More recently, F. F. Bruce, writing on Col 2:11–13, claims that, contrary to the normal first-century Jewish view that heart circumcision was linked to physical circumcision,

> the work of Christ has so thoroughly exhausted the significance of the original ordinance (as of the whole ceremonial law) that it is henceforth superseded. . . . No longer is there any place for a circumcision performed by hands . . . ; the death of Christ has effected the inward cleansing which the prophets associated

---

4. Calvin, *Galatians, Ephesians, Philippians and Colossians,* 331–32, emphasis original. Note that Calvin's view on Eph 2:11 is more nuanced than his view on Col 2:11. Calvin argues that Eph 2:11 does not "throw contempt on outward circumcision" but rather simply acts to prevent undue boasting in physical circumcision (ibid., 148).

with the new covenant, and of this Christian baptism is the visible sign.[5]

Paul Foster also writes on Col 2:11:

> In effect the author of Colossians is stating that believers have been divinely circumcised through their union with Christ. From this perspective physical circumcision is emptied of value, and the image is redefined from being a concrete and physical action, instead being transformed into a metaphorical and spiritual state.[6]

Corresponding claims have also been made about Eph 2:11–12. Andrew Lincoln, for example, who is one of the most forthright modern exponents of the existence of a replacement theology in Ephesians,[7] reads Eph 2:11 to be describing an old order that is now entirely done away with in Christ:

> [The readers] are asked to reflect on their former condition in terms of categories valid at a prior stage in the history of salvation in order to appreciate all the more their present privileges. ... Describing the circumcision as not only "in the flesh" but also χειροποίητος, "made by hands," adds to the distancing and the negative evaluation. This term and its opposite are frequently used in the NT for the contrast between external, material aspects of the old order of Judaism and the spiritual efficacy of the new order (e.g., Mark 14:58; Acts 7:48; Col 2:11; Heb 9:11,24).[8]

This is a key part of Lincoln's argument that Ephesians has a different perspective on Israel's advantages than that of the historical Paul:

> The thought of v 12 appears to be dependent on Rom 9:4,5, where Paul could say, "To them belong the sonship, the glory, the covenants, the giving of the law, the worship, and the promises; and of their race according to the flesh is the Christ. . . ." But whereas in Romans 9–11 the advantages of Israel still play a role in the time after Christ, in Ephesians, in contrast—as will

---

5. Bruce, *Colossians, Philemon, Ephesians*, 103–4. See also Boyarin, *Radical Jew*, 27.

6. Foster, *Colossians*, 263.

7. For Lincoln, in both Galatians and Ephesians, "Israel's role is replaced by that of the church" ("Church and Israel," 621).

8. Ibid., 609; Lincoln, *Ephesians*, 136. Cf. Ridderbos, *Paul*, 335.

become even clearer—they pertain only to the time prior to Christ.[9]

Thus for Lincoln, physical circumcision in Ephesians is part of an old order that has been superseded by the new spiritual reality in Christ.

Circumcision Replaced by Baptism

Another, related,[10] line of interpretation understands Col 2:11–13 to be implying that circumcision has been entirely replaced by Christian baptism as the sign of a deeper spiritual reality. For example, Joachim Jeremias writes:

> Paul here names baptism "the Christian circumcision" (ἡ περιτομὴ τοῦ Χριστοῦ) and describes it thereby as the Christian sacrament which corresponds to Jewish circumcision and re-places it.[11]

More recently, David Gibson has argued that:

> spiritual circumcision fulfills and replaces physical circumci-sion, but baptism replaces physical circumcision as the sign of the spiritual reality.[12]

Circumcision Set Aside as an Invalid "Boundary Marker"

Another view of circumcision in Col 2:11–13 focuses on its role as a community-defining and social boundary-marking practice. Some inter-preters claim that with the coming of Christ, circumcision and ethnic Jewish identity has now been "set aside" because it is no longer a valid boundary-marking practice for the Christian community. N. T. Wright, for example, writes:

> The point once again is that baptism defines the community of the Messiah's people in the way that circumcision defined the people of Israel according to the flesh. Identity "according to

9. Lincoln, "Church and Israel," 610.

10. Cf. the above quotation from Bruce, *Colossians, Philemon, Ephesians*, 103–4.

11. Jeremias, *Infant Baptism*, 39–40.

12. Gibson, "Sacramental Supersessionism," 204.

the flesh" is set aside: you and your community are no longer defined by who your parents were.[13]

Jewish Law-observance Abolished? (Eph 2:14–15a; Col 2:13–23)

A second category of supersessionist over-reading of Ephesians and Colossians involves the claim that Christ, through his crucifixion, has abolished all forms of observance of the law of Moses, including Jewish observance. The claim arises from interpretations of Eph 2:14–15a and Col 2:13–23. Ephesians 2:14–15a speaks of Christ "having abolished the law of the commandments in decrees" (τὸν νόμον τῶν ἐντολῶν ἐν δόγμασιν καταργήσας). The ESV renders this:

> For he himself is our peace, who has made us both one and has broken down in his flesh the dividing wall of hostility by abolishing the law of commandments expressed in ordinances, ...(Eph 2:14–15a)

Colossians 2:13–23 speaks of God and/or Christ "having canceled the record of debt against us [in] the decrees" (ἐξαλείψας τὸ καθ᾿ ἡμῶν χειρόγραφον τοῖς δόγμασιν, v. 14); it describes issues concerning food, drink, feasts, new moons, and Sabbaths as a "shadow" (σκιά) whose "substance" (σῶμα) is Christ (v. 17); and it states that the readers have "died to the elements of the world" (v. 20). Although the word "law" (νόμος) does not appear in Colossians, there are strong traditions identifying both the "elements of the world" (cf. Gal 4:3, 9) and the "record of debt" with the law of Moses.[14] Hence, Col 2:13–23 has been linked with the abolition of Jewish law-observance.[15]

Several interpreters take these passages in Ephesians and Colossians to mean either that Christ has abolished the Jewish ritual elements of the law of Moses for all people (including for Jewish believers in Christ), or that Christ has abolished the law of Moses in its entirety. In either case, since first-century Jewish identity was normally expressed in some form of concrete law-observance, this claim carries with it the implication that any meaningful distinctive Jewish identity has been "abolished" by Christ.

13. Wright, *Paul and the Faithfulness of God*, 425. Cf. a suggestion by Gupta, *Colossians*, 94, 106.

14. Weiss, "The Law," 294–96.

15. See, e.g., Bevere, "Cheirograph," 199–206.

The "Ceremonial" Law Abolished

Some significant medieval and Reformation interpretations of Eph 2:14–15 and Col 2:13–23 understood these passages specifically to be about the abolition of the "ceremonies" of the law of Moses. Thomas Aquinas in the thirteenth century, for example, understood Eph 2:14–15 in this way:

> The Old Law contained both moral and ceremonial precepts. The moral commandments were not destroyed by Christ but fulfilled in the counsels he added and in his explanations of what the Scribes and Pharisees had wrongly interpreted. . . . He abolished the ceremonial precepts with regard to what they were in themselves, but he fulfilled them with regard to what they prefigured, adding what was symbolized to the symbol.
>
> It should be understood, therefore, that in saying *breaking* he refers to the observance of the carnal law. To break down this barrier of partition is to destroy the hostility between the Jews and Gentiles. The former wanted to observe the law and the latter had little inclination to do so, from which anger and jealousy sprung up between them. But certainly, Christ has abolished this animosity . . . .[16]

Even more explicitly, John Calvin in the sixteenth century, while wrestling with the issue of Roman Catholic "ceremonies" in his own day, identifies the "law" that is "abolished" in Eph 2:14–15 with Jewish "ceremonial" law-observance:

> Paul means not only that the Gentiles are equally admitted to the fellowship of grace, so that they no longer differ from the Jews, but that the mark of difference has been taken away; for ceremonies have been abolished. Just as, if two contending nations were brought under the dominion of one prince, he would not only desire that they should live in harmony, but would remove the badges and marks of their former enmity.
>
> . . . Paul is here treating exclusively of the ceremonial law; for the moral law is not a wall of partition separating us from the Jews, but it includes teaching which concerns us no less than the Jews. From this passage we refute the error of some, that circumcision and all the ancient rites, though not binding on the Gentiles, still remain today for the Jews. On this principle there would still be a middle wall of partition between us, which is proved to be false.[17]

16. Aquinas, *Ephesians*, 105–6.

17. Calvin, *Galatians, Ephesians, Philippians and Colossians*, 151.

Calvin understands Col 2:14, 16–17 in a similar way, seeing it as abolishing *all* kinds of ceremonies:

> Now Paul contends that ceremonies have been abolished; . . . Hence it follows, that all those who still press for ceremonies diminish the benefit of Christ, as though absolution were not procured for us through Him. For they restore its freshness to the hand-writing, and hold us still under obligation . . . .[18]
>
> Now, the reason is, that all the Mosaic ceremonies had in them some acknowledgment of guilt, which bound those that observed them more firmly, as it were, to God's judgment. . . . The Son of God has not only by His death delivered us from the condemnation of death, but in order that absolution might be made more certain, he abrogated those ceremonies, that no monument of obligation might remain . . . .[19]
>
> For the substance of those things which the ceremonies once figured is now presented before our eyes in Christ, in that He contains in Himself everything that they pointed to as future. Hence, anyone who calls back the ceremonies into use either buries the manifestation of Christ, or robs Christ of His power, and makes Him as it were empty.[20]

The Boundary-Marking Function of the Law Abolished

A more recent view concentrates on the abolition (by way of fulfillment) of the specifically Jewish *boundary-marking* functions of the law of Moses. N. T. Wright, for example, sees Col 2:16–23 as speaking primarily about the Jewish "rules of diet and ritual" which "marked out the Jew from his pagan neighbour."[21] It is these rules that have been "abolished":

> Christianity is the *fulfilment* of Judaism. Christians are members of the "age to come" for which Israel had been waiting. But "when the perfect is come, the partial is abolished" (1 Cor. 13:10): or, as he puts it here, *these are a shadow of the things that were to come; the reality, however, is found in Christ.*[22]

18. Ibid., 334.

19. Ibid., 335.

20. Ibid., 337.

21. Wright, *Colossians and Philemon*, 119. See also Dunn, *Beginning from Jerusalem*, 1113.

22. Wright, *Colossians and Philemon*, 119, emphasis original.

Further:

> The regulations of Judaism were designed for the period when
> the people of God consisted of one racial, cultural and geo-
> graphical unit, and are simply put out of date now that this
> people is becoming a world-wide family. They were the "shad-
> ows" that the approaching new age casts before it. Now that the
> reality is come, there is no point in clinging to the shadows. And
> the reality belongs to Christ.[23]

The Entire Law Abolished

Many modern interpreters reject the idea that it is only one aspect of the
law (i.e., the ceremonial or boundary-marking function) that has been
"abolished." For Andrew Lincoln, the *entire* law has been abolished in
Eph 2:15:

> Torah as an impenetrable fence protecting Israel from the impu-
> rity of the Gentiles (see, e.g., *Letter of Aristeas* 139,142) became
> such a sign of Jewish particularism that it alienated Gentiles and
> became a cause of hostility. For the writer of Ephesians, Christ
> has neutralized this negative effect of the law by doing away with
> the law.[24]

For Lincoln, this is a key point of difference between Ephesians
and Paul's genuine letters. In Rom 3:31, for example, Paul denies that
"we abolish" (καταργοῦμεν) the law through faith; whereas in Eph 2:15
(according to Lincoln), Christ's work involves "abolishing" (καταργήσας)
the law entirely.[25]

Similarly strong statements about the abolition of the law in its
entirety, for both Jewish and gentile believers, are made by many other
modern commentators on Ephesians.[26] For example, on Eph 2:15a, Harold Hoehner writes:

> Since the whole Mosaic law has been rendered inoperative for
> Jewish and Gentile believers in Christ, it is a false dichotomy

23. Ibid., 120.

24. Lincoln, "Church and Israel," 611. Cf. Lincoln, *Ephesians*, 142.

25. Lincoln, "Church and Israel," 611–12.

26. In addition to the commentators quoted here, see Martin, *Ephesians, Colossians and Philemon*, 36; Perkins, "The Letter to the Ephesians," 399–400; Talbert, *Ephesians and Colossians*, 81; Arnold, *Ephesians*, 163; Thielman, *Ephesians*, 170.

to distinguish between the moral and ceremonial laws, making only the ceremonial laws inoperative . . . . Christ has fulfilled it [i.e., the Mosaic law] and it is no longer operative, and this applies to both Gentile and Jewish believers who are in Christ.[27]

Allan Bevere argues that a similar abolition of the law in its entirety is being described in Col 2:14.[28]

If this were true—i.e., if Ephesians and Colossians were advocating a wholesale abolition of the law of Moses in all respects—then Harlow would be correct in claiming that Ephesians advocates "a unity that effectively erases Jewish distinctiveness."[29] A similar point may be made with respect to Colossians.[30]

Jewish Distinctiveness Nullified in a New Humanity? (Eph 2:14–16; Col 3:11)

The third category of supersessionist over-reading involves the idea that Christ, by forming a new kind of humanity, has nullified all forms of Jewish distinctiveness. This claim arises from interpretations of Eph 2:14–16 and Col 3:11. Ephesians 2:14–16, situated within a discussion of the relationship between Israel and the nations (cf. 2:11–12), speaks of Christ making "two" (δύο) or "both" (ἀμφότερα) entities into "one" (ἕν) entity:

> For he himself is our peace, who has made us both one and has broken down in his flesh the dividing wall of hostility by abolishing the law of commandments expressed in ordinances, that he might make the two into one new humanity in himself,[31] so making peace, and might reconcile us both to God in one body through the cross, thereby killing the hostility. (Eph 2:14–16, modified ESV).

---

27. Hoehner, *Ephesians*, 376–77.

28. Bevere, "Cheirograph."

29. Harlow, "Early Judaism and Early Christianity," 269.

30. Shkul, "New Identity," 384–85.

31. I have modified this phrase from the ESV, removing the rendering "in place of," since it inclines the reader toward a supersessionist interpretation (see below). I have also rendered the term "man" (ἄνθρωπον) as "humanity," since, as Lincoln argues, in the context this is referring to "a corporate new humanity ('one new person') which is embraced in Christ's own person" ("Church and Israel," 612).

Colossians 3:11 states that the pairs "Greek and Jew, circumcised and uncircumcised" are not relevant in the "new humanity" (cf. Col 3:9–10):

> Here there is not Greek and Jew, circumcised and uncircumcised, barbarian, Scythian, slave, free; but Christ is all, and in all. (Col 3:11)

Several interpreters take these passages in Ephesians and Colossians to mean that Christ has nullified the value of Jewish distinctiveness in all respects.

Chrysostom: Jewish Distinctiveness as an Obstacle to Peace

An early, yet influential, view of the meaning of the "two" becoming "one" in Eph 2:14–16 can be found in the writings of John Chrysostom in the late fourth century. Chrysostom's interpretation of this passage is shaped by two factors. The first factor is his disputes with Judaizers (or perhaps actual Jews),[32] which led him to adopt "an unfriendly attitude toward the Jewish people [that] affected his approach to the passage."[33] The second factor is his view that Eph 2:11–22 is a lesser, "earthly" illustration of the more profound "heavenly" truths contained in Eph 2:1–10.[34] Due to these factors, when Chrysostom approaches Eph 2:11–22, he is less interested in concrete relationships between Jews and gentiles, and more interested in emphasizing the superabundance of God's grace in raising gentiles to a high position.[35] Thus, Chrysostom can speak of the "two" becoming "one" in ways that appear to eradicate any possibility for distinct Jewish identity. For example, he uses the illustration of the melting down of two metal statues to form a single statue:

> I will give you an illustration. Let us suppose there to be two statues, the one of silver, the other of lead, and then that both shall be melted down, and that the two shall come out gold. Behold, thus hath He made the two one.[36]

---

32. Rader, *Racial Hostility*, 33; cf. Stark, *Rise of Christianity*, 66–67.

33. Rader, *Racial Hostility*, 33–35, quotation from 34.

34. Chrysostom, *Galatians and Ephesians*, 148.

35. Ibid., 149.

36. Ibid., 149–50.

Chrysostom also describes Jewish distinctiveness as an inferior condition that created an insuperable obstacle to "peace" and had to be overcome:

> Peace for them both towards God, and towards each other. For so long as they continued still Jews and Gentiles, they could not possibly have been reconciled. And had they not been delivered each from his own peculiar condition, how had they ever arrived at another and a higher one? For the Jew is then and not till then united to the Gentile when he becomes a believer. It is like persons being in a house, with two chambers below, and one large and grand one above: they would not be able to see each other, till they had got above.[37]

As Rader notes, Chrysostom's view of Eph 2:11–22 was highly influential in the centuries that followed.[38]

Calvin's Opposition to "Ceremonies"

The sixteenth-century Reformer John Calvin, as we saw above, understood the New Testament discussions concerning Jewish identity in light of questions concerning external religion and "ceremonies," which in his own context were pressing issues with significant soteriological implications. With these controversies in mind, Calvin understood Ephesians and Colossians to be teaching that maintaining Jewish ethnic identity was antithetical to the gospel of Christ. So Eph 2:15–16 means

> that in Christ neither circumcision, nor uncircumcision, avails anything, that nothing external is of any value, but that a new creature holds the first and last place. Therefore there is one spiritual regeneration which joins us. If then we are all renewed by Christ, let the Jews cease to congratulate themselves on their ancient conditions, and let them, both for themselves and for others, allow Christ to be in all (as he says elsewhere).[39]

On Col 3:11 Calvin writes:

> *Where there is neither Jew.* He added this deliberately, to draw the Colossians away from ceremonies. For the words mean that Christian perfection does not need those outward observances;

37. Ibid., 152.
38. Rader, *Racial Hostility*, 35.
39. Calvin, *Galatians, Ephesians, Philippians and Colossians*, 151–52.

in fact, they are altogether alien to it. For under the distinction of circumcision and uncircumcision, Jew and Greek, he includes, by synecdoche, all externals.[40]

"Third Race" Interpretations

The twentieth century saw the rise of "third race" terminology and concepts in the interpretation of New Testament passages. This is the view that Christians form a new "race" of people in distinction from the "races" of Jew and gentile. A key proponent of this racial interpretation was Adolf von Harnack.[41] In chapter 7 of *The Mission and Expansion of Christianity in the First Three Centuries*, Harnack seeks to demonstrate that the concept (if not the terminology) of "the third race" was central to early Christian consciousness.[42] According to Harnack, Christians saw themselves as "the *true Israel*, at once the *new* people and the *old*," having a status that involved "the transference of all the prerogatives and claims of the Jewish people to the new community as a new creation which exhibited and realized whatever was old and original in religion."[43] So Harnack states that according to places in Paul's letters, including Col 3:11 and Eph 2:11, Christians

> represent the new grade on which human history reaches its consummation, a grade which is to supersede the previous grade of bisection, cancelling or annulling not only national but also social and even sexual distinctions.[44]

A "third race" interpretation of Eph 2:11–22 can also be discerned in some of the popular sermons published in *The Speaker's Bible* (1925). Several of these sermons exposit the passage in terms of a Darwinian evolutionary theory in which Jews are regarded as a lower race that has evolved along with gentiles into a higher race.[45] For example:

40. Ibid., 350.

41. Rader, *Racial Hostility*, 228–29 n. 185. As Rader notes, although "third race" terminology was occasionally used in the early Christian centuries, it was almost exclusively as a term of abuse levelled at Christians by their opponents rather than a term owned by Christians themselves.

42. Harnack, *Mission and Expansion*, 240–65. German: "das dritte Geschlecht."

43. Ibid., 240.

44. Ibid., 243.

45. Rader, *Racial Hostility*, 203–4.

Moreover, the method by which Jesus Christ secures this new type conforms perfectly to what we recognize as God's law of development [i.e., through Darwinian evolution]. It is not secured by giving an arbitrary victory to some earlier type, but by the fusion of existing types in a higher and nobler unity. Consider this matter historically, and ask what exactly Jesus Christ has done. Before He appeared there were two clearly-marked models, the Jew and the Gentile. The Saviour did not destroy these, nor did He select one of them for supremacy. He used both of them in creating a new man—the Christian. This Christian was neither a Jew nor a Gentile.[46]

"Third race" interpretations of Eph 2:11–22 have appeared in various commentaries throughout the twentieth century.[47] For example, Ernest Best writes:

In the first of these contrasts between "two" and "one" (v. 14)—ὁ ποιήσας τὰ ἀμφότερα ἕν—the neuter is used; it is natural to assume the omission of some such word as γένη [race]; the two races, Jew and Gentile, are made one; no longer is there a distinction between them. . . . [T]he new group, the ἕν [one], is, of course, the Church, which is the new race. . . . [T]he two types of men—Jews and Gentiles—have given way to a third type, the "new man", the Christian. . . . There are Jews and there are Gentiles; but the Jews that become Christians lose their Jewishness and are not Jewish Christians, and the Gentiles that become Christians lose their Gentileness and are not Gentile Christians; both are simply Christians—a third and new type of man distinct from the old twofold classification of Jew and Gentile. There are now three races of men, Jews, Gentiles, and Christians.[48]

Andrew Lincoln writes:

It must be underlined that the nature of Christ's accomplishment is described as a creation and its product as something new. In its newness it is not merely an amalgam of the old in which Gentiles have been combined with the best of Judaism.

46. Hastings, *Speaker's Bible*, 109.

47. In addition to the authors cited below see the term "third race"/"das dritte Geschlecht" used in Gnilka, *Der Epheserbrief*, 139 (with modifications); Bruce, *Colossians, Philemon, Ephesians*, 295–96; Hoehner, *Ephesians*, 379–80; Talbert, *Ephesians and Colossians*, 82. Cf. Shkul, *Reading Ephesians*, 90–91 esp. n. 35.

48. Best, *One Body*, 152–54. Cf. Best, *Ephesians*, 269.

The two elements which were used in the creation have become transformed in the process. This is "the third race" which is different from both Jews and Gentiles.[49]

Whatever the dangers for the relationship between Christians and Jews which arose from later abuse of the concept, there is no escaping the conclusion that Ephesians 2 depicts the church in terms of a new, third entity, a third race which transcends the old ethnic and religious identities of Jew and Gentile.[50]

Lincoln uses this conclusion concerning the "third race" concept in Ephesians to highlight a contrast with undisputed Pauline epistles, particularly Galatians and Romans:

The situation of the addressees [of Ephesians], like that of most later readers of Paul, was one in which one of the primary contexts of Paul's work, the struggle over circumcision and the law in order to forge unity between Jewish Christians and Gentile Christians, was no longer immediately relevant. In the letter as a whole, therefore, the writer treats the unity between Jew and Gentile achieved by Christ's reconciling death and proclaimed by Paul to the Gentiles as a past event which has placed its stamp on the very nature of the church. . . . It is because the church is the one new humanity in place of two that it can be depicted as providing the powers with a tangible reminder that their authority has been decisively broken and that everything will be made one in Christ. In this way, the writer skillfully combines the Jew/Gentile concerns of Galatians and Romans with the cosmic concerns of Colossians in his interpretation of Paul for a new day.[51]

Ralph Martin, who similarly interprets Eph 2:11–22 in terms of a "third race," also sees it as evidence for a contrast between Ephesians and the undisputed Pauline writings:

Another unusual emphasis here is the way the church takes the place of national groups in verse 15 ("one new person in place of the two") instead of merely existing alongside the ethnic divisions that persist (as in I Cor. 10:32). . . . [B]oth Jews and Gentiles in losing their ethnic and racial claims gain something

49. Lincoln, "Church and Israel," 612; cf. Lincoln, *Ephesians*, 144.

50. Lincoln, "Church and Israel," 616; cf. Lincoln, *Ephesians*, 163. See also Dunning, "Strangers and Aliens," 14.

51. Lincoln, "Church and Israel," 619.

in return which is said to be far better, namely, a place in Christ's body, as Christ's body, thereby forming a new race of humanity. Later writers therefore call the church "the third race"—neither Jews nor Gentiles but Christians.[52]

"Replacement" Terminology in Bible Translations

Considering the popularity of the "third race" concept in the twentieth century, it is interesting to note the decision of the Revised Standard Version translators (1946) when they came to Eph 2:15b. The Greek text of Ephesians 2:15b reads: ἵνα τοὺς δύο κτίσῃ ἐν αὐτῷ εἰς ἕνα καινὸν ἄνθρωπον. This is literally, "that he might create the two, in him, into one new human[ity]." The Greek text is ambiguous, and leaves open the possibility that the "two" still retain their distinctiveness within "one new human[ity]." The King James Version reflects this ambiguity:

> for to make in himself of twain one new man (Eph 2:15b KJV)

However, the Revised Standard Version resolves the ambiguity in a supersessionist direction, with the addition of the English phrase "in place of":

> that he might create in himself one new man *in place of* the two
> (Eph 2:15b RSV, emphasis added)

This clarification, of course, implies that the new humanity is to be understood as a "replacement" of distinct Jewish and gentile humanity. It rules out the possibility that Jewish and gentile distinctiveness may be an ongoing feature of identity in Christ. Subsequent translations in the tradition of the RSV—i.e., the NRSV and ESV—retain the "replacement" terminology.[53]

Extreme "Abolition" Language

There is also a tendency among some commentators to over-read Col 3:11 as implying a total abolition of any kind of ethnic or other distinctiveness within the body of Christ. It is not simply that ethnicity is no longer a barrier to unity in the Christian community; rather all ethnic

52. Martin, *Ephesians, Colossians and Philemon*, 31.

53. The NRSV simply changes "man" to "humanity" in line with its gender-inclusive language policy; the ESV is identical to the RSV.

distinctives have been "abolished" and have "lost their meaning." So Eduard Lohse writes:

> What separates men from one another in the world—which of course still exists—has been abolished in the community of Jesus Christ. . . . For in Christ there is no longer any validity either to the boundaries between different nations or to the distinction between Israel and the Gentiles. Consequently, even "circumcision" (περιτομή) and "uncircumcision" (ἀκροβυστία) have lost their meaning . . . .[54]

Paul Foster also speaks of Col 3:11 as an "emancipatory Pauline charter that abolishes social distinctions." He sees it as a "radical outlook" deriving from Paul, that soon afterward is "greatly softened (perhaps even undermined)" by the author of Colossians with the non-Pauline idea that social distinctions should continue in the household code (Col 3:18—4:1).[55]

James Dunn claims about this verse that:

> Not simply particular ethnic distinctions have been abolished, but the very possibility of such distinctions having any continuing meaning has ceased to exist.[56]

Summary

As we have already noted, most of the interpretations cited in this section are not primarily driven by a desire to nullify Jewish identity. Nevertheless, they are effectively supersessionist, because they place Jewish distinctiveness, along with its key markers—circumcision and law-observance—in antithetical contrast to Christian identity. Such interpretations undermine the possibility that there might be some positive value for Jewish distinctiveness in relation to Christ, whether advocated or assumed, within these letters. These interpretations also distance Ephesians and Colossians from the concerns of the historic Pauline mission at this point, since in Paul's undisputed letters, distinct Jewish

---

54. Lohse, *Colossians and Philemon*, 143–44; cf. O'Brien, *Colossians, Philemon*, 192.

55. Foster, *Colossians*, 48, 110, cf. 338–343.

56. Dunn, *Colossians and Philemon*, 223.

identity and the law retain a significant, albeit relative, role in relation to the gospel of Christ (e.g., Rom 1:16; 3:1–2; 9:4–5).

However, as we have noted, these supersessionist readings are not simply straightforward readings of the relevant texts. Rather, they are *over*-readings. That is, they extrapolate from the texts to reach conclusions that are not necessarily made by the texts themselves. There are other ways to read Ephesians and Colossians. Indeed, in the case of Ephesians, there have been several significant, deliberately post-supersessionist readings. It is to these readings that we now turn.

Post-supersessionist Readings of Ephesians

In chapter 1, I noted the rise of various *post-supersessionist* perspectives in New Testament interpretation. Post-supersessionist interpreters (i) reject the view that the Christian church has superseded or replaced Israel without remainder, (ii) see a special place or calling for Israel within God's purposes through Christ, and (iii) usually see a positive value for Jewish distinctiveness. Post-supersessionist perspectives have been brought to bear on Ephesians by several modern interpreters. In this section, I will summarize some of the key post-supersessionist interpretations, and discuss their significance for the concerns of this book.

Markus Barth

Markus Barth is a highly influential figure in twentieth-century scholarly discussion of Ephesians.[57] As Rader notes, Barth's discussion of the letter arises in part from several key scholarly questions that were significant in his own context. Firstly, Barth emphasizes scriptural and Jewish roots for concepts in Ephesians, over against earlier emphases on a gnostic background.[58] Secondly, Barth emphasizes the social dimensions of the gospel in Ephesians—especially the reconciliation of Jew and gentile—over against earlier individualistic interpretations.[59] Thirdly, Barth has a special interest in providing a nuanced view of the relationship between Christian unity and Jewish particularity. This interest was in part a response to earlier attempts in Nazi Germany to drive Jewish Christians

---

57. Rader, *Racial Hostility*, 177–246, esp. 222–28.

58. Ibid., 192.

59. Ibid., 201–8.

into separate congregations,[60] and in part related to the need to provide theological underpinnings for Jewish-Christian dialogue and discussions surrounding the modern state of Israel.

Barth's views on Ephesians can be found in several key works written over a period of approximately twenty-five years. *The Broken Wall: A Study in the Epistle to the Ephesians* (1960) is a pastorally-motivated introduction to Ephesians, which includes a discussion of the relationship between the church and Israel.[61] *Israel and the Church: Contribution to a Dialogue Vital for Peace* (1969) is a scholarly work aimed at providing theological reflections for Jewish-Christian dialogue. It includes a substantial section titled "Israel and the Church in Paul's Epistle to the Ephesians."[62] Barth's *Ephesians* commentary (1974) is his major work on the epistle.[63] *The People of God* (1983) is a series of lectures that concentrates on the relationship between Jew and gentile in Rom 9–11, but that also discusses Eph 2 in relation to Romans.[64]

For Barth, the description of Jew-gentile reconciliation in Eph 2:11–22 is "the key and high point of the whole epistle."[65] Barth interprets other passages in light of this central passage. For example, Barth understands the distinction between "we" and "you also" in Eph 1:11–14 as a distinction between Jews and gentiles. For Barth, the passage is describing a historical sequence in which the gentiles were included in Israel's election.[66] Furthermore, Eph 3:5–6 is a description of God's great purpose that gentiles are adopted into "one body, brotherhood, and covenant life together with Israel."[67]

Barth's interpretation of Eph 2:11–22, and thus of the entire letter, is explicitly Israel-centric and non-supersessionist:

---

60. Ibid., 213–22.

61. Barth, *The Broken Wall*, 115–27.

62. Barth, *Israel and the Church*, 79–117. Cf. his earlier *Israel und die Kirche im Brief des Paulus an die Epheser* (1959), summarized in Rader, *Racial Hostility*, 222–28.

63. Barth, *Ephesians*.

64. Barth, *People of God*, 45–49. See also Barth's 1979 discussion of Jewish identity in the Pauline epistles ("A Good Jew").

65. Barth, *Ephesians*, 275. Note the contrast with Lincoln, "Church and Israel" (see above).

66. Barth, *The Broken Wall*, 116; Barth, *Israel and the Church*, 85–86; Barth, *Ephesians*, 130–35.

67. Barth, *Israel and the Church*, 85–95, quotation from 92.

> The baptized Gentiles are, according to this epistle, not the legal successors of God's chosen people, Israel. Only together with Israel are they worshippers of one Father, citizens of God's Kingdom, members of God's household (2:18–19). No one can call himself a Christian and forget that he shares in the privilege that first has been accorded to Israel alone. There is only *one* Christian church: the church from Israel and from the Gentiles.[68]

Barth believes that Ephesians is describing the gentiles' "incorporation into Israel." Indeed, salvation itself derives from such an incorporation:

> Through his incorporation into Israel a Gentile finds communion with God.[69]
>
> "To be saved" means, for Gentiles, to be grafted into the people of Israel, to have part in the heritage which was pledged to the Fathers, and to rejoice in the fulfilment of the promise and hope which God gave to that people (Eph. 1:12–14; 2:1–6, 11–22; 3:6).[70]
>
> So they [the Gentiles] "have" nothing—whether redemption, forgiveness, peace, access to God, or hope (1:7, 18; 2:14, 18, etc.)—which they do not have together with Israel. Alienated from Israel they were "bare of hope and without God" (2:12). Joined to Israel they partake in "the life of God" (cf. 4:18; 2:14; 3:6).[71]

However, although the gentiles are "incorporated into" or "joined to" Israel, this does not imply that the distinctions between the gentiles and Israel have disappeared. On the contrary, in the "new man" of Eph 2:15, these differences must be maintained. It is only the "dividing-wall of hostility" between Jew and gentile that is destroyed (cf. Eph 2:14):

> Their [i.e., Jews' and Gentiles'] historic distinction remains true and recognized even within their communion. According to Paul, the first may continue to observe the law as long as it is not used for a hostile division or imposition (I Cor 9:20, etc.). The Gentiles need not be forced under its "yoke"—as Paul untiringly stressed, and as Peter pointed out according to Acts 15:10. Eph 2:15 proclaims that the people of God is different from a

---

68. Ibid., 83.

69. Barth, *Ephesians*, 270.

70. Barth, *People of God*, 20.

71. Barth, *The Broken Wall*, 120.

syncretistic mixture of Jewish and Gentile elements. The members of the church are not so equalized, leveled down, or strait-jacketed in a uniform as to form a *genus tertium* [third race] that would be different from both Jews and Gentiles. Rather the church consists of Jews and Gentiles reconciled to one another by the Messiah who has come and has died for both.[72]

For Barth, the breaking down of the dividing-wall between Jews and gentiles is an irreducibly particular phenomenon. It should not be understood simply as one historical instance of a more generalized "peacemaking" ministry of Christ toward any "partition between races and classes, nations and neighbours, ages and cultures."[73] Rather, it is a unique event in history. Nevertheless, provided it retains its particularity, the Jew-gentile reconciliation described in Eph 2 can become the source and standard for all other kinds of human peacemaking.[74] Within the church itself, it becomes "[t]he great example, the test of unity in difference and of distinctiveness in unity."[75] Thus, the removal of the dividing-wall between Jew and gentile is the key for shaping the church as a mutually dependent communion of those who are and remain different.[76]

> Abolition and peace—these great words will keep us from dreaming of, or scoffing at, a sexless, raceless, homeless, neuter superman, whom Christianity allegedly ought to promote or to produce. . . . [Words such as those found in Gal 3:28; Col 3:11; 1 Cor 12:13] by no means wipe out or deny distinctions between nations, sexes, classes and occupations. . . . But, faith in Christ, even Christ himself, means that the two—whatever their distinctions are—can and do live together: those who were formerly opposed, mutually exclusive, separated by what seemed to be an insurmountable wall. To say "Christ" means to say community, co-existence, a new life, peace (2:14).[77]

For Barth, the fact that Israel is not superseded by gentile Christianity, but rather shares its prior privileges with Christian gentiles, highlights Israel's divine vocation in the world as a bearer of revelation.

---

72. Barth, *Ephesians*, 310.

73. Barth, *The Broken Wall*, 116.

74. Ibid., 117.

75. Barth, *Israel and the Church*, 89.

76. Ibid., 103–5.

77. Barth, *The Broken Wall*, 38.

Fundamentally, Israel's salvation from sin teaches the gentiles what it means to be saved by grace alone:

> The pre-existence of a commonwealth and house, of a plan, of covenants and promises of God in the history of Israel reminds the Gentiles to look at their own history and to appreciate that only by sheer grace they are no longer dead in sins and strangers (2:5, 8, 12, 19). . . . [B]y looking at Jews the Gentiles realize which kind of man is confronted by God: Man is a sinner.[78]

Thus, the church is dependent on Israel. This dependence also has implications for the use of the Scriptures in the New Testament and beyond:[79]

> If community with Israel is essential and basic to the church's foundation, life, and order, then references to the fulfilment of the Old Testament are not primarily an academic or literary trick comparable to the footnote strategy. . . . In the New Testament, Scripture quotations and allusions belong to the very core of the matter that is announced. They are proclamation and exhortation rather than mere reasonings; they deal with the fulfillment of the Old Covenant, not with reflections about an old book.[80]

The priority of Israel in God's dealings with humanity also means that Israel is God's primary "missionary." Thus, all Christian mission depends on this prior "mission" of Israel to the world—a dependence and priority that needs to be acknowledged:

> Yet denominations and congregations, synods and boards, world councils and individuals can be ambassadors of the Gospel, evangelists carrying an urgent message, and missionaries equipped with good credentials only when they realise what thankful and responsible conversation with Israel means. Israel is the original and logical missionary of God. The mission of the Church is carried out only in fulfilment of Israel's calling and privilege.[81]

Barth therefore sees the idea of Christian "mission to the Jews" as a denial of Israel's missional priority. Rather, he argues that gentile Christians should maintain an attitude of gratefulness to Israel for her mission

78. Barth, *Israel and the Church*, 101–2.

79. Ibid., 105–8.

80. Ibid., 106–7.

81. Barth, *The Broken Wall*, 126–27.

to *them*. Granted, Christians cannot keep silent on the truth that the Law and Prophets are fulfilled in Christ, and need to speak of this matter to Jews. For Barth, however, this should not be seen as "mission" but rather as "testimony," given in a spirit of humility. Hence, Barth prefers the concept of "dialogue" or "conversation."[82]

Barth's insights concerning Israel's distinctiveness and priority, along with the ecclesiological, hermeneutical, vocational, and implications he draws, are valuable and often under-appreciated. I will make use of several of Barth's observations in this book.

There are, however, some problematic elements in Barth's reading of Ephesians. The key problems arise from Barth's view of the place of *faith in Christ* vis-à-vis Israel according to Ephesians. Admittedly, Barth's understanding of Ephesians is explicitly Christocentric. He affirms in the strongest terms that Israel's election was always "in Christ" as Israel's Messiah (Eph 1:3–10, cf. 2:12);[83] and their reconciliation can only take place "in Christ."[84] However, for Barth, Israel's status of being "in Christ" does not necessarily imply Jewish *faith* in Christ. Barth argues that while "faith" in Ephesians is predicated of gentile Christians (e.g., Eph 1:13), it is not necessarily predicated of Israel. Thus, Barth refuses to limit the "Israel" referred to in Ephesians to Christ-believing Jews. For Barth, all Jewish people—whether Christ-believing or non-Christ-believing—are God's instrument to demonstrate God's grace in adoption. Indeed, even in its worst apostasy, Israel has always been God's people, with an inalienable privilege and role.[85] Hence, for Barth, Ephesians' call to unity between the church and "Israel" is applicable to every possible definition of "Israel": past and present, believing and unbelieving.[86]

Elements of this view do have Pauline precedents, for example, in Rom 9–11. However, Barth's view ultimately downplays the role of faith in the overall structure and argument of Ephesians—a role that applies to Jews as much as gentiles. While it is true that election "in Christ" is presented as a reality that exists prior to any response of faith (Eph 1:4, 11), the concrete call to unity in Ephesians is nevertheless predicated on such

82. Barth, *Israel and the Church*, 108–15.

83. Barth, *Ephesians*, 132; cf. Barth, *Israel and the Church*, 97–100.

84. Barth, *The Broken Wall*, 118–19.

85. Barth, *Ephesians*, 132–33.

86. Barth, *The Broken Wall*, 116–27; Barth, *Israel and the Church*, 94–95; Barth, *Ephesians*, 132. Barth believes the call to unity implies that the church today must affirm and support the modern state of Israel (*People of God*, 72).

faith. This can be seen most clearly in Eph 4:4–5. Here the "one body" in which both Jews and gentiles are reconciled (cf. Eph 2:16) and the "one Spirit" through which both Jews and gentiles have access to the Father (cf. Eph 2:18) is placed in parallel with "one Lord, one faith, one baptism." In other words, Ephesians' explicit call to unity (Eph 4:1–3) is based on a common confession of faith in Christ (Eph 4:4–5).[87] It is therefore reasonable to infer that when Eph 2:11–22 speaks of the reconciliation between Israel and the nations, it is referring primarily to Christ-believing Jews and gentiles. While in places Ephesians shows an awareness of the existence of Jews living without faith in Christ, and presumably values their Israelite status, the assumption appears to be that they also need to hear the gospel of Christ in order that they might believe in him (Eph 2:3, 17–18).[88] This emphasis on faith in Christ as a call to both Israel and the nations will guide our exegesis in the following chapters.

Donald Robinson

In chapter 1, I noted that the approach taken in this book is most strongly indebted to the biblical theology of Donald Robinson. As we saw, Robinson highlights the prophetic eschatological expectation that Israel would act as a priestly nation, becoming a channel of God's blessing to the nations. He sees this expectation fulfilled in three ways in the New Testament: through 1) the incarnation, death, and resurrection of Christ 2) the Israel-centered preaching of the gospel of Christ to the nations, and 3) the coming together in fellowship of believing Jews and gentiles. Robinson's writings on Ephesians—and to a lesser extent on Colossians— reflect these concerns.[89] Robinson summarizes his perspective on Jew-gentile unity in Ephesians as follows:

> The Epistle to the Ephesians is the coping stone of Paul's theo-
> logical position. In it is set forth the most striking statement
> of the unity of Jew and Gentile in Christ. It is all the more
> remarkable that it does not overlook the priority of Israel as God's
> instrument of evangelism in the dispensation of the gospel, nor

---

87. Rader, *Racial Hostility*, 226.

88. See the discussion of Barth in chapter 2; cf. Shkul, *Reading Ephesians*, 82 n. 7.

89. See various references throughout Robinson, *Selected Works*, 5–194.

go so far as to say that believing Gentiles become Israelites when they embrace the promise of salvation.[90]

For Robinson, Ephesians is intensely interested in the local church as the place where this Jew-gentile unity-in-distinction is actualized:

> What Ephesians does emphasise more than other letters is that this new creation, the new mankind made in the image of God, is *already* being embodied in actual churches of mixed Jewish and Gentile membership, where the middle wall of partition has been broken down and a foretaste of the ultimate new humanity is already present, a place where it meets together in a single *ecclesia*. The OT picture behind this is Jerusalem, the centre of universal pilgrimage and worship, where all nations may assemble. The heavenly church of Ephesians is a transcendent body, but its focus on earth is wherever Jew and Gentile meet together in the same local *ecclesia*.
>
> At the same time, there is no epistle in which the actual distinction between Jews and Gentiles is more of a practical reality than Ephesians. . . . [T]he people addressed in Ephesians are made acutely aware that they are uncircumcised Gentiles who need special grace to comprehend the nature of the spiritual blessings which, through Christ, they have been enabled to share with their Jewish Christian brethren.[91]

Robinson also had a special interest in the question of the identity of "the saints" in Ephesians, seeing the phrase as a reference to Jewish Christians.[92] We will return to this question below.[93]

Tet-Lim Yee

The most comprehensive recent study of Jewish identity in Ephesians is Tet-Lim Yee's *Jews, Gentiles and Ethnic Reconciliation*.[94] Yee seeks to understand Ephesians within the framework of the "New Perspective," following the work of Sanders and Dunn:

90. Robinson, "Jew and Greek," 107.

91. Robinson, *Faith's Framework*, 114–15, emphasis original.

92. Robinson, "The Saints."

93. See chapters 3–6.

94. Yee, *Ethnic Reconciliation*.

> The present study seeks to bring the significance of the "new perspective" to bear on Ephesians, in the hope of being able to read Ephesians within the context which it provides. . . . It is my contention that previous work on Ephesians has seriously undermined the degree of continuity between Israel and the church which it expresses. The "new perspective" mentioned above has given us an opportunity to look at some of the old issues afresh.[95]

Yee contends that questions surrounding Jewish ethnic identity and ethnic reconciliation are central to Eph 2:11–22, and that Eph 2:11–22 in turn is integral to the overall argument of the letter. He maintains that the principal issue being addressed in Ephesians is Jewish "covenantal ethnocentrism." This is an attitude that identifies "religious identity" too closely with a single "ethnic group," thus making gentile "inclusion" impossible. The author of Ephesians is seeking to counter such covenantal ethnocentrism by redefining "Israel" to allow for gentile inclusion.[96] Yee summarizes his thesis as follows:

> The thesis of the present study is that Jewish attitudes toward the Gentiles had become the main factors which had led to Gentiles being excluded from the purpose of God before the latter had any positive connection with Christ. The Gentiles were excluded from Israel's God-given blessings on the basis of a particular *ethnos*. To make sense of these exclusive attitudes and of a self-confident Judaism which is bold enough to reduce the Gentile "other" to the category of the false or "out of place," the author does not just expose the Gentiles to these attitudes, but also re-presents what the Jews perceived about the Gentiles in such a way as to make it interpretable and usable for his own communicative purposes. His representation of the Gentile "other" from a Jewish perspective is meant to underscore the exclusivistic Jewish attitude which has led to ethnic alienation. The antidote to the alienation or ethnic estrangement is that the Messiah Jesus, who is eulogised as the peace-maker, and whose reconciling work is marked by his undisguised inclusivism, has come disinterestedly between Jews and Gentiles to overcome the barrier between the two and to create a people that is marked by the acceptance of the ethnic "other."[97]

95. Ibid., 2–3.
96. Ibid., 71.
97. Ibid., 31–32.

For Yee, the author of Ephesians does not cast any doubt on Israel's election itself. Indeed, the author remains entirely Jewish in his view that God's blessings were given to Israel so that the gentiles could come to know God (see esp. Eph 1:3–14).[98] Instead, the author has in his sights an "ethnocentric" view of Israel's election held by certain influential Jews.[99] The author, in a number of ways, seeks first to present this ethnocentric view (e.g., in Eph 2:1–2 and 2:11–12), then to deconstruct and critique it (e.g., in Eph 2:3–10 and 2:13–22). By using the "one new man" concept (Eph 2:15), the author aims to "subvert the social implications embedded in the Jewish notion of humanity."[100] His ultimate aim is replace this "ethnocentrism" with a new conception of a community in which ethnicity is irrelevant.

Yee's work shares the New Perspective's ambiguity with respect to the question of supersessionism, an ambiguity we highlighted in chapter 1. On the one hand, Yee refutes the kind of supersessionist over-readings we identified in the previous section of this chapter. He views the discussion of the law in Eph 2:15 simply as "an acknowledgement of the fact that the law has played a substantial role in leading to the strains between two ethnic groups rather than as an overt attack on the law itself";[101] he explicitly rejects the idea that Ephesians represents "a levelling and abolishing of all ethnic differences,"[102] and he sees the supersessionist idea that "the 'Church' has stepped in to become the 'true Israel'" as "[o]ne of the most unfortunate features in the Christian history of interpretation."[103] On the other hand, Yee argues that the author of Ephesians is seeking to redefine "Israel" so that it is no longer understood in "ethnic" terms.[104] Thus, for Yee, the principal problem in Ephesians is the "ethnic factor,"[105] and the principal solution is to promote a "non-ethnic religion, one with no ethnic ties whatsoever."[106] In this way, Yee's view that "ethnocentrism" is the overarching error in Ephesians tends to obscure or undermine the notion of Israel's distinctiveness. Thus, although Yee affirms in various

98. Ibid., 35–45.
99. Ibid., 110.
100. Ibid., 164.
101. Ibid., 157.
102. Ibid., 166.
103. Ibid., 187.
104. Ibid., 176.
105. Ibid., 187.
106. Ibid., 102.

places that Ephesians is not opposing the notion of "Jews and Gentiles as two ethnic groups of distinct background,"[107] he assigns no positive value to this distinctiveness. He even states that the "distinctiveness and separation" of the Jews simply represents a problem that needs to be overcome.[108]

Despite this overemphasis on "covenantal ethnocentrism," however, Yee's book contains many valuable insights. These insights flow from Yee's careful reading of Ephesians as a document reflecting a fundamentally Jewish and Israel-centered perspective. In this perspective, "'Gentile Christianity' cannot understand itself except in terms of the category of Israel and of Israel's blessing."[109] I will return to and make use of several of Yee's insights in this study.

William S. Campbell

William S. Campbell is a significant contemporary post-supersessionist interpreter of Paul's letters. In his work on the undisputed Pauline epistles, Campbell has demonstrated that according to Paul, Jewish ethnic identity is relativized and transformed "in Christ," but not eradicated.[110] Campbell has also sought to apply these insights to Ephesians.[111] He sets out to examine

> whether Paul's stance on retaining one's ethnic identity (remaining in the calling in which one was called) which eventually was lost when the church became predominantly gentile was already lost by the time the letter to the Ephesians was written around 90 CE at the latest.[112]

Against the view that in Eph 2:11–22, "ethnicity has no longer any actual significance in the church" and that "Israel's privileges, responsibility and identity [have] been transferred to the gentiles," Campbell argues that Christ is presented as a peacemaker between concrete ethnic groups—particularly between Jews and gentiles. This reconciliation between Jews and gentiles is not simply a past event but an "ongoing

---

107. Ibid., 164.

108. Ibid., 165.

109. Ibid., 221.

110. Campbell, *Christian Identity*, 104–20.

111. Campbell, "Unity and Diversity."

112. Ibid., 16.

process."[113] Campbell provides some plausible explanations for "the lack of explicit reference to actual problems between Jews and gentiles in the church" and emphasizes the fact that the removal of hostility is still a *"basic assumption of the text."*[114] He observes that 1) the *syn*-compounds (i.e., compound verbs beginning with the preposition σύν, "with") in Ephesians imply reconciliation between concrete groups rather than simply between individuals 2) gentile Christ-followers are depicted as being weak and unstable and so in need of fellowship with Jewish Christ-followers, and 3) Ephesians contains varying metaphors denoting "unity in diversity."[115] On this basis, Campbell claims that Ephesians is seeking to address actual Jew-gentile tensions:

> Thus we are led to the hypothesis that Ephesians, like Romans, though addressed to gentiles in Christ, nevertheless envisages contacts with synagogues or household assemblies of Jewish Christ-followers.[116]

On this basis, Campbell argues that for the author of Ephesians, "Christian identity is not a substitute for previous Jewish and gentile identities. . . . The Israelite symbolic universe is foundational to his thinking and Christ is not depicted in opposition to it."[117] In Ephesians, Paul's mission is "not to make the gentiles Israelites like himself, but co-heirs as gentiles with Israel."[118] Thus, Campbell concludes:

> The preferred identity which the author seeks to construct is one based on resolution of ethnic enmity by depicting Christ as the peace-maker between those who are alienated from one another due to ethnically significant issues. His solution is not to downplay ethnic awareness or to ignore the hostility usually associated with it, but to seek resolution in that reconciliation and peace with difference, which he presents as the outcome of the Christ-event.[119]

Campbell's observations here will inform my own reading of the text of Ephesians at several points.

113. Ibid., 19.
114. Ibid., 20, emphasis original.
115. Ibid., 21–22.
116. Ibid., 22.
117. Ibid., 23. Citing Esler, *Conflict and Identity*, 276.
118. Campbell, "Unity and Diversity," 23. Citing Esler, *Conflict and Identity*, 276.
119. Campbell, "Unity and Diversity," 24.

Mark Kinzer

In chapter 1, I reviewed Mark Kinzer's post-supersessionist interpretation of the New Testament and his proposal for a "Bilateral Ecclesiology in Solidarity with Israel."[120] I noted the value of Kinzer's approach, while highlighting a few specific areas in which his argument was less convincing. Here I will focus on Kinzer's reading of Ephesians, highlighting some of Kinzer's particularly insightful observations concerning the nature of Israel's distinctiveness.[121]

Kinzer's discussion of Ephesians in *Postmissionary Messianic Judaism* is relatively brief.[122] He points out that Ephesians seems to be addressed to gentile Christians. On this basis, he argues that the exhortations toward local and concrete unity in Eph 4 do not undermine his vision for bilateral ecclesiology. Rather, Eph 4 offers support for bilateral ecclesiology. This is because the "translocal officials" in Eph 4:11—i.e., the "apostles," "prophets," etc.—were Jewish. Thus, "the local Gentile ekklesia would be able to express its unity with the Jewish ekklesia by honoring the Jewish apostles and prophets who linked them to Israel."[123]

In *Searching Her Own Mystery*—addressed to Vatican II's "Declaration on the Relation of the Church to Non-Christian Religions" (*Nostra Aetate*)—Kinzer discusses Ephesians in more depth.[124] Like Barth, he argues that Eph 2:11–22 is central to Ephesians, and thus should act as a lens for reading the entire letter. He highlights four key features of Eph 2:11–22 that are linked to other features of the letter as a whole: 1) first- and second-person plural pronouns are used to distinguish Israel from the nations; 2) *syn*-compounds are used to refer to a communion of two different groups (Jew and gentile) in the one body; 3) the term "saints" is used to refer to Jews in distinction from gentiles; and 4) Israel is described as already being "in Christ" before Christ's birth.[125]

Kinzer concentrates on Israel's priestly vocation—that is, on Israel's role as a particular nation through whom God brings blessing to all the other nations. According to Kinzer, Ephesians 1 describes a priestly

---

120. Kinzer, *Postmissionary Messianic Judaism*, 151–79.

121. Kinzer does not discuss the key texts from Colossians, an omission noted by Blomberg, "Non-Supersessionist Alternative," 46.

122. Kinzer, *Postmissionary Messianic Judaism*, 165–71.

123. Ibid., 171 n. 51.

124. Kinzer, *Searching Her Own Mystery*, 65–82.

125. Ibid., 67–69.

dynamic in which blessing extends through Israel to the nations via the "apostolic community" who originally proclaimed the "word of truth" (Eph 1:13). This dynamic is expressed partly through the interplay between first- and second-person plural pronouns.[126] Israel's priestly vocation is also prominent in Eph 2:11–22.[127] The "one new human being" consists, not in a third entity distinct from Jews and gentiles, but in a new expanded Israel, which incorporates both Jews and gentiles in a way that retains the distinct identity of each group. The passage reaches a crescendo in the temple imagery, with clear priestly connections. Furthermore, because the temple is built on the foundation of the "apostles and prophets" (Eph 2:20), there is an *inextricable connection between the apostolic office and the people of Israel.*"[128] In discussing Eph 3:1–6, Kinzer again highlights the use of *syn*-compounds. He believes that these compounds are used to present the Israelites as already close to God, and the gentiles as joining "with" them through Christ.[129] Thus:

> What we have seen in Ephesians 1–3 could be described as the "catholicization" of Israel, accomplished in principle in the death and resurrection of Israel's Messiah, and realized in history through his prophetic apostles and the work of the Holy Spirit. Catholic Israel remains "one" people, yet it now consists of a twofold reality—gentiles united to Jews, but always as "co-sharers" of the inheritance, as one of the two parties who "both" have priestly access to God through the Messiah in one Spirit.[130]

This implies that the connection between Israel and the apostles is crucial to understanding Ephesians overall:

> If we are reading Ephesians correctly, then the Jewish identity of the apostles is crucial. They represent the Messiah of Israel, and thus they also represent Israel itself. This connection to Israel is evident in the Gospel tradition concerning the Twelve, who are appointed and destined to rule over the twelve tribes of Israel (Matt 19:28; Luke 22:28–30). But Ephesians suggests that this connection applies equally to the entire company of apostles, including Paul. When Paul goes to the gentiles, he represents

---

126. Ibid., 69–73.

127. Ibid., 73–79.

128. Ibid., 79, emphasis original.

129. Ibid., 80–81.

130. Ibid., 81.

not only the Messiah but also the people who were chosen in the Messiah before the foundation of the world.[131]

These insights into the positive, vocational element of Israel's distinctiveness and the connection between Israel's "priestly" ministry and the apostolic mission will inform my reading of Ephesians at many points.

Stephen Fowl

The final post-supersessionist interpretation to be discussed here is that of Stephen Fowl, in his 2012 commentary.[132] Fowl's theological reading of Eph 2:11–22 is thoroughly Christological, yet also thoroughly Israel-centric. Fowl titles his discussion of Eph 2:11–22 "Remember that you were Gentiles," from the opening words of Eph 2:11.[133] He argues that the command to the addressees to "remember" their gentile past is not incidental. Rather, it highlights a key feature of their new identity in Christ: they must adopt an Israel-centered perspective on their salvation.[134] Discussing the "one new person" of Eph 2:15, Fowl writes:

> It is clear that participation in this new person does not require the Ephesians or any other Gentile to become Jews in the sense of needing to be circumcised and so forth. Nevertheless, vv. 11–13 demand that the Ephesians rethink their pre-Christian identity as a Gentile identity. Conceiving of their pre-Christian past as simply pagan is not enough. They must understand their alienation from God as Gentile alienation. That is, their alienation from God must also include an understanding of their alienation from Israel and God's particular dealings with Israel.[135]

Thus, there is a redefinition of gentile identity inherent in the command to "remember" in Eph 2:11. This also, of course, implies a redefinition of Jewish identity:

> Though Ephesians does not devote much space to this matter, one should acknowledge that Jews, like Paul, needed to radically reconceive their perception of their own Judaism. . . . For now let

131. Ibid., 81–82.

132. Fowl, *Ephesians*.

133. Fowl obviously understands the verb "you were" (ἦτε) to be implied in Eph 2:11.

134. Ibid., 88–89.

135. Ibid., 95.

it suffice to say that the new person created in Christ brings Jews and Gentiles together into one body without requiring them to submit to a homogenizing erasure of their identity as Jews and Gentiles. Nevertheless, participation in this new creation requires changes from both of them. Erstwhile pagans must come to understand themselves as Gentiles; Jews must come to understand their Judaism in Christ, the telos of the torah. It is only in this way that peace is truly made.[136]

Fowl points out that Israel-centered identity for gentiles is not simply a polemical device that arises from the kinds of conflicts that are evident in Romans and Galatians. It is more fundamental than this, because it can arise even in the absence of "Judaizing pressures":

It appears that whether or not Christians in Ephesus or elsewhere are subject to Judaizing pressures, they must understand themselves as Christians in relation to Israel and Israel's God. They must understand their past as a Gentile past because that is God's understanding of their past. Moreover, this understanding makes sense only in the light of God's call of Israel; if there are no Jews, then there are no Gentiles. Christian identity requires the taking on or remembering of Gentile identity because Christian identity is always tied to Israel.[137]

Summary

The foregoing discussion of key post-supersessionist interpreters of Ephesians has brought to light several insights. These insights include:

- The observation that Eph 2:11–22 is integrally related to the letter as a whole, which raises the possibility that the explicit concerns of Eph 2:11–22 regarding Jewish and gentile reconciliation may be implicit in many other parts of the letter.

- The possibility that underlying Ephesians is a Jewish understanding of Israel's "priestly" role in bringing God's blessings to the nations (e.g., Eph 1:3–14).

- The likelihood that in certain places the distinction between the first- and second-person plural pronouns—i.e., "we" and

136. Ibid.
137. Ibid., 101.

"you"—indicates a distinction between Jews and gentiles (e.g., Eph 1:11–14; 2:1–3).

- The possibility that "the saints" in Ephesians at certain points is a reference either to Jews in general, or to Jewish Christ-believers in particular (e.g., Eph 2:19).

- The observation that Eph 2:11–12 describes the priority of the promises and hope given to Israel, in which Christ-believing gentiles are graciously enabled to participate.

- The observation that the command to "remember" in Eph 2:11 implies that gentile Christ-believers must understand themselves in terms of Israel's prior blessings.

- The observation that while reconciliation in Eph 2:11–22 involves the removal of ethnic hostility, it does not necessarily involve the removal of all ethnic distinctiveness.

- The likelihood that *syn*-compounds (e.g., Eph 2:6, 19, 21–22; 3:4, 6, 18) are being used to describe a communion of two distinct groups rather than a flat unity in which distinctions have been erased.

- The inference that Israel's priority indicates a vocation for Israel as a bearer of divine revelation to the world, which gives it a "missionary" role toward gentiles.

- The observation that there is a link between Israel's "priestly" vocation and the missionary vocation of Jewish apostles or the Jewish apostolic community as a whole (e.g., Eph 2:20; 3:5–6).

- The possibility that the author of Ephesians is seeking to address concrete relationships between Jews and gentiles.

These insights will be important for the reading of Ephesians (and, by extension, of Colossians) in the chapters that follow.

Critical Questions Concerning Ephesians and Colossians

There are several critical questions surrounding Ephesians and Colossians that are relevant to the discussion in this book. We will briefly survey them here.

Some of the critical questions surrounding the letters are not particularly controversial nor crucial for this study. It is likely that Ephesians was written to Christ-believers in Asia Minor, perhaps within a region centered on Ephesus.[138] If Paul is the author or was directly involved in the authorship of Ephesians, we can say that it was most likely written during Paul's Roman imprisonment (cf. Acts 28:16–31), in 60 C.E. at the earliest.[139] If Pauline authorship is not accepted, then we can at least say that it was written prior to 90 C.E.[140] Colossians is addressed to Christ-believers in the city of Colossae in the Lycus Valley. If Pauline authorship or involvement in the authorship of Colossians is accepted, we can say that it too was probably written during Paul's Roman imprisonment, in or soon after 60 C.E.[141] If Pauline authorship is not accepted, then, like Ephesians, it was written in 90 C.E. at the latest.[142]

The more significant questions for our study concern the authorship, setting, and purpose of the letters.

Ephesians

Authorship

One of the most commonly discussed critical questions relating to Ephesians is that of authorship. While the letter itself depicts the apostle Paul as its author (Eph 1:1; 3:1)[143] and Pauline authorship had "strong and widespread geographical attestation in the early church,"[144] there have been numerous critical objections against Pauline authorship. Here I will summarize some of the most common objections, along with common counters to these objections.

The first objection is that, unlike Paul's undisputed letters, Ephesians lacks concrete detail—it is thus not explicitly aimed at any obvious

---

138. Best, *Ephesians*, 6.

139. Hoehner, *Ephesians*, 92–97.

140. Best, *Ephesians*, 19.

141. Many scholars also see reasonably good evidence for composition during an imprisonment in Ephesus in the mid 50s. O'Brien, *Colossians, Philemon*, xlix–liv; Pao, *Colossians & Philemon*, 23–24; Dunn, *Colossians and Philemon*, 39–41 see Rome as marginally more likely; Bird, *Colossians & Philemon*, 19–23 sees Ephesus as marginally more likely.

142. Foster, *Colossians*, 73–81.

143. Hoehner, *Ephesians*, 38.

144. Ibid., 2–6, quotation from 6.

church, person, or situation.[145] This objection is often countered by the suggestion that Ephesians may have been a letter with a wide circulation, which would explain its lack of concrete detail. Some suggest, for example, that Ephesians was an encyclical in which a space was left in the prescript for each destination to be inserted; others suggest the letter was simply intended for a wide region which included but was not restricted to Ephesus.[146]

The second, related, objection is based on the likelihood that the original designation for the addressees of the letter (Eph 1:1) probably did not contain the words "in Ephesus" at all, and read "to the holy ones, to those who are also faithful [or believers] in Christ Jesus" (τοῖς ἁγίοις τοῖς οὖσιν καὶ πιστοῖς ἐν Χριστῷ Ἰησοῦ). Kümmel argues that it is "inconceivable" for Paul to have written such a salutation.[147] Against this objection, it has been argued by some that "in Ephesus" was original, despite the textual issues.[148] We will return to this question in chapter 3, when we discuss Eph 1:1 in more detail. We will conclude that, while it is likely that the words "in Ephesus" were not original, a post-supersessionist reading provides a plausible explanation for why Paul would have written the salutation in this way.[149]

The third objection against Pauline authorship is that Ephesians exhibits a distinctive, pleonastic style that differs significantly from the style of Paul's undisputed letters.[150] Several commentators, however, have pointed out that the stylistic differences, while real, are inconclusive for the question of authorship. They suggest that the differences can be explained in other ways, for example by a different situation, or a development in Paul's style over time.[151]

The fourth objection involves the close relationship between Ephesians and Colossians. Many scholars have discerned both a literary dependence by Ephesians on Colossians, and also key theological differences between the two letters. The literary dependence and theological

145. Kümmel, *Introduction*, 352; Dahl, "Gentiles, Christians, and Israelites," 38; Dunn, *Beginning from Jerusalem*, 1106–7.

146. Hoehner, *Ephesians*, 21–24.

147. Kümmel, *Introduction*, 355.

148. Thielman, *Ephesians*, 11–16.

149. See chapter 3.

150. Kümmel, *Introduction*, 358; Best, *Ephesians*, 27–42; Dunn, *Beginning from Jerusalem*, 1107.

151. Hoehner, *Ephesians*, 21–29; cf. Best, *Ephesians*, 27–32.

differences together suggest that Ephesians was written by someone other than Paul.[152] However, this dependence is not as clear-cut as is sometimes assumed. Best, for example, argues that the evidence does not necessarily point to a literary dependence. Rather, it simply indicates an association between the two letters. Best suggests that the two letters may have been penned by two authors from the same "Pauline school."[153] Others claim that the evidence is consistent with Paul having written both letters for different audiences within the same time period,[154] and that the conceptual differences between Ephesians and Colossians are too easily exaggerated.[155]

The fifth objection involves the claim that pseudonymity was an accepted practice in first-century Christian circles, and that its use did not involve any intention to deceive. This would make non-Pauline authorship *a priori* possible, and even likely.[156] This objection has been countered by pointing out that the problems with assuming the likelihood of pseudonymity are greater than is often assumed. For example, Jewish pseudepigrapha used the names of figures from the distant past, whereas Ephesians, if non-Pauline, is attributed to a recently deceased figure.[157]

The sixth objection is that certain theological perspectives in Ephesians seem to be more developed than those in the undisputed Pauline letters. For example, there is a more pronounced and universal ecclesiology and a more realized eschatology in Ephesians than that found in the undisputed letters.[158] Furthermore, concepts and vocabulary that are central to Paul's soteriological discourse in Romans and Galatians, such as justification and the law, are absent or downplayed in Ephesians. For example, while Paul in Romans and Galatians opposes concrete "works of the law" as a means of justification, Ephesians simply opposes "works" as a means of salvation.[159] This objection has been countered by argu-

152. Kümmel, *Introduction*, 358–60; Lincoln, *Ephesians*, li–lviii; Dunn, *Beginning from Jerusalem*, 1107.

153. Best, *Ephesians*, 20–25, 36–40; see also Best, "Who Used Whom?"

154. Hoehner, *Ephesians*, 38; Cohick, *Ephesians*, 14–15.

155. Thielman, *Ephesians*, 8–10.

156. Best, *Ephesians*, 10–13.

157. Hoehner, *Ephesians*, 38–49; Cohick, *Ephesians*, 19–27.

158. Kümmel, *Introduction*, 360–61; Best, *Ephesians*, 32–35; Dunn, *Beginning from Jerusalem*, 1108.

159. Kümmel, *Introduction*, 361; Dunn, *Beginning from Jerusalem*, 1108. Cf.

ing that these distinctive theological emphases can be explained either as developments of Paul's thought, or as simply a drawing out of elements within Paul's thought for a new situation. Thus, they need not imply a different author.[160]

The seventh objection is based on the observation that the "apostles" and "prophets" in Ephesians are described as foundational (Eph 2:20) and "holy" (Eph 3:5). Many take this to indicate a second-generation perspective in which the first-generation apostles have accrued an exalted, semi-legendary status.[161] Against this objection, it is pointed out that the adjective "holy" can be used to speak of certain persons who have been set apart for a particular ministry, and therefore does not imply a second-generation perspective (cf. Paul's self-designation as "set apart" in Rom 1:1).[162]

The eighth objection is that Paul's description of his own apostolate in Eph 3:1–13 seems to go beyond the claims he makes for himself in the undisputed letters.[163] However, even Best, who ultimately prefers non-Pauline authorship for Ephesians, argues that "it is easily conceivable that Paul could have developed his thinking in these ways."[164]

A ninth objection is that Ephesians' perspective on the issue of supersessionism is different from that of the undisputed Pauline letters. Interestingly, both Käsemann and Lincoln raise this objection, but for opposite reasons. Käsemann maintains that the historical Paul is supersessionist and Ephesians is not supersessionist. For Käsemann, Paul "insist[s] that the church, in contrast with Judaism, is the true Israel"; whereas Ephesians (and Acts) adopt the perspective that the gentiles have been joined to Israel.[165] Lincoln, on the other hand, maintains that the historical Paul was non-supersessionist and Ephesians is supersessionist. For Lincoln, Paul depicts the gentiles as being "added to a given Jewish base," "incorporated into Israel," and "joining a renewed Israel of Jewish Christians"; whereas Ephesians depicts them as "being made members of

Barclay, *Paul and the Gift*, 570–71.

160. Hoehner, *Ephesians*, 49–58; cf. Marshall, "Salvation, Grace and Works."

161. Käsemann, "Ephesians and Acts," 291–92; Best, *Ephesians*, 19–20; Dunn, *Beginning from Jerusalem*, 1107.

162. Hoehner, *Ephesians*, 443; Barth, *Ephesians*, 335. For more on the priestly nature of Paul's ministry in Romans, see Windsor, *Vocation of Israel*, 112–19.

163. Kümmel, *Introduction*, 361; Dunn, *Beginning from Jerusalem*, 1107–8.

164. Best, *Ephesians*, 44; cf. Cohick, *Ephesians*, 18–19.

165. Käsemann, "Ephesians and Acts," 296.

a new community which transcends the categories of Jew and Gentile."[166]
The difficulty with this objection is, of course, that it appears to be
entirely dependent on the interpreters' reading of supersessionism in the
respective texts, such that diametrically opposed arguments have been
used to reach the same conclusion.

A final objection is that there is a lack of evidence in Ephesians for
any concrete struggle between Jews and gentiles, such as is evident in
Romans and Galatians. For Lincoln, this demonstrates that Ephesians
was written *after* the Pauline mission from Israel to the nations:

> In the latest epistles of Paul, he was still engaged in a life-and-
> death struggle with rival Jewish Christian groups, but Ephesians
> looks back on an achieved unity between Jew and Gentile in
> the Church as the one body (cf. 2:11–22). Gone are the heated
> struggles with rival groups about the terms of Gentile admis-
> sion and about the law and gone also is the apostle's personal
> agony, expressed in Romans, about the relation of believers to
> ethnic Israel. Ephesians exhibits a detachment from such issues,
> reflecting its setting toward the end of the first century C.E.
> when Paul's position on admission of Gentiles had been firmly
> established, Jerusalem had fallen, and Gentile Christians in
> terms of influence and numbers were dominant in the churches
> of Asia Minor.[167]

Against this objection, it has been suggested that the lack of ethnic strug-
gle between Jews and gentiles in Ephesians may simply be evidence that
Ephesians was written at a later date in Paul's ministry, at a time when
Jewish and gentile hostility was a matter of the recent past.[168]

These objections will not be fully resolved here. While I favor Pauline
authorship, and my reading may even contribute in a small way toward
the case for Pauline authorship, for the purposes of this book, the identity
of the "real" author of Ephesians is not absolutely critical. This is because
my reading will focus most attention on the "implied" author. That is, I
will be exploring how Ephesians depicts the apostle Paul and his relationship to Israel and the nations. Thus, in the rest of this book, I will follow
Fowl's lead and for simplicity's sake refer to the author of Ephesians as
"Paul," rather than as "the author."[169] This is on the understanding that

166. Lincoln, *Ephesians*, xciii.

167. Ibid., xcii–xciii. Cf. Dahl, "Gentiles, Christians, and Israelites," 37–38.

168. Percy, *Die Probleme*, 284–86.

169. Fowl, *Ephesians*, 27–28.

"Paul" is the implied author, even though I acknowledge that the identity of the real author is still an open question for many scholars.

Occasion and Purpose

The occasion and purpose of Ephesians are also significant critical questions. Various possibilities have been proposed. I will overview a selection of these possibilities before reaching a conclusion that will guide my own reading.

For several scholars, Ephesians represents a conservative attempt by a post-Pauline author to draw the church back to its Pauline (and thus Jewish) roots, in order to reinforce present structural unity. Käsemann argues that Ephesians is evidence of "the transition from the Pauline tradition to the perspectives of the early Catholic era."[170] Ephesians, like Acts, exhibits a selecting, solidifying, and structuring of church tradition. The letter is responding to the situation that Paul saw as a possibility in Rom 11:17–24, i.e., "Jewish Christianity is pushed aside and despised by the steadily growing Gentile Christianity."[171] In the face of this problem, Käsemann argues, the author of Ephesians seeks to draw gentile Christians back to their roots and to the Jewish origins of the gospel. Kümmel similarly argues that Ephesians is addressed to "a general spiritual crisis in post-Pauline Gentile Christianity in which it must be stressed that the church of the Gentiles includes also the Jewish past of the church because it is in every sense a universal church."[172] For Lincoln, Ephesians is responding to a church situation in which gentile Christians "have a deficient sense of what it means to belong to the church and an accompanying diminishing awareness of the church's origins and place in history." In the face of this problem, the author of Ephesians, a "Jewish-Christian disciple of Paul," seeks to "updat[e] Paul's teaching in order to reinforce these Christians' identity as the church and to underline their distinctive role in the world."[173] This will enable his readers to appreciate the greatness of their new status, to be assured of salvation, to understand the

---

170. Käsemann, "Ephesians and Acts," 288.

171. Ibid., 291.

172. Kümmel, *Introduction*, 364.

173. Lincoln, "Church and Israel," 618.

historical nature of their salvation, and to look back to a paradigm for their own efforts at unity.[174]

Arnold points to the general religious environment of Ephesus and the existence of various magical practices. He maintains that Christians in Ephesus and its surrounds would have feared spiritual powers which manifested in magical practices. In light of these fears, they needed their identity and security "in Christ" to be affirmed above the spiritual powers. Arnold includes Jew-gentile unity and the transformation of believers' lifestyles as purposes of Ephesians alongside this affirmation of Christian identity.[175]

For Yee, the author of Ephesians is writing to deconstruct a Jewish "ethnocentric" attitude. He therefore describes the place of gentiles in the purposes of God, explaining firstly why they had been excluded from Israel, and secondly why they are now, in Christ, included in a renewed and expanded Israel. In this way, the gentiles can understand their "true identity."[176]

Other authors see Ephesians as having a more general purpose. For Barth, Ephesians has "many purposes."[177] This is because Ephesians is not an occasional letter, but is written to gentile Christians in Ephesus, many of whom Paul did not know personally because they had been converted after his departure.[178] Barth maintains that "Ephesians represents a development of Paul's thought and a summary of his message which are prepared by his undisputed letters and contribute to their proper understanding."[179] Best notes that the occasion of Ephesians is quite general, and that we lack any more specific information. Hence the purpose of Ephesians is difficult to state with much specificity. However, the purpose appears to be to establish and reinforce Christian identity, particularly in relation to Christ and Israel.[180] For Dunn, Ephesians is written by a disciple of Paul who is seeking to celebrate Paul's legacy and

174. Ibid., 618–19.

175. Arnold, *Ephesians*, 41–46.

176. Yee, *Ethnic Reconciliation*, 219–21.

177. Barth, *Ephesians*, 58.

178. Ibid., 3–4.

179. Ibid., 4.

180. Best, *Ephesians*, 63–75.

to update and adapt it to the situation post-60s, possibly using Colossians as a model.[181]

As we can see from this selection, most interpreters understand the letter as in some way seeking to establish and reinforce Christ-believing identity, particularly in relation to Israel, among a group of predominantly gentile believers. I will take this consensus as my starting point. However, I consider this view of Christ-believing identity in Ephesians to be too static. I will argue that the *dynamics* of the Pauline mission, through Israel to the nations, are integral to this identity. Thus, I will explore how the letter seeks to catch its readers up in the ongoing apostolic dynamic—a dynamic in which Israel plays a key role. I will also take up a suggestion by Thielman and argue that the description of the apostle's imprisonment and sufferings in Eph 3:1, 13 provides a plausible occasion for the letter.[182] The apostle is concerned that his readers see his imprisonment as a failure of God's global purposes.[183]

We should not discount the possibility that some form of concrete relationship with Jewish Christ-believers is also on view in Ephesians, even though Jewish Christ-believers are not the primary focus of the letter. As Campbell points out, the language of reconciliation between Jew and gentile needs some basis in social reality.[184] I will argue that the connection between Jewish and gentile Christ-believers is best understood in terms of the early mission through Israel to the nations in which the Jewish apostolic community, especially Paul, played a key role. The discussion of the unity of Israel and gentiles is thus aiming to affirm and advocate an inter-congregational unity, grounded in the apostolic mission.[185] In this reading, the notion of "peace" between the gentiles and Israel (Eph 2:14–18) is not limited to peace within congregations or between local Christ-believing congregations and local synagogues; rather it is the worldwide "peace" between Israel and the nations, ground-

---

181. Dunn, *Beginning from Jerusalem*, 1108; cf. Dahl, "Gentiles, Christians, and Israelites," 38.

182. Thielman, *Ephesians*, 19–28. Thielman here highlights the dynamics of Paul's apostolic ministry as significant for the letter's purpose (cf. Eph 3:13), along with Paul's aim to remind the readers of their role in God's plan for the world.

183. See esp. chapter 5.

184. Campbell, "Unity and Diversity," 21–23; *pace* Dahl, "Gentiles, Christians, and Israelites," 36; cf. Moritz, who regards the "subtle use of Israel's Scriptures" as evidence of a concrete relationship with Jewish Christ-believers (*A Profound Mystery*, 216–17).

185. See esp. chapter 6.

ed in Christ's sacrifice, and established primarily through the gospel-preaching mission of the early Jewish apostolic community (Eph 2:17).

Colossians

Authorship

The Pauline authorship of Colossians, like that of Ephesians, is also commonly disputed, although less often.[186] Again, I will summarize some of the most common objections to Pauline authorship, along with some counters to these objections.

The first objection is based on the observation that there are differences in vocabulary and style between Paul's undisputed letters and Colossians. However, given the very small sample from which these observations are made (Colossians has ninety-five verses), it is normally conceded that such conclusions are too reliant on subjective factors and are not by themselves conclusive.[187] The differences may, for example, be explained by use of an amanuensis or greater involvement of the co-author Timothy.[188]

The second objection, which we also noted above in relation to Ephesians, is that Colossians contains theological perspectives that appear to be developed beyond the undisputed Pauline letters. There is, for example, a strikingly "cosmic" Christology evident in Colossians: "it is upon the core teaching of the centrality, uniqueness, and supremacy of Christ that all the theological themes of the letter are constructed."[189] There is also a more "universal view of the church" which Foster claims "is more developed than what is found in the earlier letters .... The emphasis falls heavy [sic] upon Christ's primacy over the church, which is a corporate entity constituted of Christ-followers."[190] Furthermore, Foster notes, the greater emphasis on realized eschatology (e.g., 2:11–12; 3:1) with less explicit reference to the second coming of Christ, while in continuity with Pauline thought, appears to be too domesticated to have

186. E.g., Dunn argues for Paul's involvement alongside Timothy in the authorship of Colossians but against Pauline authorship of Ephesians in any direct sense (*Beginning from Jerusalem*, 1038–40, 1106–9).

187. Foster, *Colossians*, 67–69.

188. Dunn, *Beginning from Jerusalem*, 1038–39.

189. Foster, *Colossians*, 24.

190. Ibid., 39–40, cf. 69–71.

been penned by Paul himself.[191] As with Ephesians, however, it has been argued that these distinctive emphases may be understood in light of the particular situation to which the letter was written.[192] Indeed, as we will see, Colossians stresses the place of the Colossian community within the context of the worldwide progress of the gospel (e.g., Col 1:5–8, 24–49; 4:3–4); in such a context a special emphasis on the supremacy of Christ and the universal nature of the church is understandable.[193]

A third objection involves the social perspective reflected in the household table (Col 3:18—4:1) which, it is claimed, has a non-Pauline character. Foster, as we saw above, sees a strong dissonance between the apparent abolition of social distinctions evident in 3:11, which he regards as an "inclusive and emancipatory Pauline charter," and the apparent desire to maintain social norms in 3:18—4:1, which he regards as "a social conservatism that is not representative of wider Pauline theology."[194] However, the same kind of views also exist alongside each other in the undisputed Pauline epistles (cf. e.g., 1 Cor 12:13 with 1 Cor 7:17–24).[195]

There are a few other factors that seem to weigh in support of Pauline authorship of Colossians. Firstly, there is the mention of various people known from his letter to Philemon to have been involved with Paul (Col 4:7–17; cf. Phlm 23–24).[196] This is sometimes explained by positing that the non-Pauline author of Colossians is seeking deliberately to portray the letter as written to the same life-setting as that of Philemon.[197] Others counter that such a hypothesis is unnecessarily complex, and that it is difficult to discern the precise function of such an elaborate device.[198] In addition, the lack of any reference to a major earthquake in Lycus Valley, which occurred some time between 60–64 C.E., may also suggest an early date for Colossians.[199] However, caution is needed here since, as

191. Ibid., 46–49, 70.

192. Pao, *Colossians & Philemon*, 20–21.

193. See chapter 7.

194. Foster, *Colossians*, 48.

195. On 1 Cor 7:17–24 see further Tucker, *Remain in Your Calling*.

196. Dunn, *Beginning from Jerusalem*, 1039.

197. E.g., Foster, *Colossians*, 84–85.

198. Pao, *Colossians & Philemon*, 22–23; Dunn, *Beginning from Jerusalem*, 1039.

199. Ibid.

Foster demonstrates, "the case for the abandonment of Colossae [after the earthquake] has recently been shown to be questionable."[200]

As with Ephesians, then, I will in this book refer to the author of Colossians as "Paul," who is at least the implied author of the letter (along with Timothy), and quite likely the real author also.

Setting and Purpose

What exactly is the situation to which Colossians is written? Paul does seem to be reacting to a real issue or perceived threat to the community (see e.g., Col 2:4, 8, 20).[201] The threat could arise from a range of sources including, for example, actual false teachers in Colossae, the attraction of the community to the views of outsiders, or differing understandings of Christ within the community.[202] This is a significant question for our purposes, since as we have seen, elements of Jewish identity such as circumcision and Sabbaths appear to be at least part of the mix that Paul regards as a threat to the Colossians. Thus, it is important to understand the perceived threat, so that we can better discern what Paul is or is not asserting about Jewish identity in Colossians.

The concrete nature of the threat is perhaps most clearly outlined in Col 2:16–23.[203] Paul fears that the community is in danger of adopting a "philosophy" (cf. v. 8) that is aligned with the "elements of the world" (v. 20, cf. v. 8), forbids certain bodily actions including eating and drinking certain foods (vv. 16, 21), advocates the "worship of angels" (v. 18), and places great weight upon the observance of certain ceremonies such as festivals, new moons, and Sabbaths (v. 16). The final element in this list of ceremonies—i.e., Sabbaths—is clearly Jewish. The other elements, while they could be Jewish, were also features of many other religious traditions of the time and place.[204] What, then, is the nature of this threat?

Some scholars locate the source of the threat in the local Jewish synagogue or synagogues.[205] Dunn, for example, argues that there is evi-

---

200. Foster, *Colossians*, 3–8, quotation from p. 4.

201. Ibid., 106–7.

202. Shkul, "New Identity," 378–79.

203. Foster, *Colossians*, 107–8.

204. Cf. ibid., 280–82.

205. E.g., Wright, *Colossians and Philemon*, 23–33; Dunn, *Colossians and Philemon*, 29–33.

dence for a substantial Jewish population in the vicinity of Colossae (see e.g., Josephus, *Ant.* 12.147–53), from which he concludes that there was most likely a significant Jewish presence in Colossae itself.[206] He notes that "[t]he implication of several passages in Colossians [i.e. Col 1:12, 27; 2:13; 3:11; 4:11] is that the readers were predominantly Gentiles who through the gospel had now been given to share in privileges hitherto known only to Israel."[207] Furthermore, the letter seems to be concerned with various elements of Jewish identity including food laws, circumcision, and the rejection of idolatry (Col 2:11, 13, 16; 3:5, 11; 4:11); in addition the "worship of angels" seems to be aligned to Jewish mystical traditions.[208] Dunn does not believe that the Jews of Colossae were "vigorously evangelistic," but rather that the Colossian Christ-believing community would have been attracted to the synagogue's way of life and were in danger of being persuaded by Jewish apologetic endeavors.[209] Bird, on the other hand, argues that the references to circumcision in Colossians "could hardly be heard as any other than an intra-Jewish debate stemming from factional rivalries over the nature and boundaries of Jewish identity" and that the philosophy being referred to "arguably represents an attempt by one or more Jewish individuals to recruit Christian Gentiles to a form of Jewish belief and practice through a highly contextualized missionary approach."[210] In either case, Colossians is understood by these scholars to be directed against concrete Jewish practices.

However, when examined more closely, the evidence of a specifically Jewish threat to the Colossian believers is far from convincing. Foster notes that "there is no conclusive evidence either for the presence or absence of Jews in Colossae during the mid- to late first century."[211] He also observes that "in contrast to several of the other Pauline letters there is a relative lack of interest in Jewish matters in Colossians."[212] Foster proposes that the nature of the threat in Colossae is a more generalized

206. Dunn, *Beginning from Jerusalem*, 1036.

207. Ibid., 1037.

208. Ibid., 1043–45. Smith identifies the source of the teaching as a form of Jewish Merkabah mysticism (*Heavenly Perspective*).

209. Dunn, *Colossians and Philemon*, 32.

210. Bird, *Colossians & Philemon*, 34.

211. Foster, *Colossians*, 10–14, quotation from p. 10.

212. Ibid., 10. The scarcity of direct use of Jewish Scriptures (ibid., 52–60) also suggests a situation where the readers are not in direct contact with Jewish synagogue teachers.

"syncretistic . . . religious pluralism."[213] For Foster, this best accounts for the religious environment in Colossae:

> [P]agan religion throughout Phrygia (and the rest of Asia Minor) was largely syncretistic in nature . . . . Given that the Colossian believers were drawn from the majority Hellenistic culture of the region with syncretistic religious practices, it appears likely that some of the recent believers in Christ at Colossae saw nothing untoward in combining elements of their new faith with their earlier commitment to some of the mystery cults that perhaps offered more ecstatic rites than Christianity. This may have also entailed drawing elements from Judaism, although that remains less certain.[214]

Thus, it is quite likely that Colossians is seeking to counter a perceived threat from a general milieu of syncretistic religious pluralism, rather than from specifically Jewish sources. Nevertheless, the Jewish elements we noted above need to be accounted for. The most satisfactory way to account for this evidence is to assume that the threat involves "a syncretism with Jewish elements providing the controlling framework."[215] If this is the case, then Colossians is not seeking directly to undermine Jewish identity or distinctiveness. Rather, it is seeking to counter a situation in which certain Jewish practices or beliefs have been co-opted into a syncretistic mix that has the potential to draw the Colossians away from their allegiance to Christ. This understanding of the background to the letter will be significant when we come to examine its discussion of circumcision, Sabbaths, and other practices in detail.[216]

While the nature of the religious threat has received a great deal of attention in discerning the purpose of Colossians, there is another feature of the letter that has received far less consideration in this regard: the frequent references to the ongoing mission and ministry of Paul and his co-workers (e.g., Col 1:1, 5–7, 23–29; 2:1–5; 4:2–4, 7–18), including various references to Paul's hardships, struggles, and imprisonment (Col 1:24, 29; 2:1; 4:3, 18). The references to the Pauline mission are often understood as a further means to counter the threat in Colossae: if the teaching about Christ's supremacy can be shown to be widely accepted,

213. Ibid., 16. Cf. Lohse, who regards it as a "pre-gnostic" syncretism (*Colossians and Philemon*, 2–3, 127–31).

214. Foster, *Colossians*, 109.

215. Pao, *Colossians & Philemon*, 31.

216. See chapter 7.

including by many authority figures known to the Colossians, then the Colossians will be more likely to accept it.[217] While this may well be the case, it does not explain the emphasis on Paul's imprisonment, which (as in Eph 3:1, 13) seems to be raised by Paul as a problem in need of explanation. Esler, on the assumption that Ephesians, Colossians, and 2 Timothy are "pseudo-Pauline,"[218] sees the reference to Paul's imprisonment as a "memorialization" designed to provide an example of steadfastness for communities facing persecution.[219] However, there is no reference in either Ephesians or Colossians to the readers being persecuted. Both letters speak only of *Paul's* imprisonment. The imprisonment is not mentioned as an example, but as an issue that needs to be resolved because it imperils the gospel message itself. There is an explanation that fits this evidence: as in Ephesians, Paul is concerned that the Christ-believing readers in Colossae, on hearing of Paul's imprisonment, might lose confidence in the gospel message and the mission through which it came. The gospel message had proclaimed Christ as supreme, and yet the great proclaimer of that gospel, Paul, had been imprisoned by secular powers. In Colossae, this seeming dissonance may well have led the believers to turn back to more familiar syncretistic religious practices for security. In such a scenario, the believers needed to be persuaded to have confidence *both* in the supremacy of Christ *and* in the success of the worldwide mission through which the gospel had come, and of which Paul played a key role. Thus, Paul needed to explain his imprisonment in terms of the success of the ongoing gospel mission—which is precisely what he does here (e.g., Col 1:23–25; 2:4–5; 4:3).

This survey of the nature and purpose of Colossians provides us with two guiding principles for our post-supersessionist reading of the letter. Firstly, since the threat to the Colossians is most likely a syncretistic religious pluralism incorporating certain Jewish elements, we cannot assume that statements in the letter are straightforwardly directed against features of Jewish identity. Secondly, we should be alert to the possibility that a feature in the foreground of Ephesians may also be in the background of Colossians: i.e. that the apostolic mission is closely connected with a priestly ministry through Israel to the nations.

217. E.g., Foster, *Colossians*, 93–95.

218. Esler, "Remember My Fetters," 231.

219. Esler, "Remember My Fetters."

Christ through Israel to the Nations
in Ephesians and Colossians

The approach in the following chapters will be primarily exegetical, but with a focus on how Ephesians and Colossians portray the dynamics of divine blessing "in Christ" proceeding through Israel to the nations. Throughout the exegesis, I will seek to highlight the connection between Israel's divine vocation and the apostolic mission to the nations. I will conduct a sustained engagement with Ephesians (chapters 3–6), followed by a briefer application of the insights gained to the text of Colossians (chapter 7).

As the exegesis proceeds, especially in Ephesians, we will see how the relationship between Israel and the nations is caught up in a *movement* toward blessing and unity. This "unity" needs to be understood rightly. While unity is an important feature of the letter, it is not portrayed as a monochrome unity in which distinctions are erased. Indeed, in Ephesians, unity is achieved *through* diversity, not despite it nor against it. Thus, the concept of a distinct ethnic Jewish identity is an important element in the argument of the letter. Jewish distinctiveness in Ephesians is not portrayed merely as a problem to be overcome, but as a key means for God to achieve blessing for the nations "in Christ." Furthermore, Ephesians does not portray a static vision of unity, but a dynamic vision. By means of the apostolic mission, Christ's blessings are shared through Israel with the nations, resulting in mutual blessing. This dynamic forms a key part of God's cosmic purposes through Christ. It also has implications for the everyday speech and the lives of gentile Christ-believers as they are caught up in and live out this gospel dynamic.

In sum, I will present a positive case that Paul in Ephesians assumes that the distinct identity and calling of Jewish people has an ongoing value, because he regards Israel as the original bearer of divine blessing and links Israel's vocation with the apostolic ministry to the nations. Although Paul argues for the supreme value of finding one's identity in Christ, which implies equality between Jews and gentiles in Christ, this equality does not negate the positive value for Israel's distinct calling within the divine plan. This special calling for Israel is a key factor in the argument of Ephesians; it is also a plausible background assumption for the argument of Colossians.

3

Christ's Blessings through Israel
to the Nations (Ephesians 1)

IN CHAPTER 2, WE saw the potential of a post-supersessionist perspective
for highlighting the dynamics of the apostolic mission within Ephesians
and Colossians. I will now commence a sustained engagement with
Ephesians, paying special attention to those elements of the text that
are relevant to the apostolic mission, and seeking to discern their connection to any Jew-gentile dynamic. In this chapter, focusing on Eph
1, we will see how the apostolic mission is portrayed as the means by
which Christ's blessings have come through Israel to the nations. We will
examine the significance for this theme of: Paul's introduction of himself
as an "apostle" (Eph 1:1a), Paul's complex designation of his readers as
"the holy ones, who are also believers in Christ Jesus" (Eph 1:1b), the
Jewish context of the "blessing" (Eph 1:3), the dynamic movement of
"blessing" from "us" to "you" through the preaching of the gospel (Eph
1:4–14), and the apostolic prayer (Eph 1:15–23).

Paul's Apostolic Mission (Eph 1:1a)

In the opening words of Ephesians, Paul[1] introduces himself as an
apostle of Christ:

> Paul, an apostle of Christ Jesus by the will of God . . . (Eph 1:1a)

---

1. See chapter 2 for my defence of the use of "Paul" to describe the author of
Ephesians, despite the fact that historical Pauline authorship is disputed by many
scholars.

The term "apostle" is often understood primarily in terms of *authority*. Several interpreters argue that the author's main purpose in using the term is to claim the authority that derives from the office of apostle, in order to lend weight to the commands in the rest of the letter.[2] Admittedly, the term "apostle" does imply an authoritative status, and can indeed be described as an "office." However, this emphasis on authority can obscure the term's more fundamental significance. In Paul's undisputed letters, when he refers to himself as an "apostle" (ἀπόστολος) or as possessing an "apostolate" (ἀποστολή), he is speaking of his role as an envoy or a *foundational missionary*—an individual commissioned by God to bring the gospel of Christ to the nations (see e.g., Rom 1:1, 5; 11:13; Gal 2:8; 1 Cor 4:9).[3] Indeed, as Best points out, in these instances he tends *not* to use the term "apostle" primarily to assert his authority. Rather, he uses the term when defending his ministry, or in "contexts in which there is some connection with either the truth or the proclamation of the gospel."[4] Hence, as we approach Eph 1:1, we should at least begin with the assumption that the term is being used primarily as a way of referring to Paul's ministry of gospel proclamation.[5]

When we examine Paul's self-references in the rest of the letter, we find that his gospel ministry to the nations is indeed a key motif. In Eph 3:1–13, Paul maintains that his imprisonment and its associated sufferings are not an obstacle to such gospel ministry; rather, they are a significant element of this ministry. His role is to take the "mystery" (Eph 3:4) which has been revealed to the "apostles and prophets" (Eph 3:5) and to bring it to the world—that is, "to evangelize the nations" (τοῖς ἔθνεσιν εὐαγγελίσασθαι, Eph 3:8). In Eph 6:19–20, Paul asks for prayer that he might be able to "make known the mystery of the gospel" for which he is an "ambassador in chains." Furthermore, his prayers for his readers are directed at an increase in love and knowledge arising from this gospel message (Eph 1:15–23, cf. 1:13; 3:14–21). Paul's later self-references in Ephesians, then, are consistent with understanding the term "apostle" in

2. Lincoln, *Ephesians*, 6; Best, *Ephesians*, 96–97; Hoehner, *Ephesians*, 135; Thielman, *Ephesians*, 32–33; Arnold, *Ephesians*, 68.

3. Cf. Caird, *Letters from Prison*, 30.

4. Best, "Apostolic Authority?," quotation from 36. Cf. Barnett, "Apostle."

5. *Pace* Best, *Ephesians*, 96–97 who, despite his conclusions elsewhere about the undisputed Pauline epistles ("Apostolic Authority?"), takes the term in Eph 1:1 to be primarily a statement of Paul's "authority," which lends weight to the commands in the letter.

Eph 1:1 primarily in terms of Paul's gospel-preaching mission. The word is thus intended to invoke Paul's role as a foundational missionary "of Christ Jesus," commissioned to bring the gospel of Christ to the nations. Although this does of course also imply an authoritative status, its use at the beginning of the letter implies that we should expect Paul's *missionary* role, not simply his authority, to be significant for what follows.

Paul's self-reference as "apostle" anticipates the three further references in Ephesians to plural "apostles." These "apostles" (along with the "prophets") are described firstly as the foundation on which Israel and the gentiles are united (Eph 2:19–20); secondly as the initial recipients of divine revelation concerning gentile inclusion in divine blessings (Eph 3:5–6); and thirdly as the first and second in a series of unfolding gifts from the ascended Christ to his church ("the body") which enable the body to grow together in knowledge, love, and unity (Eph 4:11–16). In the immediate context of each reference, there is a movement of God's blessings in which the key agent is Christ (Eph 2:17, 20; 3:11; 4:11, 15–16), the key instrument is a message (Eph 2:17; 3:6–7; 4:11, 15), and the key result is that gentiles are brought in to share in God's blessing (Eph 2:13–22; 3:6; 4:13–16).[6] In other words, the use of the term "apostle" in the body of Ephesians is associated with a dynamic involving Christ's blessing, through a message, going to the nations. The use of the term "apostle" at the start of the letter, therefore, leads us to expect this dynamic to be significant to the concerns of a letter.

Paul's apostleship is "by the will of God" (Eph 1:1). Again, many commentators take this phrase primarily as a claim that the author's authority to issue commands has divine backing.[7] However, the phrase may be understood more broadly, considering the use of the term "will" (θέλημα) in the rest of the letter. In Ephesians, God's "will" is his "larger purpose"[8] for the entire creation; a purpose that he is currently working out in the human sphere. It undergirds his predetermination to bring the blessings of adoption and inheritance to his people (Eph 1:5, 11); it has now been revealed (Eph 1:9); and it will finally be achieved when all things are united in Christ (Eph 1:10). Because God's "will" takes concrete shape within history, and because it involves a particular purpose and future hope, it can be used as a basis for admonitions to understand the

6. See the discussion of "apostles and prophets" in chapter 5.

7. Lincoln, *Ephesians*, 5; Best, *Ephesians*, 97; Hoehner, *Ephesians*, 136–37; Arnold, *Ephesians*, 68.

8. Caird, *Letters from Prison*, 30.

nature of the current time (Eph 5:16–17), and as a ground for right action in light of future reward (Eph 6:6–8). In Eph 1:1, this "will" or purpose of God is said to undergird Paul's apostolic ministry. The implication is that Paul's gospel-preaching role has a key part to play in bringing about these purposes.

Thus, considering the use of similar terminology in the rest of Ephesians, Paul's introduction of himself as "an apostle of Christ Jesus by the will of God" is not simply a claim to a kind of static authority to issue commands to an individual congregation. The phrase is rich with connotations of a dynamic mission. This mission is intended by God to enact his purposes for the world, is proceeding apace, and presumably has significant implications for the readers of the letter.

Who, then, are these readers, and what is their relationship to Paul's apostolic mission?

Holy Ones—Who Are Also Christ-believers (Eph 1:1b)

Paul specifies his addressees with a nuanced phrase that has generated a great deal of discussion:

> to the holy ones, who are also believers in Christ Jesus (Eph 1:1b, my translation)

Most modern translations of Eph 1:1 also include the phrase "in Ephesus" (ἐν Ἐφέσῳ). However, the phrase is absent from key early manuscripts.[9] The most probable original reading is: "to the holy ones [i.e., saints], who are also believers in Christ Jesus" (τοῖς ἁγίοις [τοῖς] οὖσιν καὶ πιστοῖς ἐν Χριστῷ Ἰησοῦ).[10] However, many modern interpreters

---

9. Best, "Ephesians 1.1"; Barth, *Ephesians*, 67. The phrase ἐν Ἐφέσῳ is absent from key early witnesses such as 𝔓⁴⁶ ℵ* B*, as well as from minuscules 6, 1739, the corrector of 424, and many or all of the older manuscripts known to Basil. Without the phrase, the syntax seems a little awkward; Origen and Basil appear to struggle with it. However, this syntactical awkwardness is a point in favor of its originality. It is easy to see how a scribe might have added a destination for the letter after οὖσιν to smooth out the syntax and to conform it to other Pauline epistles (cf. Rom 1:7; 1 Cor 1:2; 2 Cor 1:1; Phil 1:1). However, it is very difficult to see why ἐν Ἐφέσῳ would be omitted to create such apparent awkwardness. Various conjectural solutions have been proposed—e.g., a space was included so individual destinations such as ἐν Ἐφέσῳ could be added later—but these all lack any concrete evidence. For further discussion see Best, "Ephesians 1.1 Again."

10. ℵ* B* 6 1739 etc. τοῖς is omitted in 𝔓⁴⁶.

regard this reading as too difficult to admit as original. The first problem is that the syntax seems awkward.[11] This syntactical difficulty is taken as evidence against its originality, despite the external textual evidence in its favor. Nevertheless, the syntax is not impossible, and so syntax alone cannot be used to discount the reading.[12] The more substantial issue raised by modern interpreters is that the reading does not seem to make any sense.[13] Best, for example, sees it as tautological, since "almost by definition the saints are those who are faithful in Christ Jesus."[14] Hoehner believes it "utterly lacks sense and is out of keeping with the style of the author."[15]

However, the possibilities raised by a post-supersessionist perspective helps us to make sense of this early reading, in a way that coheres with the letter as a whole. It is possible that, in using such nuanced phraseology for his addressees, Paul is introducing one of the themes of the letter: Christ-believing gentiles have, remarkably, been made participants in the holiness that had once been the prerogative of God's ancient people Israel.[16] By designating his gentile addressees in this precise way—as "the holy ones, who are also believers in Christ Jesus"—Paul emphasizes the fact that the designation "holy ones" is not only applicable to God's

11. Best, "Ephesians 1.1," 5. Cf. Arnold, *Ephesians*, 26.

12. The construction is in the form: article-substantive-article-participle of εἰμί-additive adverb καί-adjective. While complex, it is not impossible. Individual elements of the construction have parallels elsewhere. For example, the construction article-substantive-article-participle of εἰμί-qualifying phrase is quite common (e.g., John 12:17; Acts 11:1; Rom 7:23; Eph 4:18; and many others). A participle of εἰμί followed by an additive adverb καί, while less common, is also possible (Luke 23:7). In Ephesians, the additive καί is used extensively, especially when comparing groups of people (e.g., Eph 1:11, 13 [2x], 15; 2:3, 22; 4:4, 17; 5:2; etc.), which increases the probability that an additive καί is being used at this point.

13. Best maintains that "the real difficulty commentators have with the B text is its meaning" ("Ephesians 1.1," 7). Thielman maintains that "the text without ἐν Ἐφέσῳ . . . produces almost unintelligible Greek" (*Ephesians*, 36).

14. Best, "Ephesians 1.1," 5. Cf. Best, "Ephesians 1.1 Again," 21. See also Lincoln, *Ephesians*, 2.

15. Hoehner, *Ephesians*, 147.

16. So Caird, *Letters from Prison*, 31; Kümmel, *Introduction*, 355. Kümmel here sees the second part of the phrase as a "more precise designation" for the first, which refers to the "old people of God." He regards this as evidence against Pauline authorship: for Kümmel, it is "inconceivable" for Paul to have thought of the old people of God as holy, although an "unknown author" might have done so. Kümmel's view appears to arise from an assumption that the historical Paul's thought is supersessionist—a perspective which, as we have seen, is far less common today (see chapter 2).

ancient people Israel, as might perhaps be assumed by those familiar with the Scriptures (cf. e.g., Exod 19:6; Deut 7:6; Ps 68:35 LXX; Dan 7:18), but that it is *also [or even]* applicable to those who believe in Christ Jesus.[17] There are several good reasons to adopt this interpretation.

Firstly, this perspective—i.e. that gentile participation in holiness through faith in Christ is true yet remarkable—is found elsewhere in the New Testament. For example, it is the burden of Peter's speech to the Council of Jerusalem in Acts 15:

> And after there had been much debate, Peter stood up and said to them, "Brothers, you know that in the early days God made a choice among you, that by my mouth the Gentiles should hear the word of the gospel and believe. And God, who knows the heart, bore witness to them, by giving them the Holy Spirit just as he did to us, and he made no distinction between us and them, having cleansed their hearts by faith." (Acts 15:7–9)

The fact that the early Jewish Christ-believers needed a council to discuss the possibility that Christ-believing gentiles, too, could be "cleansed" and receive the "Holy Spirit" demonstrates that it was a remarkable concept for them. Indeed, Paul's defense before Agrippa in Acts 26 highlights this remarkable truth concerning gentile inclusion in holiness by faith, portraying it as the climactic element in Paul's own commissioning. Jesus sends Paul to "the gentiles" (Acts 26:17)

> so that they may receive forgiveness of sins and a portion (κλῆρον) among those who are made holy (ἐν τοῖς ἡγιασμένοις), by faith (πίστει) in me (Acts 26:18, my translation).

Secondly, Ephesians itself often emphasizes this amazing-but-true fact that gentile Christ-believers "also" (καί) participate in various aspects of "holiness," including the Holy Spirit and the holy temple:

> In him *you also* (καὶ ὑμεῖς) when you heard the word of truth, the gospel of your salvation, and believed in him, were sealed with the promised Holy Spirit, ... (Eph 1:13 ESV, emphasis added).

> ... in whom the whole structure, being joined together, grows into a holy temple in the Lord. In him *you also* (καὶ ὑμεῖς) are

17. This view is both predicated upon and supports the understanding that πιστοῖς should be understood in its active sense as "believers" rather than as "faithful." See Lincoln, *Ephesians*, 6; Thielman, *Ephesians*, 34; Arnold, *Ephesians*, 69.

being built together into a dwelling place for God by the Spirit.
(Eph 2:21–22 ESV, emphasis added).[18]

Thirdly, this interpretation of the earliest textual witnesses explains the alternative textual witnesses. Later Christians came to see the holiness of Christ-believers as commonplace. Thus, the phrase "to the holy ones—to those who are also believers in Christ Jesus" seemed redundant to a reader such as Origen who, while a Greek speaker, was living two centuries after the apostolic era.[19] Although we have seen that the phrase is not redundant according to the perspective found elsewhere in the New Testament, or indeed in the rest of Ephesians, it may well have been puzzling for scribes in the post-apostolic era. It is entirely conceivable, then, that they added the phrase "in Ephesus" (ἐν Ἐφέσῳ) to conform the letter to other Pauline epistles in which the phrase "to those who are" (τοῖς οὖσιν) or "to [the church of God] which is" (τῇ οὔσῃ) is followed by a phrase specifying the location of the readers ("in Rome," ἐν Ῥώμῃ, Rom 1:7; "in Corinth," ἐν Κορίνθῳ, 1 Cor 1:2, 2 Cor 1:1; "in Philippi," ἐν Φιλίπποις, Phil 1:1). However, the earliest witnesses to Eph 1:1 do not specify a geographical location. The only "location" for the readers that matters is their place "in Christ" (ἐν Χριστῷ Ἰησοῦ). The text therefore emphasizes the fact that the readers' holiness is connected to their place and status as Christ-believers.

Understanding the text in this way also provides insight into the occasion and purpose of Ephesians. It strengthens the view that the letter has a wider scope, beyond the concerns of any particular congregation or congregations. This is consistent with features of the rest of the letter. For example, it is difficult to see how the historical Paul would write a letter intended primarily for congregations "in Ephesus," whom he knew and had worked among for so long according to his letters and traditions about his ministry (e.g., Acts 18:19–21; 19:1—20:2; 20:17–38; 1 Cor 15:32; 16:8–9; 1 Tim 1:3; 2 Tim 1:18; 4:12), and yet in that letter state that he had simply "heard" of their faith and love (Eph 1:15), that he is "assuming" (εἴ γε) that they have "heard" of his ministry (Eph 3:2), and that he is "assuming" (εἴ γε) that they had "heard" of Christ and been "taught" in him (Eph 4:21). Nor is it easy to see how somebody writing in

18. In both passages the additive adverb καί ("also") is used, as it is in Eph 1:1; cf. Eph 2:3.

19. Origen saw the participle οὖσιν as syntactically redundant and sought to explain it in ontological terms. See Heine, *Origen and Jerome*, 80; Best, "Ephesians 1.1," 6–7.

the name of Paul but with knowledge of his letters and the traditions concerning his apostolic ministry could write in such a way.[20] However, if we understand the letter as having a deliberately broad scope, this difficulty disappears. Granted, the antiquity of the traditional superscription "to [the] Ephesians" (πρὸς Ἐφεσίους),[21] along with the fact that Tychicus is named as an emissary and so presumably was the letter-bearer (Eph 6:21, cf. Col 4:7),[22] makes it likely that Paul envisaged that the letter would be received and read by churches in a general region that included Ephesus. Nevertheless, as we noted in chapter 2, the letter has broad horizons, and does not seem to be intended to address particular congregational issues. This is important to bear in mind as we approach the rest of the letter.

This emphasis on gentile *inclusion* in holiness in Eph 1:1 is seen even more clearly when it is contrasted to the parallel designation of addressees in Col 1:2. Colossians as a whole does not lay the same stress on the inclusion of gentile Christ-believers in Israel's privileges. Accordingly, Col 1:2 simply states that the believing brothers in Colossae are holy: it is written "to the holy and believing brothers in Christ in Colossae" (τοῖς ἐν Κολοσσαῖς ἁγίοις καὶ πιστοῖς ἀδελφοῖς ἐν Χριστῷ; Col 1:2, my translation). This does not mean there is an irreconcilable contradiction between the two letters; it simply indicates different perspectives and thrusts. In both Colossians and Ephesians, faith in Christ is connected with holiness. In Colossians, the connection is simply stated; in Ephesians, the connection is stressed and its existence becomes significant for the rest of the letter.[23]

This discussion raises a question that often arises in the interpretation of Ephesians: What is the referent of the term the "saints" (i.e., the "holy ones") in this letter? Often the question is framed in terms of two simple alternatives: either "the saints" refers to all believers, or it refers to Jewish believers.[24] Yet, the perspective on holiness we have seen is more subtle than can be conveyed by this simple "either-or" dichotomy. The burden of Ephesians is not that one group or another has the right to the name "the saints." Rather, the burden of Ephesians is that, in Christ, there has been a dynamic *movement* of holiness through Israel to the nations. The point is this: *not only* can Israel be called holy, *but also* gentile

---

20. Thielman, *Ephesians*, 15.

21. Best, "Ephesians 1.1," 3–4.

22. Collins, *Diakonia*, 222–23.

23. See further chapter 7.

24. See e.g., Thielman, *Ephesians*, 33–34.

Christ-believers can be called holy. Thus, the distinctive holiness of Israel is assumed in Ephesians, while the remarkable holiness of gentile Christ-believers is asserted and celebrated. This is the thrust of Eph 1:1, 13, 18; 2:19, 21–22; 3:18; 5:27. We will return to this question of the identity of "the saints" again when we examine Eph 2:19.[25]

We see, then, how adopting a post-supersessionist reading allows us to bring forward a possible explanation for a textual issue which has been deemed unfathomable by many other interpreters. Indeed, if we understand Eph 1:1 in this way—which, after all, is simply seeking to make sense of the most likely original reading—we can see how it sets up some key themes that will recur throughout Ephesians. The apostle, the missionary of Christ, is enacting the purposes of God in the world. He is writing to Christ-believing gentiles who, indeed *as* Christ-believers, can be called "holy ones," and he implies through his phraseology that this fact is remarkable. These points will prove to be significant for the dynamics that arise in the rest of the letter.

Israel's Blessing Fulfilled in Christ (Eph 1:3)

In Eph 1:3, the apostle praises the God who has "blessed us in Christ":

> Blessed be the God and Father of our Lord Jesus Christ, who has blessed us in Christ with every spiritual blessing in the heavenly places . . . (Eph 1:3)

The phrase "Blessed be God" (Εὐλογητὸς ὁ θεὸς) introduces a single, syntactically complex sentence (Eph 1:3–14),[26] whose dominant tone is one of praise for the abundance of blessing God has poured out "in Christ." These blessings include election to holiness (v. 4), predetermination for adoption (v. 5), redemption through the blood of Jesus Christ (v. 7), forgiveness (v. 7), the knowledge of God's purposes (vv. 9–10), the "obtain[ing] of an inheritance" (v. 11), and sealing with the Holy Spirit (v. 13). The blessings in this opening passage introduce many of the key themes of the letter as a whole.[27]

---

25. See chapter 4.

26. O'Brien notes that Eph 1:3–14 contains "an accumulation of relative clauses, participial and infinitival constructions, a large collection of prepositional expressions . . . and instances of synonymous words linked together with the genitive case, as well as other genitival constructions" ("Unusual Introduction," 506).

27. Ibid., 510–12.

Most commentators agree that Eph 1:3–14 has many formal similarities to the Jewish *berakhah* (בְּרָכָה, "blessing").[28] In the Hebrew Scriptures, the term "blessed" (בָּרוּךְ/LXX εὐλογητός) is frequently used to introduce discourses praising God for acts of protection and salvation. Often in the openings of such *berakhoth*, God is blessed as "the God of Israel" (e.g., 1 Sam 25:32; 1 Kgs 1:48; 8:15; Pss 41:13 [MT 41:14, LXX 40:14]; 68:35 [MT 68:36, LXX 67:36]; 72:18 [LXX 71:18]; 106:48 [LXX 105:48]; 1 Chr 16:36; 29:10; 2 Chr 2:12 [MT/LXX 2:11], 6:4) or of Israel's progenitors (e.g., Gen 9:26; 24:27; Ezra 7:27); these terms emphasize God's particular protection or salvation for his special people. The *berakhah* form also appears in various places in Second Temple literature; there too, God is often described as the God of Israel or Israel's progenitors (e.g., 1QM 13.2; Tob 8:5; 1 Macc 4:30; 3 Macc 7:23; cf. Luke 1:68).

In Eph 1:3–14, a comparable Jewish "blessing" formula is used, but with a strongly Christological thrust. God is not here named as the "God of Israel" or of Israel's progenitors, but rather as the "God and Father of our Lord Jesus Christ" (v. 3). Furthermore, God's blessing itself is said to have been given "in Christ" (v. 3), an expression that is repeated in various forms throughout the passage ("in Christ," v. 10; "in him," vv. 4, 9, 10; "in the beloved," v. 6; "in whom," v. 7, 11, 13). This raises the question of whether "Christ" is being portrayed as a *replacement* for Israel within this *berakhah*, or whether the relationship between Israel and Christ should be understood in some other way.

A key to answering this question is found in scriptural antecedents to the concept of "blessing in." Although, as we have seen, scholars often discuss the Jewish background to the phrase "blessed be God" (Εὐλογητὸς ὁ θεός), less attention has been paid to echoes of Jewish ideas in the claim that God is "the one who has blessed us . . . in Christ" (ὁ εὐλογήσας ἡμᾶς . . . ἐν Χριστῷ). Yee argues that the background to this expression is "the Jewish wisdom tradition in which such concepts as 'wisdom' or 'Logos' were often employed to speak of God's activity and his nearness to his creation."[29] However, exemplars of the wisdom tradition do not tend to speak of being "blessed in" wisdom or the Logos. Thus, the wisdom

---

28. Barth, *Ephesians*, 77–78; Caird, *Letters from Prison*, 32–33; Lincoln, *Ephesians*, 10–11; Best, *Ephesians*, 104–8; Hoehner, *Ephesians*, 157–59; Yee, *Ethnic Reconciliation*, 35–38; Dunn, *Beginning from Jerusalem*, 1109; Arnold, *Ephesians*, 77–78; Thielman, *Ephesians*, 45–46. See also Mouton, "Memory in Search of Dignity?" 137–38; Starling, *Not My People*, 187.

29. Yee, *Ethnic Reconciliation*, 36–38.

background to this expression is by no means certain. However, there is another, closer, verbal parallel to the phrase in the Scriptures. Expressions in which people are "blessed" (verb בָּרַךְ/[ἐν]ευλογέω and cognates) "in" (בְּ/ἐν) an individual, while rare in the Scriptures generally, feature prominently in Genesis. They occur in several passages concerning Israel's progenitors—i.e., Abraham, Isaac, Jacob, and their "seed"/"offspring."[30]

In the Genesis narrative, God promises both that he will "bless" Abraham, and that all the nations of the earth will be "blessed in" Abraham:

> Now the LORD said to Abram, "Go from your country and your kindred and your father's house to the land that I will show you. And I will make of you a great nation, and I will bless (LXX εὐλογήσω) you and make your name great, so that you will be a blessing (LXX εὐλογητός). I will bless (LXX εὐλογήσω) those who bless (LXX εὐλογοῦντάς) you, and him who dishonors you I will curse, and in you all the families of the earth shall be blessed (LXX ἐνευλογηθήσονται)." (Gen 12:1–3)

This is a programmatic statement in Genesis, and it is returned to frequently throughout the subsequent narrative.[31] Six chapters later, God promises that all the nations of the earth "will be blessed in" (LXX ἐνευλογηθήσονται) Abraham (18:18). Close to the end of the Abraham sequence, after Abraham has been willing to sacrifice Isaac, God promises that the nations will be "blessed in" Abraham's "seed"/"offspring" (σπέρμα, Gen 22:17–18). In the subsequent patriarchal narrative, God promises that all nations will be "blessed in" Isaac's and Jacob's offspring (Gen 26:3–4; Gen 28:14). Furthermore, God's goodness to Abraham in protecting and providing offspring for him is used as a basis for returning blessing to God (Gen 14:20; 24:27, 48). The theme of Abraham's blessing is further developed in the prophetic tradition (Isa 51:2) and echoed in several Second Temple writings (e.g., Sir 44:21; Tob 4:12). Given that the theme of the nations being "blessed in" Abraham is such a distinctive scriptural theme, and given that elsewhere in Ephesians, Paul cites directly from Genesis (Eph 5:31, citing Gen 2:24), it is likely that in Eph 1:3 the mention of blessing "in Christ" is an allusion to this prominent scriptural theme. If this is the case, it implies that Christ is not here being

---

30. For the Abrahamic background see Barth, *Ephesians*, 28; Hoehner, *Ephesians*, 171; Fowl, *Ephesians*, 39–41.

31. Williamson, *Abraham*, 220–34.

portrayed as a *replacement* for Israel, but rather as the *fulfillment* of God's purposes *for* Israel—and further as the fulfillment of God's purposes for the nations *through* Israel.[32] Ephesians 1:3, in other words, is implying that Christ—or the "Messiah"—fulfills the role of the "seed" of Abraham, "in" whom the nations are "blessed."

This concept of the universal fulfillment of God's promises to Israel coheres with the other descriptions of God's blessing in Eph 1:3. Firstly, God is described as the one who has blessed us "with every spiritual blessing" (ἐν πάσῃ εὐλογίᾳ πνευματικῇ). The use of the term "spiritual" is not here evoking an ontological dualism between material and immaterial realities. Rather, it is indicating that the blessings received "in Christ" pertain particularly to the "Spirit."[33] In Ephesians, the Spirit is associated with the age of fulfillment of God's promises, in which Israel and the nations are united in Christ (1:13; 2:18, 22; 4:3), God's purposes are revealed (1:17; 3:5, 16), and believers are oriented toward future redemption and encouraged to exhibit speech and behavior appropriate to the new age (1:13–14; 4:30; 5:18–19; 6:17). Thus, the blessings are blessings of the new Messianic age in which God's promises have been fulfilled (cf. e.g., Isa 11:1–5). Secondly, the blessing is said to be located "in the heavenly places" (ἐν τοῖς ἐπουρανίοις). This indicates that the fulfillment of God's promise of blessing in Christ has cosmic significance. The heavenly places are the arena of Christ's victory (1:20), a victory that is shared with believers who themselves are "in the heavenly places in Christ Jesus" (2:6, cf. 6:12). The victory is also demonstrated in the united church of Jews and gentiles (3:10).[34] Ephesians 1:3 is, then, indicating that "in Christ," God's promises to Israel, and through Israel to the nations, have reached their eschatological fulfillment. Furthermore, this fulfillment has far-reaching implications, not only for the readers of the letter, but for the cosmos itself.

A similar concept is found in Galatians.[35] In Gal 3, Paul cites the promise in Genesis that all the nations would be "blessed in" Abraham

---

32. I am grateful here to Benjamin Hudson who, in a personal conversation in January 2016, suggested that the *berakhah* in Eph 1:3–14 contains a number of allusions to scriptural themes to demonstrate that in Christ, expectations for Israel are being fulfilled, and also that the gentiles are being included in those expectations.

33. Thielman, *Ephesians*, 46–47.

34. Fowl, *Ephesians*, 37–38.

35. Ibid., 39.

(v. 8), and argues that this promise has been fulfilled "in Christ" (vv. 28–29), who is Abraham's "seed"/"offspring" (v. 16):

> And the Scripture, foreseeing that God would justify the Gentiles by faith, preached the gospel beforehand to Abraham, saying, "In you (ἐν σοί) shall all the nations be blessed (ἐνευλογηθήσονται)." (Gal 3:8; citing Gen 12:3)

> There is neither Jew nor Greek, there is neither slave nor free, there is no male and female, for you are all one in Christ Jesus (ἐν Χριστῷ Ἰησοῦ). And if you are Christ's (Χριστοῦ), then you are Abraham's offspring (τοῦ Ἀβραὰμ σπέρμα), heirs according to promise. (Gal 3:28–29)

Johnson Hodge argues that the Pauline notion of "blessing in" can be understood in terms of ancient concepts of patrilineal descent. Against this background, Paul is claiming that Abraham's blessings have been passed down through various generations to his physical offspring, Christ. The offspring receives the blessings of the progenitor, and can pass these blessings on to others. Thus, for Paul, "Christ, as a genuine descendant of Abraham, serves as the crucial link between the gentiles and Abraham. Being 'in' Christ enables them to be 'in' Abraham" and thus receive the blessings.[36] While this understanding does not exhaust the multifaceted nature of the concept of being "in Christ,"[37] it does helpfully highlight the connection with scriptural antecedents. In Gal 3, as in Eph 1:3, the blessing of Abraham "in Christ" is a spiritual blessing, since it involves the reception of the "Spirit" (Gal 3:14). Furthermore, as the frame of Galatians demonstrates, this blessing "in Christ" has far-reaching implications, since it involves deliverance from "the present evil age" (Gal 1:4) and the coming of "new creation" (Gal 6:15).[38] This is comparable to the statement in Eph 1:3 that the blessings "in Christ" are "in the heavenly places," which as we have seen is the arena of Christ's victory, shared with believers.[39] These verbal and conceptual similarities

36. Johnson Hodge, *If Sons, Then Heirs*, 93–107, quotation from 103. Cf. Barth, *Ephesians*, 28.

37. Cf. Lincoln, *Ephesians*, 21–22.

38. Despite many assertions by modern commentators, it is not necessary to read the "new creation" language in Gal 6:15–16 in a supersessionist manner. See further my argument in Windsor, *Vocation of Israel*, 55–61.

39. Cf. Romans 4, in which the promise to Abraham and his offspring is universalized to become a promise that "he would be heir of the world" (Rom 4:13).

between Gal 3 and Eph 1:3 help to strengthen our argument that Eph 1:3 is alluding to the programmatic statements of Genesis, in which God promises worldwide blessing through a particular people.

To summarize our findings from Eph 1:3: Paul is implying that Christ fulfills the role of the "offspring" of Abraham "in" whom the nations are "blessed" (cf. Gen 12:3). In Christ, God's promises through Israel to the nations have reached their eschatological fulfillment. This fulfillment has far-reaching implications for the gentile readers of the letter, since it means they have been caught up in God's eternal, cosmic purposes.

The Priestly Dynamic of Blessing (Eph 1:4–14)

Blessing for Whom?

With the causal particle "even as" (καθώς, Eph 1:4), Paul begins to spell out the nature of the blessings from God that have prompted his *bera-khah*.[40] At this point a question arises for us: to whom do these blessings pertain? Or to put it another way: What is the identity of the first-person plural "we" whom God has blessed (v. 3), elected to holiness (v. 4), predetermined for adoption (v. 5), etc.?

At first glance, the flow of the letter suggests that the "we" of 1:3ff. should be identified as the apostolic writer (1:1a) along with his addressees, the "holy ones who are also believers in Christ Jesus" (1:1b)—that is, all those who are "in Christ" (1:3; cf. 1:2).[41] This suggestion is strengthened by the fact that many of the characteristics mentioned in the introductory *berakhah* (1:3–14) are predicated or implied of Christ-believers elsewhere in Ephesians: e.g., their blessing in "the heavenly places" (v. 3; cf. 2:6), God's purpose to make them "holy and blameless" (v. 4; cf. 5:27, also 1:1), an "adoption" (1:5) by the Father (cf. 2:18; 4:6; 5:1, etc.), the prospect of "redemption" (v. 7; cf. 4:30); and the forgiveness of "trespasses" (v. 7; cf. 2:1, 5).[42] However, before making such a straightforward identification of the first-person plural "we" with all Christian believers, we should consider a number of factors that suggests that the situation may be a little more complex.

40. Hoehner, *Ephesians*, 175.

41. So e.g., Lincoln, *Ephesians*, 21–22; Best, *Ephesians*, 112; Hoehner, *Ephesians*, 165–66.

42. O'Brien, "Unusual Introduction," 510–12.

Firstly, at certain points within the body of Ephesians, a distinction is made between the first-person plural ("we") and the second-person plural ("you").[43] This distinction comes into view as early as Eph 1:11–14, where Paul first speaks in the first-person plural (vv. 11–12) and then turns to address "also you" (καὶ ὑμεῖς, v. 13). The distinction also emerges in Eph 2:1–3, where Paul first says that "you" once walked in sin (vv. 1–2), then affirms that "also we" (καὶ ἡμεῖς) were in the same condition (v. 3). Furthermore, in Eph 2:11–12, "you" are identified explicitly as those who were "once gentiles" in distinction from Israel. Again, in Eph 3:1, Paul speaks of himself as a "prisoner for Christ Jesus on behalf of you gentiles." Of course, there are other places in Ephesians where the first-person plural "we" clearly includes both author and readers (e.g., Eph 2:18; 3:12), and the same may be the case here. Nevertheless, there is at least a possibility that a distinction between "we" and "you" is implicit as early as Eph 1:3, and that this distinction relates to a distinction between Israel and the gentiles.

Secondly, the use of the Jewish *berakhah* form in a letter to a gentile audience (cf. Eph 2:11) suggests that a Jewish understanding of the relationship between Israel and the nations is being invoked.[44] Of particular significance are those biblical *berakhah* passages which, while speaking of God's blessings for Israel, also refer to certain benefits for the nations. For example, Solomon's prayer at the dedication of the temple (1 Kgs 8:22–53) is framed by *berakhoth* praising God for fulfilling his promises of rest and blessing to Israel (1 Kgs 8:14–21, 54–56). The prayer also envisages the "foreigner" receiving blessing through praying toward Israel's temple (1 Kgs 8:41–43). Similarly, the *berakhah* in Tob 13:1–18, which envisages Israel in exile among the nations (v. 3), praises God in expectation that he will forgive the sins of Israel and gather them back to Jerusalem to worship (v. 5). The nations are portrayed as the audience of this praise, and thus act as witnesses to God's special concern for Israel (vv. 3, 4). Although they do not enjoy the same exalted position as Israel, the nations overhear the call to turn to God (v. 6) and to join in a profession of thanks to him (vv. 8–10). They also play a role in building up Jerusalem by bringing gifts (v. 11). In both cases, while the emphasis is on praising God for his special blessing for "us" (i.e. Israel, in distinction

---

43. Barth, *Ephesians*, 130–35; Kinzer, *Searching Her Own Mystery*, 67–69.
44. Yee, *Ethnic Reconciliation*, 35–38.

from the other nations), God's blessing for these other nations *through* Israel is also envisaged.

In Eph 1:3ff., the blessing comes about "in Christ." However, as we have seen, this does not imply that "Christ" (or the church) is to be understood simply as a *replacement* for "Israel." Rather, the allusion to Gen 12:1–3 indicates that Christ is being presented as the *fulfillment* of God's purposes for Israel, and thus for the nations *through* Israel. As Soulen has pointed out in relation to the Abrahamic promises in Genesis:

> God's promise to Abraham links God's blessing not to some generic feature of human identity that all people share but to an encounter between those who are and who remain genuinely different. As a result, there are no "general" or "universal" paths that lead to the God of Israel. Apart from a relationship to the people Israel, no relationship to the God of Israel is possible.[45]

Speaking of the Scriptures more generally, Soulen observes that the biblical ideal for the relationship between Israel and the nations is not a flat uniformity. Rather, it involves a dynamic of mutual blessing:

> To be a Gentile is to be the other of Israel and as such an indispensable partner in a single economy of blessing that embraces the whole human family. This does not mean that Israel alone will bless the nations or the nations alone will bless Israel. God is the ultimate source of blessing for both. But God blesses both as the God of Israel, and hence in the context of the history that unfolds on the basis of the distinction between Israel and "all the families of the earth."[46]

Since this positive distinctiveness of Israel is so fundamental to and pervasive in the scriptural narrative,[47] and since such a scriptural narrative is being invoked in Ephesians through the reference to blessing "in Christ," we should expect it to inform the letter in some way. What, then, might it say about the identity of the first-person plural "we" who have received these blessings?

Kinzer, on basis of such observations, argues that the "we" in the entirety of Eph 1:3–14 refers to Israelites. For Kinzer, the *berakhah* is

---

45. Soulen, *God of Israel*, 8. See also Barth, *CD* 3/4:319. Note, however, that Soulen critiques Barth's Christocentric concentration of election, which tends to collapse the covenant history Barth earlier affirms (*God of Israel*, 89–94).

46. Soulen, *God of Israel*, 125–26.

47. Ibid., 120–21.

referring to Israel's priestly vocation as God's chosen people among the nations.[48] He argues that the divine election to "holiness" (v. 4) refers to Israel's special election in distinction from the nations (Deut 7:6). He also argues that the language of "adoption" (v. 5), which is explicitly predicated of Israel in Rom 9:4, is referring to Israel's special place as God's "son" (e.g., Exod 4:22). Kinzer does of course observe that "the letter radically recontextualizes the tradition" through use of the phrase "in Christ."[49] However, this recontextualization does not imply that Christ is a replacement for Israel. Rather, it is a reference to Christ as "the Messiah [of Israel]." For Kinzer, vv. 4–6 is asserting that Israel was always "bound to its pre-incarnate Messiah" (cf. 2:11–12).[50] Kinzer argues that in v. 7, the author "moves forward in time" to the age of the apostles, and begins to speak of Israelites who "experienced and proclaimed the redemptive work of the incarnate Messiah."[51] Verses 8ff. then describe how God has used and continues to use Israel's priestly service to bring about world-wide unity in the worship of the one God of Israel.[52]

Kinzer's argument concerning Israel's priestly vocation and its connection with the apostolic ministry is insightful. However, his argument that vv. 4–6 is referring to national Israel's prior connection with its "pre-incarnate Messiah" is not consistent with the fact that "Christ" is explicitly identified as the incarnate "*Jesus* Christ" in v. 5. Indeed, this incarnate "Christ Jesus" has already been identified as the one in whom the readers of the letter are "believers" (v. 1, cf. v. 2). At this point, then, we cannot easily draw a hard distinction between Israel and the Christ-believing gentiles. Nevertheless, as we have seen, the allusions to the Abrahamic promises and the *berakhah* form give strong indications that some form of priestly dynamic is being portrayed here.

It may be best to say that at least initially, the first-person plural "we" refers to Christ-believers, i.e., it refers to Paul along with all those who are "holy" by virtue of their faith "in Christ Jesus" (v. 1). However, the fact that the blessing is couched in the language of Abrahamic promises and Jewish *berakhoth* at least hints that a dynamic movement of blessing through Israel to the nations is envisaged. There is precedent in Romans for this nuanced way of thinking. There, the gospel is described as "the

48. Kinzer, *Searching Her Own Mystery*, 69–73.

49. Ibid., 70.

50. Ibid.

51. Ibid.

52. Ibid., 70–72.

power of God for salvation to everyone who believes, to the Jew first and also to the Greek" (Rom 1:16). In Romans, various divine benefits are predicated both of Israel in particular, and also of believers in general: for example, holiness (Rom 11:16) and adoption (Rom 9:4; 8:15, 23).[53] In all this, an Israel-centered dynamic is at work in Paul's apostolic ministry (Rom 1:1; 15:14–33).[54] Thus a priestly-style dynamic of blessing is at least plausible in the early verses of Ephesians.

The Structure of vv. 3–14

This concept of a dynamic movement of blessing becomes clearer when we consider the structure of Eph 1:3–14. It is notoriously difficult to discern the structure of this sentence from its syntax alone. While there are certain repeated patterns, the content as well as the form of the sentence needs to be considered.[55] The following structure arises from a consideration of both the form and the content of the blessing. It seeks to highlight the movement of blessings from God, through the first-person plural "we," to the second-person plural "you":

- v. 3 Blessing "in Christ" (summary)
- vv. 1:4–6a Blessing determined (ending with "to the praise of the glory of his grace")
- vv. 1:6b–7 Blessing given (ending with "according to the wealth of his grace")
- vv. 1:8–10 Blessing communicated
- vv. 1:11–12 Blessing inherited (beginning with "in whom also we")
- vv. 1:13–14 Blessing shared (beginning with "in whom also you," ending with "to the praise of his glory")

Blessing Determined and Given (vv. 4–7)

Verses 4–6a describe the origin of the blessings in the divine plan. The scope and significance of the blessings is immense. God's choice of his people is "before" (πρό) the establishment of the world (v. 4) and his

53. Windsor, *Vocation of Israel*, 46, 207.

54. Ibid., 112–19.

55. Best, *Ephesians*, 110.

determination to bring them to adoption through Christ (v. 5) is also a "prior" reality (προορίσας). These verses describe an exalted status for God's people: "holy and blameless before him" (v. 4) and adopted as sons (v. 5). However, the readers are reminded that the significance of their status does not terminate on themselves. Rather, these blessings are in accordance with the "pleasure of [God's] will," and has as its goal the "praise of the glory of his grace" (v. 6a). Already the gentile readers of the letter are reminded that God's purposes and plans stretch far beyond their own individual lives or even their own individual gentile congregations.

Verses 6b–7 describe the enacting of these blessings in history. The "grace" described in v. 6a was "given" to God's people "in the beloved" (ἐν τῷ ἠγαπημένῳ, v. 6b), a phrase which is being used here as a pointed alternative for the phrase "in Christ" (ἐν [τῷ] Χριστῷ, vv. 3, 10; cf. "in him"/"in whom," vv. 4, 7, 9, 10, 11, 13). The term "the beloved" (ὁ ἠγαπημένος) is applied to Israel in the LXX of Deut 32:15; 33:5, 26; and Isa 44:2. Several commentators note these references, but then dismiss their significance since they are not obvious "Messianic" types.[56] However, the use of the term in Isa 44:2 bears closer scrutiny. In Isa 44, Israel is designated as God's "servant" (παῖς, Isa 44:1); the servant here is a figure who is "beloved" (ἠγαπημένος, v. 2) by God, whom God has "chosen" (ἐξελεξάμην, Isa 44:2; cf. Eph 1:4), and upon whose seed God will pour out his "blessings" (εὐλογίας, Isa 44:3; cf. Eph 1:3). As the vision of Isaiah continues, this role of Israel as God's servant becomes concentrated in an individual figure—a figure who both restores Israel and extends God's salvation to the nations (Isa 49:6). The ultimate activity of the servant is his sacrificial death through which comes the removal of the people's "sins" (ἁμαρτίας) and "lawless deeds" (ἀνομίας, Isa 53:5 LXX), which in the MT are described as "our transgressions" (מִפְּשָׁעֵנוּ, Isa 53:5 MT, cf. Eph 1:7). Thus, the naming of Christ as "the beloved, in whom we have redemption through his blood, the forgiveness of trespasses" (vv. 6b–7) appears to be alluding to the role of the Isaianic Servant of the Lord. This is, significantly, a role that is intimately connected to Israel's own special place in God's plan for the world and for all the nations.[57]

---

56. See e.g., Best, *Ephesians*, 128–29.

57. See further Windsor, *Vocation of Israel*, 99–112.

Blessing Communicated (vv. 8–10)

Verse 8 states that God has "caused [his grace] to abound" (ἐπερίσσευσεν), implying that there are further dimensions to the grace described in vv. 6b–7. As Barth has noted "[t]here is a distinct emphasis placed upon the reception and communication of knowledge in Ephesians,"[58] and here we see an early example of this emphasis.

The way in which God has caused his grace to abound is by "in all wisdom and insight making known to us the mystery of his will" (vv. 8–9). This "mystery" (μυστήριον) is a key term in Ephesians (1:9; 3:3, 9; 5:32; 6:19). Caragounis draws a distinction between a cosmic use of the term in Eph 1—where it is "concerned with the final restoration of order in the universe when all revolting elements, together with those which maintained their allegiance, shall be reconstituted under Christ" (cf. 1:10)[59]—and a missiological use in Eph 3—where it has "a more limited aspect," referring to "the acceptance of the Gentiles on the same basis as the Jews," and focusing on Paul's missionary gospel-preaching.[60] While this distinction between a cosmic and a missiological use of the term "mystery" may be helpful in understanding the differing emphases between Eph 1 and Eph 3, it cannot be seen as an absolute distinction between two separate concepts. Indeed, the cosmic and missiological uses are connected, since, as Caragounis notes, the latter "forms a part of and is a prerequisite for" the former.[61] Furthermore, there are elements of both uses in Eph 1 itself. While v. 10 states that the "mystery" concerns a cosmic "summing up of all things in Christ" (ἀνακεφαλαιώσασθαι τὰ πάντα ἐν τῷ Χριστῷ), vv. 11–14, as we shall see, describe the early Christian mission through Israel to the nations. Thus, the "mystery," even as early as Eph 1:9, contains connotations of the same apostolic Jew-gentile dynamic that is described more fully in Eph 3.

The mystery has been made known "to us" (v. 9). Most commentators understand this "us" to be referring to all believers.[62] It is, of course, true that from the overall perspective of the letter, the mystery has been communicated to all believers—indeed, the very act of writing the letter communicates the mystery to the readers, who have been designated as

58. Barth, *Ephesians*, 42.

59. Caragounis, *Mysterion*, 117.

60. Ibid., 118.

61. Ibid.

62. E.g., Best, *Ephesians*, 133; Hoehner, *Ephesians*, 214; Thielman, *Ephesians*, 63.

believers in Christ (cf. 1:1). Nevertheless, as Eph 3 goes on to make clear, the particular way in which the mystery has been made known to all believers is *through* first making it known to the foundational apostles and prophets, including Paul, who in turn make it known to others (Eph 3:3–5, 7–10).[63] Thus, the "priestly" dynamic of blessing we noted above is also relevant to the description of the communication of blessing here in v. 9.[64]

In v. 10, Paul writes that God's good pleasure was set forth "with a view to the administration of the fullness of the times" (εἰς οἰκονομίαν τοῦ πληρώματος τῶν καιρῶν). Some earlier commentaries and several translations render the word *oikonomia* (οἰκονομία) in a static sense, as an "arrangement," "plan" (e.g., RSV, ESV), or "dispensation" (e.g., KJV, ASV).[65] However, more recent commentators agree that the word is better translated here with an active sense, as an "administration."[66] It refers to an active task, office, commission, or responsibility to manage the affairs of a master (cf. Luke 16:2–4; 1 Cor 9:17; Eph 3:2; Col 1:25; cf. 1 Cor 4:1; Gal 4:2). Many commentators who take this view argue that God himself is the one who performs the administrative task—primarily because God is the subject of the other verbal ideas in the immediate context.[67] However, there is a significant problem with this view. In its normal usage, the task of "administration" is carried out by a subordinate administrator, not by the master himself.[68] For this reason, Barth posits that Christ is the one who performs the task of administration.[69] However, in this passage, God's purposes are all said to take place "in" Christ, not to be put into effect directly "by" Christ (see esp. the end of v. 9).

Who, then, performs this "administration"? In Eph 3, it is the apostolic community. The "administration of the grace of God" (τὴν οἰκονομίαν

63. Robinson, "The Saints," 52.

64. Kinzer, *Searching Her Own Mystery*, 70.

65. See Barth, who writing in 1974 comments that his decision to translate the term as "administration" is a minority position (*Ephesians*, 86).

66. Ibid., 86–88.

67. Caird, *Letters from Prison*, 38; Lincoln, *Ephesians*, 31–32; Best, *Ephesians*, 138–39; Hoehner, *Ephesians*, 216–18; Thielman, *Ephesians*, 64.

68. Reumann notes that even in late Hellenistic literature where the term οἰκονομία is "regularly applied to God's ordering and administration of the universe," the divine administration tended to "operate through administrative subordinates like Fate, the heavenly bodies, nature, or λόγος" ("Oikonomia-Terms," 150–51).

69. Barth, *Ephesians*, 88.

τῆς χάριτος τοῦ θεοῦ, 3:2) refers to a task that has been given to Paul and, by implication, to the other "apostles and prophets" to whom the "mystery" was originally "revealed" (vv. 3, 5). We should assume that the same is true in Eph 1. That is, by using the term "administration" (οἰκονομία) in Eph 1:10, Paul is in fact foreshadowing the apostolic ministry that he will explain more fully in Eph 3. In Eph 1:10, it is called the "administration of the fullness of the times." This is not only because it is an administration of a mystery that was formerly hidden but now in Christ has been revealed (Eph 3:5; cf. Gal 4:4), but also because, as the rest of Eph 1:10 indicates, it is an administration that plays a central and decisive role in God's cosmic plan to sum up all things in Christ (cf. Eph 3:11). Thus, in both Eph 1 and Eph 3, Paul is directly linking the apostolic mission with God's cosmic purposes in Christ. This is consistent with the fact that he has introduced his apostleship as one that takes place "through the will of God" (διὰ θελήματος θεοῦ, 1:1; cf. 1:5, 9, 11).

Furthermore, since Paul's apostolic ministry involves preaching Christ to the nations and including them as equal participants in God's blessings with Israel (3:6, 8), the mention of the apostolic "administration" in v. 10 provides a logical transition to the section immediately following (vv. 11–14).[70] In these verses, the temporal movement of blessing from "us" to "you" comes into clear focus. This, as we will now see, is best understood as a movement from the original Jewish apostolic community—"we who have first hoped in Christ" (v. 12)—to the gentile believers—"you also who heard . . . and believed" (v. 13).

Thus, vv. 8–10 are best read as a concise summary of the dynamic communication of Christ's blessings through Israel to the gentiles by means of the apostolic mission. This foreshadows a theme that Paul will later return to and explain in far more detail (Eph 3).[71] Of special note are the terms "mystery" (μυστήριον) and "administration" (οἰκονομία). These terms are mentioned briefly here in 1:8–10, but are applied directly to the apostolic mission to the nations later in Eph 3.

Blessing Inherited and Shared (vv. 11–14)

The flow of divine blessing from one group to another, which has been at most implicit in vv. 3–10, becomes the focus of attention in vv. 11–14.

70. Kinzer, *Searching Her Own Mystery*, 72.

71. See chapter 5.

Syntactically, these verses are governed by two parallel clauses, each of which begins with the words "in whom also" (ἐν ᾧ καί, vv. 11, 13).[72] In vv. 11–12, a first-person plural subject ("we") is in view. "We" are said to have "obtained an inheritance," an outcome which is in accordance with God's predetermining activity (v. 11) and which results in praise of God (v. 12). In v. 13, however, there is a conspicuous transition ("in whom also") to a second-person plural subject ("you"). "You also," having "heard" and "believed" the "gospel of your salvation," have been "sealed" with the "Spirit of promise" (v. 13), which in turn is the guarantee of "our inheritance" (v. 14). Several interpreters regard the transition between "we" and "you" in v. 13 simply as a stylistic variation in which the *berakhah* form momentarily shades into a sermonic style of address.[73] However, these interpreters fail to explain adequately why an otherwise coherent *berakhah* would change its style of address for just one verse (v. 13). Even more significantly, since the transition from "we" to "you" in v. 13 is strongly marked,[74] it requires an explanation more substantial than that of a stylistic variation.

"We" and "You" in vv. 11–14

Who, then, are the "we" and "you" being spoken about in vv. 11–14, and why is there such a marked transition between the two? On the one hand, there is no indication at the start of v. 11 that the "we" in v. 11 are any

72. Each of these are relative clauses with αὐτῷ ("him," i.e., "Christ," v. 10) as their antecedent. The first relative clause Ἐν ᾧ καὶ ἐκληρώθημεν ("in whom we also received an inheritance") is qualified by a participial phrase (v. 11) and an infinitival phrase (v. 12). The second relative clause Ἐν ᾧ καὶ ὑμεῖς . . . ἐσφραγίσθητε . . . ("in whom also you . . . were sealed . . .") is qualified by two participial phrases, the second of which also begins with ἐν ᾧ καί ("in whom also," v. 13). The πνεῦμα ("Spirit") of v. 13 is also qualified by a further relative clause in v. 14.

73. Percy, *Die Probleme*, 266–67 n. 16; Dahl, "Gentiles, Christians, and Israelites," 33, 35; Lincoln, *Ephesians*, 37–38; Best, *Ephesians*, 148; Hoehner, *Ephesians*, 231–35.

74. The transition to the second-person plural subject is marked in several ways: by the use of the additive καί ("also"), by the existence of the personal pronoun ὑμεῖς ("you"), and by the placement of this personal pronoun at the beginning of the clause, before the two participial phrases. Kinzer observes: "The pronominal switch is sudden and jarring, and cannot lack significance" (*Searching Her Own Mystery*, 71). The existence of several variant readings which change the second person plural into a first person plural pronoun (ℵ[2a] A K L Ψ 326 629 630 1241 2464) suggests that the second person plural at this point was unexpected from the point of view of post-apostolic Greek speakers.

different from the "we" in vv. 3–10.[75] Yet a distinction between "we" and "you" does begin to emerge at the end of v. 12. At this point, the "we" who are to be "to the praise of his glory" are more precisely specified as "those who have first hoped in Christ" (τοὺς προηλπικότας ἐν τῷ Χριστῷ). This more precise designation of "we" is followed directly, by way of contrast, with the words "in whom also you . . ." (ἐν ᾧ καὶ ὑμεῖς, v. 13), implying that the addressees are not part of the former group "who have first hoped in Christ." Furthermore, this construction "in whom also you . . ." is conspicuously parallel with the words at the beginning of v. 11 ("in whom also [we . . .]"). This causes readers (or hearers) to reflect on what they have read (or heard) so far within the clause beginning in v. 11, and so to wonder whether "we" in the entire clause (vv. 11–12) may refer to the more limited group ("those who have first hoped in Christ").[76] Best claims that this kind of reconstruction of the intended effect on the readers is entirely implausible, and for this reason concludes that the entirety of vv. 11–14 must refer to all Christians.[77] Heil's analysis of the discourse is more nuanced. He notes that in v. 12b, Paul first raises a question for the readers as to "whether there is a distinction between the 'we,' as those 'who first hoped (προηλπικότας) in the Christ,' that may exclude from the 'we' those believers who hoped in the Christ at a later time"; then in v. 13, Paul "quickly dispels from the minds of his audience any notion that these later believers, the 'you,' are in any way excluded from the dynamics" of love described previously.[78] Heil is of course correct that Paul does not ultimately want to exclude "you" from the blessings "in Christ." However, a question remains, a question Heil does not answer: *Why* does Paul bring forward this distinction the first place?

Some understand the distinction in vv. 11–14 as a distinction between the apostles and other Christ-believers. Thomas Aquinas, for example, understood Eph 1:3–14 as a description of the "blessings offered generally to all the faithful" (vv. 3–7), followed by a description

---

75. There is no first-person pronoun in v. 11. This supports Best's view that "καί qualifies the verb and does not affect the identification of its subject: in addition to the other gifts we receive an inheritance" (*Ephesians*, 144).

76. Käsemann, "Ephesians and Acts," 295.

77. Best, *Ephesians*, 144–45, incl. n. 59. Best here appears to find it impossible for the original hearers of the letter to have allowed what they heard in v. 12 to qualify what they had just previously heard in v. 11. However, since the two verses form part of the same (albeit complex) clause, this situation is quite possible.

78. Heil, *Ephesians*, 69–70.

of blessings "especially given the Apostles" (vv. 8–12), and completed by a description of the blessings "granted to the Ephesians themselves" (vv. 13–14).[79] More recently, Shkul has argued that the "we" represents the "communal founder(s)" and the "you" represents the group being written to.[80] The view that the "we"-"you" distinction is bound up with the foundational apostolic ministry has much to commend it, given the foundational significance of the apostles in the rest of the letter (Eph 1:1; 2:20; 3:5; 4:11).[81]

Several other interpreters, however, understand vv. 11–14 to be delineating a distinction between Jews and gentiles.[82] This is consistent with the distinction between Jews and gentiles described in Eph 2:11–22 and 3:1–6.

In Eph 2:11–22, the second-person plural addressees ("you") are told to remember their former status as "the gentiles" (v. 11), who because of their separation from Israel were "without Christ" and "without hope" (v. 12). This implies that there is a strong connection between proximity to Israel on the one hand, and "Christ" and "hope" on the other hand. Thus, in Eph 1, the phrase "those who have first hoped in Christ" (1:12) is a natural designation for Christ-believing Israelites.[83] Furthermore, in Eph 2:11–22, the second-person plural addressees ("you") are described as those who were formerly estranged from the covenants "of the prom-

79. Aquinas, *Ephesians*, 64.

80. Shkul, *Reading Ephesians*, 32–33. Shkul here argues that the distinction cannot be one between Jews and gentiles, since (according to her application of social identity theory) any ethnic distinction in Ephesians would necessarily involve notions of inferiority for gentiles. However, as Tucker notes, this does not account for the kind of unity-in-distinction found within the text of Ephesians ("Continuation of Gentile Identity (SBL)").

81. See also Kreitzer's three-communities hypothesis. Kreitzer posits that the letter is written from a mother-church in Colossae (first person) to a daughter-church in Hierapolis (second person), sometimes with reference to all three churches in the Lycus Valley including that in Laodicea (first person) (*Ephesians*, 48, 62–63). At most, this view is plausible, but it cannot be established with any certainty.

82. E.g., Roels, *God's Mission*, 53–56; Barth, *Ephesians*, 85–86; Caird, *Letters from Prison*, 41; Campbell, "Unity and Diversity," 22; Cohick, *Ephesians*, 52; Starling, *Not My People*, 186–89.

83. Within the context of the verse, the prepositional prefix προ- in the compound perfect participle προηλπικότας implies that the "we" of v. 12 who first hoped are being contrasted with the "you also" of v. 13 who subsequently hoped (cf. Eph 1:18, 2:12, 4:4); *pace* Best, *Ephesians*, 147. Furthermore, the perfect tense may be indicating that their status as the "first" to put their hope in Christ continues to have some significance for the present.

ise" (v. 12) but now, having been brought near to Israel, are growing into a "holy" (v. 21) temple, a dwelling place for God "in the Spirit" (v. 22). Thus, in Eph 1, the statement that "also you . . . were sealed with the Holy Spirit of the promise" (1:13) is a natural description of the inclusion of gentiles in Israel's blessings.

In Eph 3:1–6, "you" are identified directly as "the gentiles" (v. 1). Furthermore, much of the vocabulary in Eph 3:6 is consistent with the vocabulary of Eph 1:11–14. In Eph 3:6, the addressees are designated as "the gentiles" (τὰ ἔθνη), who through the "gospel" (εὐαγγελίου, cf. 1:13), have become "co-heirs" (συγκληρονόμα, cf. κληρονομίας 1:14) and sharers "of the promise" (τῆς ἐπαγγελίας, cf. 1:13) "in Christ Jesus" (ἐν Χριστῷ Ἰησοῦ, cf. ἐν ᾧ, 1:13). Indeed, the vocabulary of "promise" is used in key places in Romans and Galatians to describe the inclusion of gentiles in divine blessings through the preaching of the gospel and faith in Christ (Rom 1:1–5; 4:13–25; 15:8–13; Gal 3:7–29).

We have thus reviewed two plausible options for understanding the distinction between "we" and "you" in Eph 1:11–14. Either it is a distinction between the foundational apostolic community and the addressees, or it is a distinction between Jews and gentiles. Which is correct? It is, in fact, possible to understand the passage in such a way that we are not forced to choose between these two options. Robinson and Kinzer, for example, have made much of the theological *connection* between the apostolic ministry and Israel's priestly ministry. In their view, it is significant that the members of the "apostolic community of Jewish disciples of Jesus" are both "apostolic" and "Jewish." They are the first to have hoped in Christ; they are also the instrument through whom the gospel is preached to the gentiles, resulting in the praise of God's glory.[84] The Jewish nature of the early apostolic community, in other words, is not an accident of history. Rather, in the theological viewpoint expressed in Ephesians, the apostolic community "in Christ" represents a renewed Israel. The members of this renewed Israel have, in Christ, entered into their inheritance (vv. 11–12), and through them God has communicated his blessing to the nations (v. 13). The nations, consequently, have received an equal share in God's blessing through faith in Christ; indeed, they have received the same "Spirit" who is the guarantee of Israel's own inheritance (v. 14).[85]

---

84. Robinson, "Jew and Greek," 107; Kinzer, *Searching Her Own Mystery*, 71–72 (quotation from 71).

85. Starling points out the way the structure of the blessings "echoes the broad

The Jewish Apostolic Mission in vv. 13–14

Both the vocabulary and the order of v. 13 indicates that it is describing the early apostolic mission through Israel to the nations.[86] There are many convergences between Eph 1:13–14 and the descriptions of this mission found in Acts.[87] The account of Cornelius' conversion (Acts 10:1—11:18) is particularly apposite. Up to this point in the narrative of Acts, the members of the Christian movement had largely confined their preaching of "the word" (τὸν λόγον) to Jews and Samaritans (Acts 8:4, 14, 25; cf. 11:19). This appears to be partly due to customary sanctions against Jewish association with gentiles (Acts 10:28). Peter, however, receives a vision that indicates to him that he should not call any person common or unclean (Acts 10:15, 28). The vision prompts Peter to respond to an invitation to visit the household of the gentile centurion Cornelius (Acts 10:23–29). Peter speaks to Cornelius "the word" (τὸν λόγον) that God had originally sent to the Israelites (Acts 10:36). This word is described in terms of "preaching the gospel" (εὐαγγελιζόμενος, Acts 10:36); it primarily concerns "Jesus Christ" (Acts 10:36–43); and it is later described as a message by which Cornelius and his household would be "saved" (σωθήσῃ, Acts 11:14). Cornelius and his household "hear" (verb ἀκούω) this word (Acts 10:44, cf. vv. 22, 33). By implication, hearing the word also prompts them to "believe" in Christ (verb πιστεύω, Acts 10:43, cf. 11:17). Upon hearing and believing, Cornelius and his household receive the "Holy Spirit" (τὸ πνεῦμα τὸ ἅγιον) in a visible and obvious way (Acts 10:44–45). The incident prompts the Jewish apostolic community to recognize that the gentiles have received the same gift they had received (Acts 11:15–18). The gift of the Holy Spirit had earlier been associated with the prophetic "promise" (τὴν ἐπαγγελίαν) of God (Acts 2:33; cf. Joel 2:28–29, Acts 2:17–21). This promise initially pertained to Israel. What

---

sweep of the scriptural story of the Exodus," which suggests that "the readers should view their salvation as the fulfilment of the second exodus and new covenant promises of the prophets" (*Not My People*, 188–89, quotation from 188).

86. For the centrality of Jerusalem in the early Christian mission according to Acts, see Bauckham, "James and the Jerusalem Church."

87. Barth, *Ephesians*, 95; Käsemann, "Ephesians and Acts," 293–95. Käsemann takes this correspondence between Acts and Ephesians to constitute evidence of an emerging "early Catholic" perspective ("Ephesians and Acts," 288) and deems the prominence of the church in Ephesians to be so great that it eclipses the theme of mission. As we have seen above, these views are not necessary implications of the text of Ephesians.

Peter finds remarkable is that "God gave to them the same gift as he had given also to us (καὶ ἡμῖν)" (Acts 11:17). As a result of this obvious pouring out of the Holy Spirit on Cornelius and his household, the apostolic community recognizes a remarkable truth: that God has granted repentance leading to life "also to the gentiles" (καὶ τοῖς ἔθνεσιν). Because of this, they "glorify" (ἐδόξασαν) God (Acts 11:18).

Ephesians 1:13–14 describes the same pattern, with very similar vocabulary, albeit in more compact form:[88]

> In whom [i.e. in Christ] also you (καὶ ὑμεῖς), having believed (ἀκούσαντες) the word (τὸν λόγον) of truth, the gospel (εὐαγγέλιον) of your salvation (σωτηρίας), and having believed (πιστεύσαντες) in him, were sealed with the Holy Spirit (τῷ πνεύματι . . . τῷ ἁγίῳ) of the promise (τῆς ἐπαγγελίας), who is the pledge of our (ἡμῶν) inheritance, unto the redemption of the possession, to the praise of his glory (δόξης). (Eph 1:13–14, my translation)

Thus, Eph 1:13–14 is best understood as a phenomenological description of the early Christian mission through Israel to the nations—a description that, as we have seen, is also evident in the accounts in Acts.[89] While Acts does not use the vocabulary of "sealing" (verb σφραγίζω) in relation to the giving of the Holy Spirit to the gentiles, the use of the term in Eph 1:13 is an appropriate one, considering the kinds of issues that arise from the early Christian mission. Seals were used as a marker to clearly identify and authenticate the ownership of property (cf. John 3:33; 6:27; 1 Cor 9:2).[90] In Acts, as we have seen, the conspicuous giving of the Holy Spirit provides an obvious sign that the gentile Christ-believers do indeed belong to God—a marker that was necessary, given that many presumed that such a gift would be given only to Israel (e.g., Acts 10:45). So here in Ephesians, the fact that these gentile readers, having heard the gospel and believed in Christ, were "sealed" with the Holy Spirit, is a clear sign that they belong to God alongside the Jewish apostolic community

---

88. Cf. Barth, *Ephesians*, 95.

89. Thus, Eph 1:13b is not, in the first instance, a claim that the Holy Spirit's indwelling is subsequent to or dependent upon the faith of the individual Christian. It does not, in other words, provide a simple blueprint for Christian experience, nor does it speak directly against a doctrine of effectual calling. Rather, it is, like Acts, a phenomenological description of the early Christian mission through Israel to the nations.

90. Best, *Ephesians*, 150.

(v. 13). According to v. 14, the Holy Spirit with which the gentile Christ-believers have been sealed is a "pledge" (ἀρραβών)—an "advance payment" guaranteeing that God will keep his promises (cf. 2 Cor 1:20–22). In this case, the Spirit acts as a pledge of Israel's own inheritance (cf. v. 11, and see Acts 1:6–8). It thus guarantees the future "redemption of the possession" (v. 14). This may refer either to Israel's acquiring of her inheritance, or to God's redemption of his people as his own inheritance.[91] In either case, the point being made is that these gentile Christ-believers, having received the same pledge as the early Jewish apostolic community, share in the same future hope, including the same "inheritance" (cf. Eph 1:18; 3:6). Here in Ephesians, as in Acts, this fact is deemed remarkable; it is emphasized (v. 13), and becomes the source of praise to God (v. 14).[92]

This has significant implications for how we should understand the notion of Israel's distinctiveness in Ephesians. Israel's distinctiveness does not consist in receiving special blessings, but rather in being the special channel *through* whom all of God's blessings in Christ are extended to the nations. As Acts 3:25–26 notes, it is precisely because Abraham is the channel of international blessing that God sends his Servant, his blessing, and his repentance to Israel "first" (πρῶτον). A similar dynamic is at work here in Ephesians.[93]

Consistent with our argument so far, then, we may see vv. 11–14 as an explication of the priestly dynamic that has been implicit from the

91. Ibid., 152–53.

92. This dynamic can be seen even more clearly when contrasted with the early second-century Epistle of Barnabas. For Barnabas, "we" Christians are heirs of God's covenant, in contrast to the Jews: "Now let us see whether this people or the first one that receives the inheritance, and whether the covenant is for us or them" (Barn. 13.1 [Ehrman]); "You see about whom he has decreed, that this people [i.e., Christians] will be first, and the heir of the covenant" (Barn. 13.6 [Ehrman]). For Barnabas, the Jews' position as the "first" has been forfeited: although they were "first" they did not receive God's inheritance and now Christians have become "first". For Ephesians, however, the inheritance flows from the "first" to others. "Those who have first hoped in Christ" do indeed obtain their inheritance, and then the blessings are extended to the gentile Christians (Eph 1:11–14). For the background to the Epistle of Barnabas, see chapter 4.

93. See also the argument of Rom 11. In Romans, Jewish rejection of the gospel of Christ (Rom 9:1–3; 10:1–4) gives rise to the question of whether God has rejected his "inheritance" (κληρονομίαν, Rom 11:1; see Given, "Inheritance" for a defense of the originality of this reading). The answer is found in the apostolic ministry of Paul, who as the paradigmatic "Israelite" (Rom 11:1) *and* as the "apostle to the gentiles" (Rom 11:13) is the guarantee that God has not rejected Israel (see further Windsor, *Vocation of Israel*, 230–46).

start of v. 3. While the blessings described in the *berakhah* are ultimately applicable to all believers in Christ, as the *berakhah* continues it becomes clearer that in God's purposes, these blessings have come to believers through a particular path. The blessings apply firstly to "us, . . . who have first hoped in Christ"; and then by extension—through the preaching of the gospel—the blessings apply equally to "you" gentile believers in Christ. Both the equality and the distinction are deemed worthy of note (cf. Rom 1:16). As we will see when we examine Eph 2:11–22,[94] this distinction will later be described as a Jew-gentile distinction (or more precisely, an Israel-nations distinction).[95] However, in Eph 1, the distinction is not described using these terms. Rather, the distinction is described in terms of the early Christian mission. Nevertheless, this mission is intimately connected to the Jew-gentile distinction, since it proceeded through Israel to the nations, and was a dynamic in which the Jewish apostolic community played a foundational role.

The Apostolic Prayer (Eph 1:15–23)

In Eph 1:15–23, the apostle turns to pray for his gentile readers. His prayer is occasioned by the fact that he has "heard" of their "faith in the Lord Jesus" and "love toward all the saints" (v. 15).[96] As we have seen, the fact that Paul only claims to have "heard" of the response of his readers to the gospel is one of the indications that the intended audience of Ephesians is wider than any single congregation or a small set of congregations in Ephesus.[97] It is better to regard Ephesians as having a broader horizon: Paul is envisaging a readership consisting of various gentile congregations that have come into being as a result of the apostolic mission through Israel to the nations. This is consistent with the fact that the prayer (vv. 15–23) is explicitly connected to the description

---

94. See chapter 4.

95. Dahl notes that "Ephesians never uses the term 'the Jews' (οἱ Ἰουδαῖοι)" ("Gentiles, Christians, and Israelites," 35).

96. Although the words τὴν ἀγάπην ("love") are missing from some key Alexandrian witnesses ($\mathfrak{P}^{46}$ א B P 33 1739 etc.), Metzger provides a persuasive case for their originality, arguing that the words were omitted as a result of homoeoarcton (*Textual Commentary*, 602).

97. See chapter 2. Paul had conducted a longstanding and well-known ministry in Ephesus, and so it is unlikely that he would only refer to reports about their faith without adding his own personal testimony to this faith.

of the mission (vv. 11–14) via the phrase "for this reason" (διὰ τοῦτο). In other words, the existence of reports about widespread "faith" and "love" among the gentile readers (v. 15) provides evidence for the success of the mission (vv. 11–14). It demonstrates that, consistent with God's purposes, the apostolic "administration of the fullness of the times" (v. 10) is being enacted, with palpable results. The gospel has been heard by the gentiles, many have "believed" (v. 13), and there are now congregations clearly displaying this "faith" in Christ (v. 15). Their faith is accompanied by "love toward all the saints" (v. 15), so that Paul does "not cease giving thanks" for them (v. 16). This phrase "love toward all the saints" (v. 15) may be a reference to various reports of tangible generosity between congregations, perhaps especially toward the Jerusalem community. In 2 Cor 8–9, for example, the collection of funds "for the saints" (2 Cor 8:4; 9:1)—which is a collection for the Jerusalem community (cf. 1 Cor 16:3)—is "proof of your [i.e., the Corinthians'] love" (2 Cor 8:24). It also results "in many thanksgivings to God" (2 Cor 9:12; cf. Eph 1:16). The parallel descriptions in Col 1:3–4 and Phlm 4–5 also occur in contexts where generosity beyond the confines of an individual congregation is in view (e.g. Col 1:6; Phlm 7, 22).

Paul's prayer in Eph 1:15–23 is, essentially, that those who have responded to the preaching of the gospel would understand the far-reaching significance of the message they have embraced. It is a prayer that they would fully share and experience the spiritual blessings of Eph 1:3–14, particularly those blessings pertaining to knowledge and insight. While these blessings were first given to the early Jewish apostolic community, they have now, through the preaching of the gospel, come to the nations. There are numerous connections between the blessing of vv. 3–14 and the prayer of vv. 15–23.[98] The "mystery" of the gospel had "in all wisdom (σοφίᾳ) and insight" been "made known" (γνωρίσας) firstly to the apostolic community (vv. 8–9); now the apostle prays that God would give his gentile readers the same "spirit of wisdom (σοφίας) and of revelation in the knowledge (ἐπιγνώσει) of him" (v. 17). The apostolic community were "those who [had] first hoped" (τοὺς προηλπικότας) in Christ (v. 12); now the apostle prays that his gentile readers would know the same "hope (ἐλπίς) of his calling" (v. 18). The apostolic community had "obtained an inheritance" (ἐκληρώθημεν, v. 11), and furthermore the gentiles had also received the Holy Spirit as the pledge "of our

---

98. Fowl, *Ephesians*, 53. Cf. O'Brien, "Unusual Introduction," 514.

inheritance" (τῆς κληρονομίας ἡμῶν) which is "to the praise of his glory (δόξης)" (v. 14); now the apostle prays that his gentile readers themselves may know the "wealth of the glory of his inheritance among the saints" (ὁ πλοῦτος τῆς δόξης τῆς κληρονομίας αὐτοῦ ἐν τοῖς ἁγίοις, v. 18). The "calling" and the "inheritance among the saints" is related here primarily to God (it is "his," αὐτοῦ) rather than directly to the gentile readers. This is not of course to deny that the gentile readers ultimately possess this "calling" (cf. 4:1, 4) and share in the "inheritance" as God's "holy ones" (cf. 1:1; 5:27). However, the emphasis here is on God's gracious *inclusion* of the gentiles in a calling, inheritance, and state of holiness that originally pertained to Israel (cf. 2:19-22).[99]

In vv. 19-23, Paul speaks in exalted terms of God's "power to us who believe" (v. 19). The apostolic community has been informed of God's plan "to unite all things in Christ, things in heaven and things on earth" (v. 10); now the apostle specifies this plan in more detail (vv. 19-23). The initial focus is on the resurrection, exaltation, and cosmic victory of Christ "in the heavenly places" (vv. 19-23a, cf. v. 3), which involves Christ reigning over "all things" (v. 22). As the prayer reaches a climax, the focus moves on to "the church, which is his body, the fullness of him who is filled with all things in every way" (v. 23, cf. v. 10).[100] This "church" which, as we have already seen, has been formed as a result of the Christian mission through Israel to the nations (vv. 11-14) and which will soon be described as the united "body" of Jewish and gentile believers (2:16), occupies a vital place in God's cosmic plans to unite all things in Christ. In this way, the "administration of the fullness of the times" (v. 10) is bound up closely with the "administration" of preaching the gospel to the gentiles (Eph 3:2, 7-10). The apostolic mission through Israel to the nations and the unity of Jew and gentile are key elements of God's wider plans for the cosmos. In all of this, Israel's priority is affirmed, as the instrument of God's blessing for his church and thereby his completion of his cosmic purposes in Christ.

99. Kinzer, *Searching Her Own Mystery*, 73. See further the discussion of "the saints" in chapter 4.

100. Taking the participle πληρουμένου as a passive, following Best, *Ephesians*, 183–89; Fowl, *Ephesians*, 63–64; Hoehner, *Ephesians*, 295–301.

Summary of Ephesians 1

In this chapter, we have seen how the apostolic mission is portrayed in Eph 1 as the means by which Christ's blessings have come through Israel to the nations. Paul's introduction of himself as "an apostle of Christ Jesus by the will of God" is rich with connotations of a dynamic mission (Eph 1:1). The apostle, the missionary of Christ, is enacting the purposes of God in the world. He is writing to Christ-believing gentiles who, indeed *as* Christ-believers, can be called "holy ones," and he implies through his phraseology that this fact is remarkable. At the beginning of the *berakhah* in Eph 1:3, Paul alludes to Gen 12:3, thereby implying that Christ fulfills the role of the "offspring" of Abraham "in" whom the nations are "blessed." In Christ, God's promises through Israel to the nations have reached their eschatological fulfillment, with far-reaching and even cosmic implications. In Eph 1:4–14, a dynamic movement of blessing from "us" to "you" through the preaching of the gospel is evident. This blessing "in Christ" (v. 3) has been divinely predetermined (vv. 4–6a), given (vv. 6b-7), communicated (vv. 8–10), inherited (vv. 11–12), and shared with "you also" through the preaching of the gospel (vv. 13–14). The fact that the blessing is couched in language of Abrahamic promises and Jewish *berakhoth* (cf. v. 3) hints that a dynamic movement of blessing through Israel to the nations is being envisaged. In Eph 1:15–23, the apostle prays that those who have responded to the preaching of the gospel would understand the far-reaching significance of the message they have embraced. While these blessings were first given to the early Jewish apostolic community, they have now, through the preaching of the gospel, come to the nations.

4

Christ's Reconciliation of Israel and the Nations (Ephesians 2)

IN CHAPTER 3, WE saw how in Eph 1, the apostolic mission is portrayed as the means by which Christ's blessings have come through Israel to the nations. While Eph 1 clearly refers to the results of the apostolic mission, it does not use explicit vocabulary relating to Jewish identity. This continues to be the case in the first main section of Eph 2 (vv. 1–10). However, in the second main section of Eph 2 (vv. 11–22), vocabulary relating to Jewish distinctiveness becomes explicit; indeed, it is central to the argument. It is my contention that this juxtaposition is not arbitrary. Rather, the question of Israel's distinctive role in God's purposes is intimately connected with the theme of the apostolic gospel-preaching mission to the nations. In vv. 1–10, Paul asserts that two distinct groups of people—designated in vv. 1–3 as "you" and "we"—are united in sin, judgment, and salvation by grace through faith in Christ. In vv. 11–22, Paul asserts that the same two distinct groups—now designated as "Israel" and "you gentiles"—have been reconciled together to God. Furthermore, this reconciliation reaches a climax in the apostolic mission: Christ has achieved "peace" through his sacrificial death on the cross (vv. 14–16), and has also "evangelized" this "peace" to Israel and to the nations (vv. 17–18).

In this chapter, we will focus on Eph 2, and will see how the apostolic mission plays a climactic role in Christ's work of reconciliation for Israel and the nations. We will examine the significance for this theme of: Paul's insistence that both "you" and "we" have been raised from death to life (Eph 2:1–10), Paul's emphasis on the fact that the gentiles have been "brought near" to Israel (Eph 2:11–13), Paul's description of

111

the peace-making activity of Christ through his sacrificial death (Eph 2:14–16), Paul's description of the gospel-preaching activity of Christ to both "near" and "far" (Eph 2:17–18), and Paul's description of gentiles being built together with the "saints" on the same apostolic foundation (Eph 2:19–22).

Israel and the Nations in Ephesians 2

As we examine Eph 2, we will need focus in some detail on those texts which have given rise to common supersessionist readings. As we saw in chapter 2, such readings fall into three general categories: (1) that Christ, by bringing a new spiritual reality, has rendered physical circumcision invalid for all (Eph 2:11–12); (2) that Christ, through his crucifixion, has abolished the Jewish observance of the law of Moses (Eph 2:14–15a); and (3) that Christ, by forming a new kind of humanity, has nullified all forms of Jewish distinctiveness (Eph 2:14–16). Andrew Lincoln, a strong advocate for a supersessionist understanding of Ephesians, and particularly of Eph 2:11–22, argues that the concept of "Israel" performs only a limited and subsidiary role in this section of the letter:

> Eph 2:11–22 is not a general depiction of the relationship between Gentiles and Jews, nor is it primarily an answer to the question, "How can Jews and Christians be the eschatological people of God?" It is not meant to be "an argument for corporate unity," nor is it even a discussion of the place of the Gentiles in the history of salvation. Instead it involves a comparison between these particular Gentile readers' pre-Christian past in its relation to Israel's privileges and to their Christian present in the church, on which attention is focused at the end of the chapter in vv. 19–22. The mention of Israel, then, only functions as part of this comparison and serves the purpose of bringing home to the readers the greatness of their salvation.[1]

Lincoln understands the supersessionist perspective held by the (post-Pauline) author of Ephesians to stand in some tension with Paul's non-supersessionist perspective as expressed in Rom 9–11. He claims that,

> whereas in Romans 9–11 the advantages of Israel still play a role in the time after Christ, in Ephesians, in contrast—as will

---

1. Lincoln, "Church and Israel," 608–9.

become even clearer—they pertain only to the time prior to Christ.[2]

Is Ephesians' perspective, then, as supersessionist as Lincoln and others claim?

To bring some context to this question, it is instructive to consider, by way of comparison, another early Christian document, which is clearly supersessionist: the Epistle of Barnabas.[3] Barnabas frequently uses the pronouns "we" and "they" to draw a distinction between Christians and Jews. For example:

> watch yourselves now and do not become like some people by piling up your sins, saying that the covenant is both theirs and ours. For it is ours. But they permanently lost it, in this way, when Moses had just received it. (Barn. 4.6–7 [Ehrman])

This "we" and "they" delineation is central to Barnabas' overall hermeneutical method. Portions of Scripture referring to misguided or sinful approaches to God are taken to refer to "them" (Jews), whereas portions of Scripture referring to right approaches to God are taken to refer to "us" (Christians). For example, when Barnabas approaches Isa 58:3–10, he claims that God speaks to two different groups in the one passage: God speaks "to them" concerning unacceptable pride-filled ritual (Barn. 3.1), whereas God speaks "to us" about true obedience, love, and righteousness (Barn. 3.3).[4] For Barnabas, the true and sole heirs of God's covenant with Israel are Christians, not Jews.[5] This explains why Christians are never described as "gentiles," since the term itself assumes an Israel-centric perspective. "The inference is simple: *We* are now the real Israel. Since the covenant belongs to Christians, the latter are not Gentiles any more."[6] For Barnabas, Christians have become the true Israel, in direct contrast with Jews. Barnabas, then, is a clear instance of

2. Ibid., 610.

3. Ehrman, *Apostolic Fathers*, 2:3. The recipients of Barnabas were almost certainly gentile Christians (cf. Barn. 3.6, 16.7). It was written between 70–135 C.E., most likely in the second half of this period, possibly in Alexandria, and probably in response to a perceived threat that the recipients would be attracted to Judaism of some form (ibid., 6, 9; Hvalvik, *Struggle for Scripture and Covenant*; pace Taylor, *Anti-Judaism*). Some scholars suggest more specific scenarios associated with the prospect of the rebuilding of the temple (Lowy, "Confutation of Judaism"; Paget, *Epistle of Barnabas*).

4. Lowy, "Confutation of Judaism," 1–2.

5. Kok, "True Covenant People," 93.

6. Lowy, "Confutation of Judaism," 29.

a supersessionist perspective in early Christianity. Can the same be said for Eph 2, as Lincoln and others have argued? As we shall see when we examine the text more closely, it cannot.

We saw in chapter 2, for example, several elements of Eph 2:11–22 that imply an ongoing value for Israel within the predominant theme of unity in Christ. These include (1) the emphatic reminder that before Christ's incarnation, Israel alone was in a positive relationship with "Christ," "God," and "hope" (Eph 2:12);[7] (2) the threefold use of the word "both" (ἀμφότεροι) to describe the ongoing state of unity between Jews and gentiles (Eph 2:14, 16, 18), so that "[t]he two corporate entities remain identifiable, and thus distinct";[8] and (3) the use of *syn*-compounds to refer to a communion of two different groups (Jew and gentile) in the one body.[9] Campbell argues that

> if gentiles are presented as joint-heirs with Israelites, this can-
> not refer merely to their being built on apostles and prophets as
> something in past history. Israelite identity cannot at one and
> the same time be presented as foundational, and simultaneously
> undermined, since it is in this direction gentiles are to proceed.[10]

Thus:

> It is presumed that gentiles, whilst remaining gentiles, instead
> of creating a new humanity in opposition to, or displacement of,
> Israel must develop a deeper understanding of their links with
> Israel and thus a more Israelite-related identity, though they are
> never identified as co-Israelites. The new *anthrōpos* is thus new
> in the specific sense that difference is no longer a cause of hostil-
> ity but a cause for celebration.[11]

In this chapter, we will examine Eph 2 with such post-supersession-ist observations in mind. We will review the overall argument of Eph 2, paying particular attention to those elements of the text that bear on the question of Israel's distinctiveness. As we do this, we will see that the theme of Israel's distinctiveness is intimately connected to the apostolic mission proceeding through Israel to the nations.

---

7. E.g., Kinzer, *Searching Her Own Mystery*, 75.

8. Ibid., 78.

9. E.g., Ibid., 78–79 cf. 73–74.

10. Campbell, "Unity and Diversity," 23.

11. Ibid., 24.

Raised Together from Death to Life (Eph 2:1–10)

Ephesians 2:1–10 is often understood as a passage designed to apply the cosmic significance of Christ described in Eph 1:15–23 to the individual Christian.[12] This "individual" turn of thought is said to be related to the language of individual desires (v. 3), individual faith (v. 8), and the mention of "anyone" (v. 9).[13] However, while Eph 2:1–10 is certainly applicable to the individual believer, the emphatic alternation between the second-person "you" and the first-person "we" at the beginning of the passage (vv. 1, 3) suggests that more is going on than an application of cosmic realities to individual believers.[14] While there are of course clear implications for individual believers, Eph 2:1–10 also highlights the past and present commonality that exists between "you" (v. 1) and "also we" (v. 3). Furthermore, the climactic statement in Eph 2:8 ("for by grace you have been saved, through faith") picks up the language that Paul had earlier used to describe the results of the apostolic mission in 1:13 ("in whom also you, having heard . . . the gospel of your salvation, in whom also having believed," cf. the foundational significance of "grace" in 1:6–7). Thus, while Eph 2:1–10 is of course concerned with the far-reaching implications of the early Christian mission for the gentile readers of the letter ("you," v. 1), it also pointedly emphasizes how "also we" (v. 3) are caught up in the same dynamic. This "we," as we shall see, is best understood as the early Jewish apostolic community.

The primary burden of Eph 2:1–10 is to recount the extraordinary transition that God's grace has effected for those "in Christ," and to draw out some of the implications of this transition. At a former point in time, they were "dead"—a highly negative portrayal of human existence in opposition to God. Now, they have been "made alive with" Christ and thus have been given a status commensurate with Christ's cosmic victory. Syntactically, vv. 1–7 form a single complex sentence, centered on the three main verbs "made alive with" (συνεζωοποίησεν, v. 5), "raised with" (συνήγειρεν, v. 6), and "seated with" (συνεκάθισεν, v. 6). The passage begins by describing the object of these verbs: "you" (ὑμᾶς) readers, who were "dead in sins and transgressions" (v. 1). The fact that the readers

12. E.g., Thielman, *Ephesians*, 118; Hoehner, *Ephesians*, 305–6; Best, *Ephesians*, 235.

13. E.g., Thielman, *Ephesians*, 118.

14. Kinzer, *Searching Her Own Mystery*, 74. *Contra* Lincoln, "Church and Israel," 607–8.

"once walked" in these sins and transgressions demonstrates that they were aligned to a spiritual power opposed to God (v. 2). However, this serious former state is not limited to "you" readers. In v. 3, "also we" are described as engaging in similar former conduct and as subject to the same plight: "we were, by nature, children of wrath, as [were] also the rest" (v. 3). In v. 4, the subject is introduced: God, who is "rich in mercy" and displays "great love." Verse 5a returns briefly to the object: "we," a pronoun which by now is being used inclusively to cover both the "you" of vv. 1–2 and the "we" of v. 3. "We" are again described as "dead in transgressions" (cf. v. 1). In vv. 5b–6 the main verbs appear: God has "made [us] alive with Christ," "raised [us] with [Christ]" and "seated [us] with [Christ]" in the heavenly realms. In v. 7, there is a clause indicating the purpose of God's action: to demonstrate in the coming ages the riches of his grace. Verses 8–10 draw out the key implications of vv. 1–7 (foreshadowed in v. 5). The activity of God in bringing sinners from death to life indicates that their salvation is "by grace" (v. 8). Negatively, this excludes boasting on behalf of "anyone" (vv. 8–9). Positively, it indicates that "we" are God's creation for the sake of "walking" in good works (v. 10).

Why does Paul highlight this distinction between "you" in vv. 1–2 and "we" in v. 3, only apparently to collapse the distinction by insisting that "you" and "we" share the same former state of being "dead" and the same present state of being "made alive with" Christ? Yee regards vv. 1–2 as an "ethnocentric" Jewish description of gentiles, which the author first presents and then undermines in v. 3 by conceding that "we" Jews too were in the same situation. In this way, the author is "turning the tables on himself and his fellow-Jews," paving the way for ethnic reconciliation.[15] However, there is no explicit indication that v. 3 is designed to undermine vv. 1–2, nor that "ethnocentrism" is the primary issue at this point. Rather, v. 3 is, to all appearances, meant to be read in parallel with vv. 1–2. Starling's analysis is insightful here:

> Having painted the blackest possible picture of the pre-conversion life of the Gentiles, the writer goes on in v. 3 to say the same things emphatically about himself and his fellow-Jews .... The "among whom" language of v. 3 (ἐν οἷς καὶ ἡμεῖς πάντες ἀνεστράφημέν) carries an implied spatial metaphor, reminiscent of the situation of Israel in exile.

15. Yee, *Ethnic Reconciliation*, 45–69, quotation from 57. Cf. the critique by Shkul, *Reading Ephesians*, 83–84.

If that is the case, then there is good reason to hear in the verse an allusion to the description of the house of Israel in Ezek 36, living "among the nations" (ἐν τοῖς ἔθνεσιν), under God's wrath and profaning his name by both their conduct and its punishment.[16]

Starling notes that the language of Israel being "among the nations" (ἐν τοῖς ἔθνεσιν/εἰς τὰ ἔθνη) as well as the concept of Israel being under God's "wrath" (ὀργή/θυμός) is particularly prevalent in Ezekiel.[17] Furthermore, Ezek 37:1–14 describes Israel as being "dead" (νεκρός, Ezek 37:9; cf. Eph 2:1) and made by God to "live" (ζάω, Ezek 37:3, 6, 9–10, 14; cf. the compound verb in Eph 2:5).[18] In addition, Paul's insistence that God's gracious activity rules out human boasting (Eph 2:8–9) may be an echo of Ezek 36:22, 32.[19]

The turn to "we also" in Eph 2:3, then, is designed to highlight a theme that is present in Israel's Scriptures, especially in Ezekiel. Israel, while distinct from the nations in certain ways (e.g., Ezek 37:28), is nevertheless subject to the same spiritual "death" as the nations and is in need of spiritual "life" from God. Although the question of Jewish sin is sometimes said to be absent from Ephesians—as opposed to, e.g., Rom 9–11[20]—Eph 2:3 demonstrates that this is not the case. The existence of Jewish sin, alongside gentile sin, is affirmed in Eph 2:1–3 and treated as a matter of spiritual "death." Nevertheless, as in Ezekiel, the affirmation of Israel's common plight with all humanity does not imply that Israel's distinctiveness has been nullified. Admittedly, as Starling rightly asserts, the distinction between Israel and the nations "recede[s] into the background for the rest of the paragraph [vv. 4–10], overshadowed by the larger story of human sin, divine grace and the exclusion of boasting."[21] In the foreground of Eph 2:4–10 is the affirmation that salvation is a divine creation or "product" (ποίημα, v. 10) that is not at all reliant on human "works" (v. 9), although it produces such works (v. 10). However, this does not mean that Israel's distinctiveness has been emptied of all meaning. It has simply been placed into a larger divine perspective—a perspective that

16. Starling, *Not My People*, 191.

17. Ibid. n. 94.

18. Hudson, "One New Humanity."

19. Starling, *Not My People*, 192.

20. Dahl, "Gentiles, Christians, and Israelites," 36.

21. Starling, *Not My People*, 192.

coheres with the prophetic witness and emphasizes God's gracious saving activity.

Brought from Far to Near (Eph 2:11–13)

Once Paul has established the primacy of God's gracious saving activity through Christ (Eph 2:1–10), he turns directly to discuss the relationship between Israel and the nations (Eph 2:11–22). In both passages, there is a "once-now" schema, indicating a transfer from a former negative state to a present positive state.[22] This has led some to conclude that the purpose of vv. 11–22 is the same as that of vv. 1–10: to highlight the greatness of the readers' individual salvation through a contrast with their former state. In this understanding, "Israel" is simply a comparative device used to achieve this end.[23] However, this conclusion does not take into account a key structural *difference* between the two passages. This difference consists in the relationship between the "we-you" distinction and the "once-now" schema in the two respective passages. In vv. 1–10, "you" and "we" are emphatically said to be in the *same* state of spiritual death before the transition to life and victory in Christ (vv. 1, 3). However, in vv. 11–22, "you gentiles" (v. 11) are said to have been in a *different* state before the transition: "you" were "those who were once far away" (ὑμεῖς οἵ ποτε ὄντες μακράν, v. 13; cf. v. 17). The transition involves "you" having been "made near" (ἐγενήθητε ἐγγύς, v. 13), as distinct from others, presumably Israelites, who were already "near" (ἐγγύς, v. 17). The distinction between these two groups is underscored by the term "both" (ἀμφότεροι). "We both"—i.e., the formerly "far" and "near"—have been given access to the Father in one Spirit (v. 18, cf. vv. 14, 16). Thus, at the end of the passage, it is emphasized that "also you" (καὶ ὑμεῖς) are being "built together" (συνοικοδομεῖσθε) into a dwelling for God by the Spirit (v. 22). In vv. 1–10, the emphasis is on "you" and "we" having the *same* plight and then receiving the *same* status; in vv. 11–22, the emphasis is on "you gentiles" having a plight *separate* from Israel and then receiving a status *equal* with Israel.

---

22. E.g., Lincoln, *Ephesians*, 86–88; Thielman, *Ephesians*, 148. The former state is indicated by the term "once" (vv. 2, 3, 11, 13); the present state is implied in the first passage (vv. 4–10) and indicated by the term "now" in the second passage (v. 13).

23. So Lincoln, "Church and Israel," 607–9.

The distinction between Israel and the "you gentiles" (v. 11), then, is a central theme throughout vv. 11–22. Before the work of Christ, this distinction was expressed in separation (v. 13) and "hostility" (v. 14). The key question for our purposes is this: how does vv. 11–22 portray the distinction between Israel and the nations *after* the work of Christ? As we have seen, several interpreters understand the distinction as having been obliterated by Christ. However, as we will now see, several elements of vv. 11–22 suggest that this is an inaccurate over-reading of the passage. The distinction between Israel and the nations has not been obliterated; rather it has been Christologically transformed in such a way that its negative aspects have been removed and it therefore no longer remains a barrier to genuine unity in Christ.

We now turn to see how this plays out in vv. 11–13. In this section, the gentile readers of the letter are told to "remember" that they have been brought from being "far" to being "near."

Remember What You Have Become (v. 11)

Ephesians 2:11 contains the first imperative in Ephesians: a command for the gentile readers of the letter to "remember" (μνημονεύετε).[24] The first thing they are commanded to remember is their prior, distinct gentile identity. The fact that they must remember this distinct gentile identity implies that it must still be relevant in some way to their present situation as believers in Christ.[25]

The command to "remember" is not necessarily assuming that each individual reader will be able to recall something he or she had once known. The command is better understood as an exercise in collective memory construction.[26] This is because gentile readers of the letter are being encouraged to understand their past, not in relation to their own

24. So the common division of Ephesians into two halves concerned with "theology" (Eph 1–3) and "ethics" or duty (Eph 4–6), while broadly useful, is imprecise. For this division see e.g., Caird, *Letters from Prison*, 70–71; Lincoln, *Ephesians*, 234; Best, *Ephesians*, 353; Hoehner, *Ephesians*, 499.

25. Barth, *Ephesians*, 253–325; Fowl, *Ephesians*, 83–102; cf. Kinzer, *Postmissionary Messianic Judaism*, 151–79; Campbell, "Unity and Diversity."

26. Cf. Esler, "Remember My Fetters." See also Shkul, *Reading Ephesians*, 79–141, although Shkul's exploration of the purpose of such "remembering" is quite different from the explanation offered here.

prior experience, but in relation to Israel. The term itself assumes an Israel-centered perspective.[27] As Fowl observes:

> That designation only had currency within Judaism or in relation to Judaism. . . . They need to remember (or reconceive) of their past as a Gentile past. They need to learn both what being a Gentile meant when they were outside of Christ and what it means now that they are in Christ.[28]

> Christian identity requires the taking on or remembering of Gentile identity because Christian identity is always tied to Israel. This is not to say that Jewish identity is untouched by the life, death, and resurrection of Christ. Far from it. Jewish identity is also radically reconceived in the light of Christ. Paul's accounts of the call of Israel, the place of the torah, and the inclusion of the Gentiles within redeemed Israel—all these are accounts that most of Paul's Jewish contemporaries rejected. Nevertheless, only in the light of this reconception can there be true reconciliation between Jew and Gentile.[29]

It is not only their gentile past that readers of the letter must remember. They must remember their *transfer* from a gentile past "in the flesh" with its negative connotations (vv. 11–12) to a new state of being made "near" through "the blood of Christ" (v. 13). The memory being constructed is, in other words, a narrative memory.[30] It is not simply that the readers must dwell on their former state of exclusion,[31] nor that they must focus on their present state of proximity while entirely forgetting their gentile identity.[32] They are not simply to remember what they *were*,

27. Best, "Christian View of Judaism," 92; Caird, *Letters from Prison*, 55; Lincoln, "Church and Israel," 609.

28. Fowl, *Ephesians*, 85–86.

29. Ibid., 101.

30. The content of the imperative "remember" (μνημονεύετε) is best taken to be the entirety of vv. 11–13 following the ὅτι in v. 11. The ὅτι in v. 12 should be taken as causal (see below).

31. *Pace* Best, "Christian View of Judaism," 92.

32. *Pace* Harrill, who takes the imperative in Eph 2:11 to "remember" their former state as gentiles as an entirely negative statement—that is, simply as a way of emphasizing their "new heritage and bloodline" by way of contrast ("Ethnic Fluidity in Ephesians," 389–401, quotation from 396). *Pace* also Yee, who regards the command to "remember" their prior status primarily as a way to evoke and undermine the divisive Jewish "ethnocentrism" that the author is seeking to oppose, and perhaps to stop it happening again (*Ethnic Reconciliation*, 72–87, 124–25). *Pace* also Dunning,

nor simply to remember what they *are*. Rather, they are to remember what they have *become*. This means that their gentile past is still relevant for their present identity. Furthermore, this present relevance cannot be limited to the concept of a negative foil[33] or a history lesson.[34] The term "gentile" is still used in a positive sense in Eph 3, where Paul addresses his readers as "you, the gentiles" (3:1), and continues to speak of "the gentiles" as fellow-heirs (3:6) as and recipients of his apostolic ministry (3:8). Being "gentiles" in relation to Israel, therefore, is not merely a past status for the readers of Ephesians; it also informs their present. They have not stopped being gentiles. Rather, in Christ, the significance of their gentile status has been radically transformed. They were once gentiles *contra* Israel; now they are gentiles *blessed alongside* Israel and blessed *through* the apostolic ministry that came first to Israel. Indeed, it is only "in Christ" that they can think of themselves as gentiles at all.[35]

The Limited Value of Jewish Circumcision (v. 11)

We now come to examine the negative descriptions of the former state of the "gentiles" in vv. 11–12. The first, and most significant for our understanding of Israelite identity, is the use of the term "uncircumcision" or "foreskin" (ἀκροβυστία, v. 11). As we saw in chapter 2, the use of this term and the corresponding term "circumcision" (περιτομή) is often taken to imply that circumcision, and thus distinctive Jewish identity, has been rendered invalid for all those in Christ, including Jews. However, a closer examination of the passage and the terminology it uses shows that this conclusion is unwarranted.

Verse 11 is worded in such a way that the element of hostility comes to the fore. The gentiles were "those called [the] foreskin" (οἱ λεγόμενοι ἀκροβυστία). This expression does not simply refer to the traditional

---

"Strangers and Aliens," 13.

33. *Pace* Lincoln, who maintains: "They are asked to reflect on their former condition in terms of categories valid at a prior stage in the history of salvation in order to appreciate all the more their present privileges" ("Church and Israel," 609). *Pace* also Dahl, who maintains: "Ephesians simply reminds Christian Gentiles of their former status as excluded aliens in order to demonstrate the magnitude of the blessings which God in his mercy has extended to them" ("Gentiles, Christians, and Israelites," 38).

34. *Pace* Best, who maintains that "perhaps as one from Jewish stock he felt Gentile Christians too easily forgot their origins" ("Christian View of Judaism," 92).

35. Fowl, *Ephesians*, 88–89.

Jewish distinction between Israel and the nations; rather it expresses the hostile purposes for which this division was often employed. The translation "foreskin" captures the strongly derogatory nature of the term ἀκροβυστία. When applied to people, "foreskin" is more than a neutral synonym for "non-Jew." Rather, it is a term of derision (e.g., Gen 34:14; 1 Macc 1:15; Acts 11:3). Paul, then, is not here simply claiming that the gentiles were once *different* from non-Jews with respect to circumcision; he is highlighting the fact that they were "called" a derogatory name by Jews, which heightened distance and promoted hostility.

This hostility was promoted on the other side also. The Jewish name-callers themselves are described as "what is called [the] circumcision" (τῆς λεγομένης περιτομῆς). As Barclay shows, when used by non-Jews to refer to Jews among the Mediterranean Diaspora, "circumcision" was normally a term of contempt or ridicule:

> Whenever it is commented on by non-Jews, circumcision is derided, either as a peculiar "mutilation" (on a par with castration, according to Hadrian's later rescript) or, perhaps, as a "barbarian" rite properly abandoned by "civilized" men. For Philo's Hellenized peers, such as Apion, the Jewish practice was laughable (Philo, *Spec Leg* 1.2; Josephus, *C Ap* 2.137).[36]

Paul, then, is not here simply critiquing the existence of a distinction between circumcised and uncircumcised.[37] Rather, he is highlighting the way in which this distinction had been used for the purposes of opposition, distancing, and hostility between Jews and non-Jews. The problem is not Jewish distinctiveness itself, but Jew-gentile *hostility*, which is here seen to be expressed in derisive language—quite literally, it was a matter of Jews and gentiles "calling" each other names.

The final three words of v. 11, literally meaning "in flesh, of hand-made [origin]" (ἐν σαρκὶ χειροποιήτου), provide a more directly theological evaluation of circumcision. Several interpreters argue that the use of these terms is intended to disparage physical circumcision to such an extent that it can retain no place whatsoever in relation to Christ. Lincoln, for example, claims that the term "flesh," especially when used in contrast with "Spirit" (v. 22), denotes inferior ethnic categories which have been "transcended" and so "no longer count as religiously significant."[38]

36. Barclay, *Mediterranean Diaspora*, 438–39.
37. *Pace* Lincoln, "Church and Israel," 609.
38. Ibid.; cf. Caird, *Letters from Prison*, 55.

Lincoln and others also point out that the term "hand-made" (χειροποίητος) is normally used in the LXX to refer to idols (e.g., Lev 26:1, 30; Jdt 8:18; Wis 14:8; Isa 2:18; 10:11; 16:12; 19:1; 21:9; 31:7; 46:6; Dan 5:4, 23; 6:28) and in the New Testament to refer to the physical temple (Mark 14:58; Acts 7:48; Heb 9:11, 24). On this basis, they argue that the term has irreducibly "negative" associations that imply that physical circumcision is no longer valid.[39]

However, while it is true that these terms do imply a degree of *relative* subsidiarity,[40] they are not intended to nullify the value of circumcision in its entirety. Rather, they indicate that physical circumcision *by itself* is insufficient to achieve the grand divine purposes spelled out in this passage. This is consonant with the scriptural perspective found, for example, in Jeremiah. Jeremiah 9:25–26 (LXX 9:24–25) brings an indictment on Israel for being circumcised merely in their "foreskin" without also being circumcised in their "heart." For Jeremiah, physical circumcision by itself makes no difference—it counts as little as shaving around the face, and so is no grounds for Israel's distinction from other nations. What is needed is an acknowledgement of God's work, which involves refusing to "boast" (verb καυχάομαι) in one's own wisdom, might, or riches, but rather to "boast" only in the knowledge of the Lord's activity (Jer 9:23–24 [LXX 9:22–23]). Jeremiah goes on to insist that Israel, despite their physical circumcision, has learned "the ways of the nations" (τὰς ὁδοὺς τῶν ἐθνῶν, Jer 10:2)—which primarily consist in making idols, described as (literally) "hand of goldsmiths, works of craftsmen" (χεὶρ χρυσοχόων, ἔργα τεχνιτῶν, Jer 10:9).

Nowhere, however, does Jeremiah nullify the value of physical circumcision entirely.[41] He merely relativizes it as a human action, insisting that beyond physical circumcision there is something greater—an acknowledgement of and "boasting" in God's saving activity. This coheres with the perspective found in Eph 2. In Eph 2:8–10, as we have seen, Paul has insisted that salvation by grace excludes "boasting" (verb καυχάομαι,

---

39. Lincoln, "Church and Israel," 609; Thielman, *Ephesians*, 160.

40. *Pace* Yee, who argues that the term "made by hands" is entirely positive from a Jewish perspective (*Ethnic Reconciliation*, 85).

41. Cf. Rom 2:25–29 and 3:1–2, which demonstrates that circumcision of the heart and the spirit fulfill, rather than cancel, Jewish circumcision (as I argue in Windsor, *Vocation of Israel*, 181–89). See also, by way of contrast, Barnabas 9.4–6, which cites this passage from Jeremiah to demonstrate that the circumcision in which the Jews trusted has been entirely "nullified" (9.4). Ephesians nowhere makes this claim.

v. 9) because it is a divine rather than a human work. Believers have not worked for their salvation; rather they are ultimately the "product" (ποίημα, v. 10) of God. However, this does not rule out the value of human actions, since Christ-believers are created to do "good works" (v. 10). Now in v. 11, Paul identifies circumcision as something "in flesh" and the "product of [human] hands" (χειροποίητος) rather than the product of God's gracious saving activity.[42] This demonstrates the limited value of circumcision. However, it is going too far to claim that Paul is ruling out any possible value for Jewish circumcision "in Christ." The point is that physical circumcision *by itself* cannot achieve the purposes spelled out in the rest of the passage. For those purposes to be achieved, the activity of Christ is necessary.

The purpose of the discussion of circumcision in Eph 2:11, then, is not to cancel the value of circumcision or Jewish distinction entirely. The purpose is more specific. Paul here refers to the way in which Jewish circumcision and distinction had been used in the context of hostility between Jews and non-Jews, and further reminds the readers that Jewish circumcision, as a human activity, would not be able to achieve the divine purposes of overcoming such hostility.

Gentile Exclusion from the Messiah and from Israel (v. 12)

We have seen that v. 11 focuses on the hostility between Jews and gentiles. The first word in v. 12 (ὅτι) should be translated "because"— i.e., v. 12 is describing the grounds for this hostility.[43] This helps us to understand the purpose of the description of the gentiles in v. 12. A key interpretive question is what it means for the gentiles to have been "at that time without Christ." Many interpreters regard this as a statement that before the coming of Jesus Christ, the gentiles were excluded from any hope of benefitting from the promises related to the Messiah.[44] This

42. Lohse, "χείρ, κτλ.," 436.

43. The ὅτι in v. 12 should be taken as causal, indicating the grounds for the hostility described in v. 11 (Yee, *Ethnic Reconciliation*, 96–97; Barth, *Ephesians*, 255–56). It is not a resumptive ὅτι (*pace* Best, *Ephesians*, 240; Thielman, *Ephesians*, 154; Hoehner, *Ephesians*, 355; Schlier, *An Die Epheser*, 120). While the phrase "at that time" (τῷ καιρῷ ἐκείνῳ, v. 12) refers back to the term "once" (ποτέ, v. 11), it does not simply resume the argument.

44. E.g., Barth, *Ephesians*, 255–56; Caird, *Letters from Prison*, 56; Best, "Christian View of Judaism," 93–94; Thielman, *Ephesians*, 154.

understanding, however, is at odds with scriptural texts that clearly hold out promises and hope for the gentiles through Israel's Messiah (e.g., Isa 11:4, 10; cf. Gen 12:1, 3). However, if we understand v. 12 in terms of real and active hostility between Jews and gentiles, the terminology of exclusion from "Christ" or the "Messiah" becomes more understandable.[45] For many Jews living in the Roman Empire, the gentiles were seen as foreign oppressors of Israel, and the coming Messiah was seen as the vindicator of Israel against the gentiles. The Psalms of Solomon well illustrate this kind of attitude. Psalm of Solomon 17 uses language that is similar to that used in Eph 2:11–12 (and cf. 2:1–3).[46] The Psalm describes the invasion of a foreign conqueror (probably the Roman general Pompey), and interprets and expands upon the Messianic hopes found in Psalm 2 and Isaiah:[47]

> 3 But we hope (ἐλπιοῦμεν) in God our savior:
> because the strength and mercy of our God will last forever,
> and the kingdom of our God will last forever
> in judgment over the Gentiles (τὰ ἔθνη)
> 4 It was you, O Lord, who chose David as king over Israel (Ισραήλ) . . .
> 5 But sinners (ἁμαρτωλοί) revolted against us because of our sins (ἐν ταῖς ἁμαρτίαις):
> they attacked us and drove us out.
> Those to whom you promised (ἐπηγγείλω) nothing,
> they violently stole from us, . . .
> 13 As the enemy (ὁ ἐχθρός) was a foreigner (ἐν ἀλλοτριότητι), and his heart was foreign (ἀλλοτρία) to our God, so he acted arrogantly.
> 14 So in Jerusalem he engaged in all the practices
> that Gentiles (τὰ ἔθνή) do for their gods (τοὺς θεούς) in their great cities (ἐν ταῖς πόλεσι)
> 15 And the people of the covenant (οἱ υἱοὶ τῆς διαθήκης) living among the many nations adopted these things. . . .
> 21 Look, O Lord, and raise up for them their king,
> a son of David, to rule over your servant Israel
> in the time that you know, O God.
> 22 Undergird him with the strength to destroy the unrighteous rulers,
> to purge Jerusalem from the Gentiles

---

45. Cf. Yee, *Ethnic Reconciliation*, 87–111.

46. I am here following up a suggestion by Williams, "Violent Ethno-Racial Reconciliation," 121–22. I am not claiming a direct literary connection between Psalms of Solomon and Ephesians; but rather claiming that the former well illustrates the *kind* of attitudes described in Eph 2:12.

47. Atkinson, "Solomon, Psalms of."

> who trample her down to destruction;
> 23 In wisdom and righteousness
> to drive out the sinners from the inheritance,
> to smash the arrogance of sinners like a potter's jar;
> 24 to demolish all their resources with an iron rod;
> to destroy the lawbreaking Gentiles with the word of his mouth;
> to scatter the Gentiles from his presence at his threat;
> to condemn sinners by their own consciences. . . .
> 32 because everyone will be holy (ἅγιοι),
> and their king will be the Lord Messiah (χριστὸς κύριος) (Ps. Sol. 17 [Wright]).

Other Jewish texts have similar concerns—particularly 1 & 2 Maccabees. The term "commonwealth" (πολιτεία) is used in 2 Macc 13:14, for example, in the context of an armed struggle against the foreign invading king Antiochus—the Jews are exhorted to "fight bravely unto death for laws, temple, city, homeland and commonwealth (πολιτεία)."[48]

These descriptions have many parallels with the description of the gentiles in Eph 2:12 who were:

> at that time separated from Christ (Χριστοῦ), alienated (ἀπηλλοτριωμένοι) from the commonwealth (πολιτείας) of Israel (Ισραήλ) and strangers to the covenants (διαθηκῶν) of promise (ἐπαγγελίας), having no hope (ἐλπίδα) and without God (ἄθεοι) in the world.

Verse 12, in other words, is a description of the plight of gentiles from the point of view of Jews who viewed gentiles primarily as enemies. This point of view is not without scriptural warrant. Psalm of Solomon 17, for example, draws heavily on texts from Isaiah and Psalm 2. However, it lacks the kind of nuance that might arise if texts about gentile hope such as Gen 12:3 or Isa 11:10 were to be drawn into the picture. It is, in other words, a description arising from the context of Jew-gentile hostility, which was quite real for many; but it is not intended to be an absolute statement that no gentile could ever benefit from Israel's privileges or Israel's Messiah before the coming of Christ.

---

48. Cf. Yee, *Ethnic Reconciliation*, 96–103.

Gentiles Made Near (v. 13)

It is significant that in Ps. Sol. 17, as in the vision of Isaiah from which it draws its imagery, the state of hostility between Israel and the nations is seen to have arisen from human sin. This sin affects both Jews and gentiles. The Psalm acknowledges that Jews, like the gentiles, have committed "sin" (ἁμαρτία) and live in "disobedience" (ἀπειθεία; Ps. Sol. 17.5, 20; cf. 17.15) and so are being judged by God. This perspective, as we have seen, is also found in Eph 2:1–3. However, there is a key difference between the perspectives found in Ps. Sol. 17 and Eph 2. According to the Psalm, God acts quite differently toward the sins of Israel and the gentiles respectively. He rescues Israel from the consequences of their sin, but judges gentiles for their sin. There is some hope held out for gentiles; however it is relatively minor: it is a hope that those gentiles willing to act as fearful subservient vassals to the Messiah will receive appropriate justice and mercy and have the opportunity to behold God's glory in Jerusalem as they stand before him (Ps. Sol. 17.29–31, 34). According to Eph 2, however, God's grace in Christ has emphatically brought about salvation from sin and its consequences for *both* Jews *and* gentiles, on equal terms, so that both of them are seated in victory with him (Eph 2:4–10). This emphasis on the equality of salvation for Jews and gentiles lies behind the logic of Eph 2:11–13. Gentile sin had previously meant that gentiles were excluded from Israel, and thereby excluded from any hope of the Messiah (v. 12). However, since *both* Jews and gentiles have been saved from sin and raised in Christ on equal terms (Eph 2:1–10), then "in Christ Jesus," gentiles have the same hope as Jews and have thus been made "near" (v. 13).

Thus, for gentiles, the "vertical" movement they have undergone—from spiritual death to being seated in the heavenly realms with Christ (Eph 2:1–10)—has created a corresponding "horizontal" movement—from being "far" to "near" (Eph 2:13; terminology that foreshadows the later reference to Isa 57:19 in Eph 2:17).[49] The distance of hostility has been replaced by closeness. This does not necessarily imply that there is no distinction between Israel and the gentiles whatsoever. The focus here

---

49. Thielman, *Ephesians*, 158. Some see the language of being "made near" in Eph 2:13 as echoing the language of proselyte conversion, but transforming the language so that it speaks, not of conversion to Judaism, but of joining the church (Lincoln, "Church and Israel," 610–11; Caird, *Letters from Prison*, 56–57; Best, *Ephesians*, 245). However, the textual evidence for these echoes is weak, and the suggestion does not seem to shed much light on the text as it stands (Yee, *Ethnic Reconciliation*, 115–16).

is not on indistinguishability, but on proximity. The question is: proximity to what? There is some ambiguity at this point, since v. 12 has described the gentiles' former state in terms of distance from a number of things: Christ, the commonwealth of Israel, the covenants of the promise, hope, and God.[50] Since, as we have seen, the primary emphasis in vv. 11–12 has been on hostility between Israel and the gentiles, it is best to understand the primary emphasis in v. 13 to be on the proximity of gentiles to Israel.[51] Nevertheless, the concept of proximity to the risen Christ himself (v. 5) remains foundational to the text.

The Blood of Christ (v. 13)

This proximity has been achieved "through the blood of Christ," i.e., through Christ's sacrificial death on the cross.[52] It is again instructive here to contrast Ephesians with the supersessionist Epistle of Barnabas. For both the Epistle of Barnabas and Ephesians, Jesus' sacrificial offering, first and foremost, achieved forgiveness of sins (Barn. 5.1; Eph 1:7). In addition to forgiveness of sins, however, both Barnabas and Ephesians describe a second outcome for Jesus' sacrificial death. For Barnabas, this second outcome is judgment against those who persecuted Jesus and the prophets, i.e. the Jews:

> Therefore, the Son of God came in the flesh for this reason, that he might total up all the sins of those who persecuted his prophets to death. And so this is why he allowed himself to suffer. (Barn. 5.11–12 [Ehrman], cf. 8.2)[53]

Thus, for Barnabas, the manifestation of Jesus creates a *division* between Jews and Christians; i.e., between "them," who are filled with sins, and "us," who receive the covenant:

---

50. Best, *Ephesians*, 245.

51. Cf. Yee, *Ethnic Reconciliation*, 111–21.

52. Best, *Ephesians*, 246–47.

53. Cf. the position of earlier anti-Judaistic writers such as Gerhard Kittel. Arnal maintains that Kittel advocated separation and discrimination against Jewish people in his own day as a "reflection of God's judgment on disobedient Israel"—a disobedience shown ultimately in their crucifixion of Jesus (*Symbolic Jesus*, 11, summarizing a key argument in Kittel's *Die Judenfrage* [1933]).

He was made manifest so that those people might be completely
filled with sins, and that we might receive the covenant through
the Lord Jesus, who inherited it. (Barn. 14.5 [Ehrman])

Barnabas, in other words, uses Christ's sacrificial death to promote a
hostile replacement theology. Ephesians, however, does the opposite. For
Ephesians, the second outcome of Jesus' blood is *reconciliation* between
Jews and gentiles (Eph 2:13, 16). Jesus' death does not result in Christ-
believers replacing Israel. Rather, it results in Christ-believers coming
near to Israel, and so being reconciled alongside Israel. The way in which
this proximity and reconciliation have been achieved are spelled out in
the following verses.

Christ Who Achieved Peace (Eph 2:14–16)

In Eph 2:14–18, Paul spells out in more detail how the gentiles have been
made "near" (v. 13) through the blood of Christ. The subject of the entire
paragraph is Christ—i.e., "he" (αὐτός), placed emphatically at the start of
v. 14 (cf. "Christ" in v. 13).[54] The key concept in the paragraph is "peace"
(εἰρήνη). Syntactically, the paragraph falls into two main sections: vv. 14–
16 and 17–18. These two sections are based on two main clauses. The first
main clause (v. 14a) pronounces that Christ *is* "our peace," and the section
that it governs (vv. 14–16) focuses on the way Christ has achieved peace
through his sacrificial death. The second main clause (v. 17a) pronounces
that Christ *proclaimed* "peace," and the section that it governs (vv. 17–18)
focuses on Christ's missionary activity.[55] In both sections, two groups
are on view, signaled by the term "both" (ἀμφότεροι, vv. 14, 16, 18). The
entire paragraph, then, is claiming that the state of "peace," which applies

54. Lincoln, following several others, argues that the author of Ephesians is here
adapting "hymnic material which originally depicted Christ as the embodiment of
peace and bringer of reconciliation for a divided cosmos" for a new situation ("Church
and Israel," 611). It is worth noting, however, the skeptical comments by Thielman
on this matter (*Ephesians*, 57). Stuhlmacher sees it as a "christological exegesis of Isa.
9:5–6; 52:7; and 57:19" ("He Is Our Peace," 187). Yee, however, rightly observes that
the passage as it stands is integral to the letter as an "amplification" of Christ's laud-
able act of ethnic reconciliation (*Ethnic Reconciliation*, 126–89). This observation is
insightful; however, Yee overstates his case that the section is written primarily to
oppose Jewish ethnocentrism (e.g., ibid., 140).

55. The ὅτι at the start of v. 18 subordinates v. 18 to the main clause in v. 17. It gives
the reason or grounds for why Christ came and preached to both far and near.

to "both" Jews and gentiles, has been brought about by a combination of 1) Christ's death on the cross and 2) Christ's missionary activity.

This first section (vv. 14–16) contains three key concepts that are significant for post-supersessionist interpretation: the breaking down of a wall (v. 14); the invalidation of the law (v. 15); and the creation of a new humanity (v. 15). The vocabulary and the syntax in which these concepts are expressed is complex, and their precise meaning is contested. We will now demonstrate how a post-supersessionist perspective helps to provide an understanding of each concept that fits into a plausible and coherent reading of the passage as a whole.

Breaking Down the Wall (v. 14)

In v. 14, Christ is described as the one

> who has made [us] both one and has broken down in his flesh
> the dividing wall of hostility . . . (Eph 2:14)

What is the "dividing wall of hostility" (literally, "the dividing-wall of the fence/wall, the hostility," τὸ μεσότοιχον τοῦ φραγμοῦ . . . τὴν ἔχθραν), and in what sense has Christ "broken down" (λύσας) this wall? There are numerous views on these questions; the most common can be grouped into three broad categories.[56]

Some interpreters understand the dividing-wall to be equivalent to "the law" (τὸν νόμον) in v. 15.[57] In this view, the law of Moses is being portrayed in terms of its role to protect Israel against gentile impurity. Those who advocate this interpretation frequently point to the Letter of Aristeas, which states that Moses the "Lawgiver" has "fenced us round with impregnable ramparts and walls of iron, that we might not mingle at

---

56. Some older interpreters understood this phrase as a fragment of traditional material describing a gnostic redeemer myth in which a redeemer-figure destroys the cosmic barrier between heaven and earth (Schlier, *An Die Epheser*, 124–25). However, this theory is now commonly regarded as untenable (Stuhlmacher, "He Is Our Peace," 186–87; Yee, *Ethnic Reconciliation*, 144). Cf. Chrysostom's interpretation of the wall (strengthened by the law) as the sin that cuts both Jew and gentile off from God (*Galatians and Ephesians*, 150–51).

57. E.g., Caird, *Letters from Prison*, 58–59; Lincoln, *Ephesians*, 141–42; Thielman, *Ephesians*, 166–67. In this view, there are actually three accusative terms in apposition: "the dividing-wall" (τὸ μεσότοιχον, v. 14), "the hostility" (τὴν ἔχθραν, v. 14), and "the law" (τὸν νόμον, v. 15). This view also requires that the two participles "broken down" (λύσας, v. 14) and "invalidated" (καταργήσας, v. 15) are being used in apposition.

all with any of the other nations, but remain pure in body and soul" (Let. Arist. 139, cf. 142 [Evans]).[58] In this view, the abolition of the entire law of Moses is central to the passage; it is Christ's pivotal accomplishment. The logic is as follows: because the law created a distinct Jewish people, it naturally became a source of hostility between Jews and others. Hence the abolition of the entire law—i.e., the breaking down of the protective wall—is the key to the removal of hostility. Lincoln thus explains the reference in Ephesians as follows:

> In functioning as a fence to protect Israel from the impurity of the Gentiles, the law became such a sign of Jewish particularism that it also alienated Gentiles and became a cause of hostility. . . . Christ neutralized these negative effects of the law by doing away with the law.[59]

However, this logic does not easily cohere with the syntax of the passage. Syntactically, the invalidation of the law is best taken as being subordinate to the breaking down of the wall, not as being in parallel to it.[60] Hence the two ideas, while connected, are not equivalent. Furthermore, the reference to the Letter of Aristeas creates more problems for this view than is commonly recognized. Within the context of the Letter of Aristeas, the mention of the law as a "fence" is not intended to engender hostility against Jewish particularism, but rather admiration for distinctive Jewish purity.[61] Interpreters too quickly assume that any mention of Jewish distinctiveness is intended to invoke hostility between Jews and non-Jews. This is not necessarily the case in the Letter of Aristeas, and cannot automatically be assumed for Ephesians.[62] Thus, the syntax, as well as the lack of unambiguous support in contemporary literature, renders this possibility unlikely.

58. Evans, *Pseudepigrapha*.

59. Lincoln, *Ephesians*, 141–42.

60. Yee, *Ethnic Reconciliation*, 147–48. The syntax of the passage is complex and contested; however, as Yee here points out, if the two participles "broken down" (λύσας, v. 14) and "invalidated" (καταργήσας, v. 15) were being used in parallel, we would expect a καί between them, as there is between "made" (ποιήσας, v. 14) and "broken down" (λύσας, v. 14). Since there is no such καί, it is more likely that καταργήσας is intended to be subordinate to λύσας (and probably to ποιήσας).

61. So Ibid., 145–47.

62. There are of course places where the concept of Jewish distinctiveness is couched in hostile terms: e.g., Jub. 22.16–18 (Williams, "Violent Ethno-Racial Reconciliation," 123). However, it is not *necessarily* the case that Jewish distinctiveness creates hostility.

Other interpreters regard the "wall" as a straightforward metaphor for hostile separation between Jews and gentiles, without seeing any need to seek a further referent.[63] Yee, who takes a "New Perspective" approach to Ephesians,[64] understands the "wall" as a "social barrier" arising directly from Jewish ethnocentrism:

> The "wall" refers to the *social* barrier which is closely associated with some of the boundary markers used by the Jews to separate themselves from the Gentiles (e.g., the mark of the covenant in the "flesh", and the ethnically based "body politic of Israel" and other indicators of Israel's God-given grace). . . . This barrier is the most immediate corollary of the Jews' reluctance to set God's grace on a broader canvas and constriction of it to a particular ethnic group.[65]

This view is supported by the fact that the terms "wall" (τεῖχος/τοῖχος) and "fence/wall" (φράγμος) are common terms for barriers erected to protect against hostile enemies. In the LXX, such terms are often used to refer to the walls of Jerusalem in the context of hostility between Israel and the surrounding nations (e.g., Ezra 4:12, 16; 9:9; 1 Macc 1:33; 4:60; 6:7, 62; Isa 5:5; etc.). However, Eph 2:14 refers not simply to a "wall" (τεῖχος/τοῖχος) but to a "dividing-wall" (μεσότοιχον), which is an architectural term for a dividing-wall internal to a building.[66] This suggests that something more specific is being referred to here. The hints of priestly imagery that have already appeared in Ephesians,[67] and the clear temple imagery that emerges by the end of Eph 2 (v. 21), suggests that the dividing-wall may be alluding to a wall within the Jerusalem temple.

This is why several interpreters see in Eph 2:14 a reference to "the balustrade, the *soreg* in the (Jerusalem) temple courtyard which separated the court of the Gentiles from the more sacred precincts which only Jews might enter."[68] Josephus, for example, refers to a "stone wall of partition"

63. Fong, "Racial Reconciliation," 573; Best, *Ephesians*, 256–57; Yee, *Ethnic Reconciliation*, 149–52.

64. See chapter 2.

65. Yee, *Ethnic Reconciliation*, 151.

66. Best, *Ephesians*, 257.

67. See chapter 3; Kinzer, *Searching Her Own Mystery*, 69–73.

68. Yee, *Ethnic Reconciliation*, 148–49; Yee himself regards this view as possible but not necessary. See also MacDonald, "Politics of Identity," 434; Campbell, "Unity and Diversity," 16; Wright, *Justification*, 148; Cohick, *Ephesians*, 76–77.

(ἑρκίον λιθίνου δρυφάκτου), which included an inscription stating that anyone from a foreign nation (τὸν ἀλλοεθνῆ) who entered through would find himself under a death sentence (*Ant.* 15.417; see also *War* 5.193–94, 6.124–26; cf. Num 1:51). Archaeological findings have confirmed the existence of this inscription.[69] The hostility that this partition and its accompanying inscription could engender is illustrated in Acts 21:27–29.[70] Here, Luke narrates an episode in which certain Jews from Asia presume that Paul has taken a Greek into the temple. On this basis, they stir up a mob against him, with the intent to kill him. Some interpreters have questioned whether it is plausible for readers in Asia Minor to have been aware of the Jerusalem partition.[71] However, since Josephus refers to this partition in multiple places, and since Luke includes "Jews from Asia" as the main protagonists in his narrative about the Jerusalem temple without feeling any need to explain the reference, it is likely that knowledge of this partition was widespread among the Jewish Diaspora, and therefore among those with whom members of the Diaspora came into contact, such as the early gentile Christ-believers in Asia Minor. Others point out that the terms used by Josephus (ἑρκίον, δρύφακτος) are different to those used in Ephesians (μεσότοιχον, φραγμός).[72] However, there are plausible reasons why these specific terms might be used in Ephesians. The architectural term "dividing-wall" (μεσότοιχον) suitably recalls the spatial division between "far" and "near" described in vv. 11–13. Furthermore, as we have already seen, the terminology used in Eph 2:14 is often used in contexts where hostility between groups of people is in view. Thus, an allusion to the partition in the Jerusalem temple is quite likely here in Eph 2:14.

Christ has broken down this dividing-wall "in his flesh," a phrase which must refer to his sacrificial death on the cross (cf. vv. 13, 16).[73] Clearly Christ did not literally destroy the temple balustrade or its accompanying inscription at the time of his death—these were in place

---

69. Yee, *Ethnic Reconciliation*, 149; Best, *Ephesians*, 253.

70. Tucker, "Continuation of Gentile Identity (Moody)."

71. E.g., Best, *Ephesians*, 254.

72. Ibid.

73. Ibid., 259. The reason Paul chose the term "flesh" in Eph 2:14 was most likely to recall his previous argument. It enables him to emphasize that Christ took human "flesh" (cf. Eph 2:3), which is subject to "death," "trespasses," and "sins" (cf. Eph 2:1), in order to achieve "forgiveness of trespasses" by his own sacrificial death (Eph 1:7).

up to the destruction of the temple in 70 C.E. (Josephus, *War* 6.124–26).[74] How, then, can Christ's death be said to have broken down this dividing-wall? Verses 14–15 answer this question. In v. 14, the "dividing-wall" is specified more exactly through the term "hostility."[75] The order of words seems chosen to have a particular effect on the reader: firstly, the image of the "dividing-wall" in the temple is brought to mind; secondly, its significance is focused not in terms of the literal dividing-wall but in terms of the "hostility" between Jew and gentile that it engendered. In v. 15, the means by which the "dividing-wall" (i.e., the hostility) is broken down is actually specified. Christ has broken down the wall "by abolishing the law of the commandments in decrees" (v. 15).[76] The reference to "abolishing the law" is not intended to stand on its own. Rather it is introduced into the discourse as an explanation of the particular means by which Christ has destroyed the "hostility" between Jew and gentile, a hostility that has already been conceived in terms of the "dividing-wall" in the temple. It is important to bear this relationship in mind as we seek to understand the meaning of the respective terms.

Abolishing the Law (v. 15a)

In v. 15a, Paul states that the way in which Christ has destroyed the dividing-wall is

> by abolishing the law of the commandments in decrees (Eph 2:15a, my translation).

This phrase has been interpreted in a wide variety of ways. As we saw in chapter 2, some understand it as a claim that the observance of the law of Moses *as a whole* has been abolished for all, including for Jews. This is either because the law is rendered obsolete by the new creation in

---

74. MacDonald suggests a possible reference to the destruction of the temple in Eph 2:14 ("Politics of Identity," 434). However, even if this were the case, it would at most be an allusion, and would not be the primary meaning of the phrase "broken down in his flesh the dividing-wall of hostility." The destruction of the wall is being envisaged as something that happened at the time of Jesus' death (v. 16), and prior to the apostolic mission which began at Pentecost (v. 17, see below).

75. "The hostility" (τὴν ἔχθραν) follows the participle and is placed in apposition with "the dividing-wall" (τὸ μεσότοιχον).

76. This is a participial phrase expressing the *means* by which the "breaking down" of the dividing-wall has been achieved (Wallace, *Grammar*, 630).

Christ,[77] or because the law creates hostility between human beings and God,[78] or because the law creates hostility between Jews and gentiles.[79] Others understand the phrase as a claim that the *ceremonial* elements of the law of Moses have been abolished for all, including for Jews; a more recent argument concentrates on the abolition of the Jewish *boundary-marking* functions of the law of Moses.[80] We saw that such claims, while common, are too broad and sweeping, and thus constitute over-readings of this phrase in Eph 2:15. As we will now see, the phrase has a specific function in the passage, and the term "law" is qualified in a specific way.

Initial Observations

There are two initial observations that will be important to keep in mind as we approach the phrase, and that should provide controls on our interpretation.

Firstly, the word "law" (νόμος) appears nowhere else in Ephesians. Unlike Romans and Galatians, Ephesians does not employ the term as a key element of its argument.[81] This means we have far less clear contextual lexical information within Ephesians to help us determine what

77. E.g., Yoder Neufeld, *Ephesians*, 131.

78. E.g., Chrysostom, *Galatians and Ephesians*, 151.

79. Caird, *Letters from Prison*, 59; Dahl, "Gentiles, Christians, and Israelites," 36; Lincoln, "Church and Israel," 611–12; Moritz, *A Profound Mystery*, 40–42, 52–53. The view of Shkul is more nuanced but moves in the same direction (*Reading Ephesians*, 79–141). For Shkul, Ephesians itself does not demand that Israel's distinctive nature and Jewish Torah-observance is abolished entirely. However, since 1) Ephesians' overarching framework involves a single Christ-based identity, 2) there is no evidence in Ephesians for continuing multiple social identities, and 3) Israelite identity and law-keeping do not seem to be live issues for the late-first-century author, it is best to view Ephesians as neither encouraging nor assuming Israelite Torah-observance. However, on point 2), as Tucker has rightly noted, the *Haustafel* in Ephesians does provide "one of the clearest examples of the way existing social identities continue in a reprioritized manner within the Christ-movement" ("Continuation of Gentile Identity (SBL)."). If this is true with respect to social identities in the *Haustafel*, there is no reason to suppose it cannot be true for Jews and gentiles also. Cf. Barth, *Israel and the Church*, 88.

80. See the various examples in chapter 2. Cf. The Epistle of Barnabas, which states that the Jewish ritual law of sacrifices is replaced by "the new law of our Lord Jesus Christ" (Barn. 2.6).

81. The term "commandment" (ἐντολή) is used in Eph 6:2, but here the context suggests that the commandment has some kind of continuing validity. This is a contrast to the use in 2:15 where abolition is in view. We will return to Eph 6:2 in chapter 6.

the term means in this one instance. By itself, the term νόμος could refer to any number of things. Even within Romans, the term has a range of meanings: it could mean, for example, the law of Moses as a whole (Rom 2:17–29), the law understood in a specific way (Rom 3:27), a specific law relating to a particular area of life (Rom 7:2–3), or a principle that stands in tension with God's law (Rom 7:23). Here in Ephesians, the term could have any of these meanings, or another meaning altogether. We need to avoid the temptation prematurely to import one preconceived notion of the meaning of the term into Ephesians. Rather, we should allow the context to guide our decision.

Secondly, this phrase "by abolishing the law of the commandments in decrees" cannot be understood in isolation. It must be read in light of its specific role in the discourse in which it is found. It is not introduced as a central element of the discourse, nor is it a key to unlocking the entire passage.[82] Rather, as we have seen, the syntax indicates that the phrase has a specific purpose in the discourse. It is intended to explain the means by which Christ destroyed the "dividing-wall," i.e., the "hostility." We should not, therefore, proceed by first interpreting the phrase as if it were an independent unit and then imposing our conclusions about the phrase on the rest of the passage. Rather, we should approach the phrase as one element of the wider discourse. That is, we should seek to discern its specific role in relation to the breaking down of the dividing-wall (cf. v. 14).

The "Law of the Commandments in Decrees"

The term "law" does not appear by itself, but is explicitly qualified by two further constructions: "of the commandments" (τῶν ἐντολῶν) and "in decrees" (ἐν δόγμασιν). Many commentators understand these qualifications simply as "a description of the nature of the law."[83] However, the qualifications perform more than a descriptive function. Rather, they perform a defining function: they specify what would otherwise be ambiguous. In other words, the qualifications indicate that what has been abolished is not necessarily the law in every sense, but rather the law *as*

---

82. *Contra* Shkul, who understands this phrase as "decisive for the textual ideology and community relations and therefore critical for Ephesians' interpretation" (*Reading Ephesians*, 79).

83. See the various commentators listed by Graham (*Exegetical Summary*, 162).

understood and used in a certain way: "the law of the commandments in decrees."[84] There is a partial parallel here with the usage of the term "law" in Rom 3:27–31. Several interpreters of Eph 2:15 point to Rom 3:31 in order to highlight the apparent contradiction between the two verses (i.e., Rom 3:31 denies that the "law" is "abolished," while Eph 2:15 affirms it).[85] However, such interpreters fail to note the complexities in the Romans passage. In Rom 3:27, the term "law" is qualified, in two contrasting ways, through genitive constructions. A "law of works" is denied validity (cf. the "law of the commandments in decrees," Eph 2:15), while a "law of faith" is said to be operative in the exclusion of "boasting" (cf. Eph 2:8–9). In Romans, then, the term "law" with a genitive qualification can be used *both* to deny the validity of the law of Moses understood in one way, and *also* to affirm the validity of the law of Moses understood in another way.[86] In this sense, Eph 2:15 is similar to Rom 3:27. Eph 2:15 denies the validity of the "law" when qualified with a genitive construction (and a further prepositional phrase). Admittedly, Eph 2:15 lacks any exposition of the nature of the law. Yet this is not particularly remarkable, given that in Eph 2 the mention of the law is briefer and intended to achieve a more limited purpose.

Thus, if we are to understand what it means for "the law" to have been "abolished" in Eph 2:15, we need to understand the nature of these qualifying constructions. The mention of "commandments" indicates that the law is being viewed here primarily in terms of its function to regulate life through specific instructions. "Commandments" appear frequently in the law of Moses (see e.g., Exod 24:12; Lev 27:34; Num 15:39–40; Deut 4:2). However, Paul is not here describing any possible view of the commanding function of law of Moses (cf. Eph 6:2). It is the

---

84. The construction noun-article-genitive noun-prepositional phrase starting with ἐν is used frequently in Ephesians; in each case the head noun is not merely described, but rather identified (e.g., Eph 2:22; 4:3, 14; 5:9, 26).

85. Dahl maintains that "Ephesians maintains what Paul denied, that the Law had been abrogated" ("Gentiles, Christians, and Israelites," 36). Lincoln maintains that in Ephesians, unlike Romans, the law is abolished "in an unqualified fashion" ("Church and Israel," 612).

86. Cranfield, *Romans*, 219–20. See Rosner: "If [Paul's] letters are marked by negative and positive statements about the law, the question to ask is not 'which bits' of the law he refers to in each case, but the hermeneutical question of 'in what sense,' or 'as what'? In my view asking the question of 'the capacity in which' or 'the force with which' the law meets the Christian resolves the tension between the negative and positive material" (*Paul and the Law*, 43).

law of "*the* commandments" (τῶν ἐντολῶν)—the article indicating that certain commandments, or certain kinds of commandments, are in view. The "law of the commandments" is then further qualified by the prepositional phrase "in decrees" (ἐν δόγμασιν).[87] A "decree" (δόγμα) is "a formal statement concerning rules or regulations that are to be observed."[88] In Luke-Acts, the word is used both of imperial declarations (Luke 2:1; Acts 17:7) and of authoritative decisions on how certain commandments from the law of Moses are to be applied (Acts 16:4; cf. 15:1–2, 19–29). It is this latter usage that makes most sense here in Eph 2:15. What has been abolished is the law, understood primarily as a set of commandments, as expressed and promulgated by authoritative formal statements concerning the observance of these commandments ("decrees").

This is where understanding the function of the phrase within the wider discourse is highly significant. As we have seen, the phrase is intended to explain the means by which Christ has "broken down" the "dividing-wall." The "dividing-wall" is most likely an allusion to the partition in the Jerusalem temple, an allusion intended to invoke the wider concept of "hostility" between Jews and gentiles (v. 14). The inscription accompanying this partition fits well with the definition of a "decree" (δόγμα): it is a formal, officially recognized regulation (Josephus, *War* 6.124–26) applying the commandments of the law of Moses to a contemporary situation (cf. Num 1:51). As Kinzer notes, it thus serves as

> an illustration of a legal decree (*dogma*) by Jewish communal authorities, an interpretive application of the Torah that sought to guard the holy things entrusted to Israel. Such interpretive decrees drew firm lines between the holy people and the nations, and (as an unintended consequence) provoked pride, envy, and mutual animosity.[89]

The way in which the contemporary Jewish observance of the law could provoke hostility can be seen in texts such as Jub. 22.16–18—which expresses Jewish hostility toward gentiles—and 3 Macc. 3:4–7—which reports gentile hostility toward Jews.[90] Paul certainly acknowledges

---

87. This prepositional phrase is omitted by 𝔓[46], vg[ms], most likely because it was considered redundant by some scribes (Best, *Ephesians*, 260).

88. BDAG, "δόγμα."

89. Kinzer, *Searching Her Own Mystery*, 77; cf. Tucker, "Continuation of Gentile Identity (Moody)."

90. Williams, "Violent Ethno-Racial Reconciliation," 123. While Williams here claims these texts evince "the enmity that Torah created," it would be more accurate

this hostility in Eph 2:11–15, and claims that the means for its reversal involves the abolition of "the law of the commandments in decrees." This is not, however, a direct attack on the law. Rather the issue being addressed is the hostility between Jews and gentiles that was provoked by *certain official contemporary applications of the law's commandments concerning Jewish distinction*.[91]

An illuminating parallel occurs in Acts 15. Luke here speaks of "a yoke . . . that neither our fathers nor we [Jews] have been able to bear," which should not be imposed on gentile believers (15:10). This "yoke" cannot be referring to distinctive Jewish law-observance *per se*, since Luke assumes that Jewish believers in Christ, including Paul, happily continued to observe the law (Acts 21:20–25).[92] The issue at hand in Acts 15 is more specific: it is a Pharisaic attempt to impose a particular decree on gentile believers: "It is necessary to circumcise them and to order them to keep the law of Moses" (15:5). It is in this context that the unbearable yoke is raised (15:10). The yoke appears to be referring to a kind of strict Pharisaic *halakhah*. Rather than placing this unbearable "yoke" on the necks of gentile believers, the apostles and elders issue more suitable "decrees" (δόγματα) concerning gentile *halakhah* (16:4). This leads to joy, encouragement, and mutual peace, and fosters further growth in the gentile mission (Acts 15:30–33; 16:4–5). Ephesians 2:15, which speaks of "the law of the commandments in decrees," is most likely referring to the same kind of stance toward the law.

Thus, Eph 2:15 is not claiming that the law of Moses has been abolished in its entirety. Rather, what has been abolished is the law understood primarily as a set of "commandments" as expressed and promulgated by certain authoritative "decrees" concerning the observance of these commandments. The law understood in this way had indeed produced hostility between Jews and gentiles—as illustrated by the officially sanctioned inscription at the dividing-wall in the temple. *This* is what Paul is claiming to have been abolished by Christ. Paul is not denigrating the law itself, nor is he ruling out any possible attempt to apply the law to

---

to speak of the enmity that Jewish observance of Torah *could* provoke. Williams also cites the Epistle of Aristeas (ibid.), but this text contains no direct evidence of enmity (see above).

91. Yee, *Ethnic Reconciliation*, 157; cf. Barth, *The Broken Wall*, 35; Barth, *Ephesians*, 287–91; Stuhlmacher, "He Is Our Peace," 189–90; Thielman, *Ephesians*, 102.

92. Bauckham, "James and the Jerusalem Council Decision," 180; cf. Soulen, *God of Israel*, 170–71.

the lives of believers. This is confirmed by the fact that Paul later quotes a Mosaic "commandment" (ἐντολή) as the basis for moral instruction of gentile believers, noting that it is (literally) "[the] first commandment in promise" (ἐντολὴ πρώτη ἐν ἐπαγγελίᾳ, Eph 6:2). The "promise" in view here involves Israel's inheritance of the promised land (Eph 6:3), an inheritance in which the gentiles have also come to have a share (Eph 1:13–14; 3:6, cf. 2:12). This demonstrates that there is a nuanced view of the value of the commandments operating in Ephesians. While the commandments of the law are invalid when understood in terms of decrees (ἐν δόγμασιν, 2:15), they are relevant and applicable when understood rightly in relation to the gospel and God's eschatological promise (ἐν ἐπαγγελίᾳ, 6:2).[93]

Christ's Death: The Means of Abolition

The abolition of "the law of the commandments in decrees" has occurred through Christ's sacrificial death on the cross (vv. 13, 16). How has this occurred? There are two elements of the context that shed light on this question.

Firstly, Christ's death has dealt with the sin of both Israel and the nations. In Eph 1:7, Christ's sacrificial death (his "blood") is introduced as the instrument of "redemption" and "forgiveness of trespasses." In Eph 2:1–3, Israel and the gentiles are said to have been subject to spiritual "death," spiritual powers, "trespasses," "sins," and God's "wrath." Verse 3 emphasizes the fact that Israel's former plight was the same as that of the nations. This viewpoint echoes the prophetic denunciation of Israel as a nation under God's curse of "death" for breaking his commandments, and so subject to exile (cf. Deut 11:26–29; 28:15–68; 30:15–20; Ezek 36:16–21).[94] A key element of the prophetic curse and exile schema is hostility between Israel and the nations.[95] If Israel had kept the law, they would have been a distinctive people, blessed by God and respected by all the nations (Deut 28:1–14). However, because of Israel's sin, this distinctiveness had turned into hostility between Israel and the nations. For the prophets, the solution to this plight was not to be found in Israel's inherent holiness, but in God's unilateral saving and life-giving activity (Ezek

---

93. See further chapter 6.

94. Starling, *Not My People*, 189–92.

95. Soulen, *God of Israel*, 143–47.

37:1–14). In Ephesians, this is said to have come about by Christ's sacrificial death (e.g., Eph 1:7), resurrection, and victorious ascension (e.g., Eph 2:4–10). Christ, through his death, has redeemed both Israel and the nations from sin and judgment. This means that the law can no longer be approached as a means for keeping Israel pure and holy, as distinct from the impure nations. This way of approaching and understanding the law (i.e., "the law of the commandments in decrees") has been rendered invalid by Christ's death.

Secondly, and conversely, Christ's death has made believers holy—believers both from Israel and the nations. The holiness of believers "in Christ" is first introduced at the start of the letter (Eph 1:1, 4), where it is implicitly connected to Christ's "blood" (1:7). In Eph 2, Christ's sacrificial death (2:13, 16) is the foundation of the description of gentile believers as "fellow citizens of the holy ones" (2:19) and growing into a "holy temple" (2:21). In Eph 5, Christ's sacrificial death (5:2) underlies the call to the gentile readers of the letter to live in a way that is "proper among the holy ones" (5:3). Later in the same chapter of Ephesians, the connection between Christ's death and holiness becomes explicit. Husbands are to love their wives

> as Christ loved the church and gave himself up for her, that he
> might sanctify her, having cleansed her by the washing of water
> with the word, so that he might present the church to himself
> in splendor, without spot or wrinkle or any such thing, that she
> might be holy and without blemish. (Eph 5:25–27).

Because Christ's death has rendered both Jewish and gentile believers "holy," there is now no longer any need for decrees that seek to guard Israel's holiness or the holy things entrusted to her. These decrees are part of the old *halakhah*. Now, "[t]he sacrificial work of the Messiah brings Jews and gentiles near to God in fellowship with one another—and new *halakhah* must reflect the transformed conditions."[96] A similar dynamic can be seen in Acts 15 (see esp. vv. 9, 11), where the gift of the Spirit by the crucified and risen Christ demonstrated that

---

96. Kinzer, *Searching Her Own Mystery*, 77. Kinzer seeks to argue that the direct object of the participle "abolishing" is not the "law" itself, but only the "hostility" *caused/stimulated by* the law (*Postmissionary Messianic Judaism*, 166 n. 35; *Searching Her Own Mystery*, 75–76). Syntactically, this does not quite work. While the accusative "hostility" is indeed in the accusative case, the term "law" is also in the accusative and is closer to the participle.

it was possible also to envisage the end of the distinction between "holy" and "profane" groups of people, that is, between Jews who were God's people and Gentiles who were not. It became possible to envisage the messianic people of God as a community of both Jews and Gentiles, the former observing Torah, the latter not. Of course, neither Peter nor any of the Jerusalem leaders entertained the idea that Jewish believers in Jesus should give up observing Torah. But Torah observance no longer constituted a barrier between Jews and Gentiles, since their fellowship was based not on Torah, but on faith in Jesus the Messiah and experience of the transformative power of the Spirit.[97]

Ephesians 2:15a is thus claiming that Christ's death renders unnecessary some of the key functions of the law's commandments as interpreted by Jewish authorities in the first century. This is because Christ's death has produced a radical change: it has dealt with the sin of both Israel and the nations, and it has rendered both Jewish and gentile Christ-believers "holy." Jews therefore no longer need to follow "the law of the commandments in decrees" to separate themselves from gentiles out of fear of contamination from uncleanness or hostility from enemies. Indeed, they no longer need to fear the enemies at all, because the erstwhile enemies have been "made near" (v. 13). Through Christ's sacrificial death, the "hostility" itself has been "broken down" (v. 14) and "killed" (v. 16). In other words, Eph 2:15a is pointing to the fact that the law's role in protecting Israel from impure and hostile gentiles has, by Christ's sacrificial death, been rendered invalid. The purpose of this phrase within the wider discourse is significant, but limited. It is simply to demonstrate how the "hostility" between Israel and the nations has been destroyed. It does not necessarily rule out other uses of the law—for example, in "demarcating Jewish identity as integral subordinate identity in Christ, or as a critical source for community praxis for Jews and gentiles alike."[98]

97. Bauckham, "James and the Jerusalem Council Decision," 180. Cf. Soulen, *God of Israel*, 170–71; Kinzer, *Postmissionary Messianic Judaism*, 66–71.

98. Zoccali, "Problem with the Law," 411. Zoccali's comments here concern Gal 3:10–12, but are just as applicable to Eph 2:15.

The "One New Humanity" out of "Both" (vv. 15b–16)

Eph 2:15b–16 describes the purpose for which Christ broke down the dividing-wall of hostility:

> that he might make the two into one new humanity in himself, so making peace, and might reconcile us both to God in one body through the cross, thereby killing the hostility. (Eph 2:15–16, modified ESV).[99]

As we saw in chapter 2, many interpreters have understood this to be implying that Christ, by forming a new kind of humanity, has nullified all forms of Jewish distinctiveness. Chrysostom could speak of the "two" becoming "one" in ways that appear to eradicate any possibility for distinct Jewish identity. Calvin understood this passage to be teaching that maintaining Jewish ethnic identity was antithetical to the gospel of Christ. The twentieth century saw the rise of "third race" concepts, involving the claim that Christians form a new "race" of people in distinction from the "races" of Jew and gentile. The translators of the RSV (followed by NRSV and ESV) added the phrase "in place of the two," implying that the new humanity is to be understood as a "replacement" of distinct Jewish and gentile humanity.

However, these constitute over-readings of the text in question. That is, they extrapolate from the explicit statements found in the text to make further conclusions that are not necessary implications of the texts themselves. Once again, this can be illustrated by contrasting Eph 2:15–16 with the explicit supersessionism found in the Epistle of Barnabas. For Barnabas, "Israel was abandoned" (Barn. 4.14). There is now a new people, a second humanity, which replaces Israel and acts in contradistinction from Israel:

> Again I will show you how he speaks to us [as opposed to "them"=Israel, cf. 6.7]. He made yet a second human form in the final days. And the Lord says, "See! I am making the final things like the first." . . . See, then, that we have been formed anew, [. . .] (Barn. 6.13–14 [Ehrman])

For Barnabas, the "church" is defined as those whom Jesus blesses and brings in to the land, in contrast to the "synagogue" who put him to death (Barn. 5.13; 6.6, 16).

99. For the nature of and reasons behind my modification of the ESV here see chapter 2.

In Ephesians, however, although there is a "new humanity," there is no reference to the replacement of Israel. On the contrary, the new humanity is comprised of "both" (ἀμφοτέρους) Jew and gentile. The emphasis in the text is on overcoming hostility, not on erasing ethnic categories. Furthermore, the "church" in Ephesians is never defined in opposition to the synagogue. Rather, the church (or "body") is envisaged as the united gathering of Jew and gentile (Eph 1:22–23; 4:4).

Thus, as we also saw in chapter 2, Eph 2:15–16 has given rise to other interpretations that do not regard Jewish distinctiveness as being nullified by the mention of the "one new humanity." Barth stresses the reconciliation between Jews and gentiles, which does not imply the eradication of differences (cf. Eph 5:21—6:9).[100] Yee concentrates on the concept of ethnic reconciliation and the overcoming of Jewish "ethnocentricity" rather than on the eradication of ethnicity altogether.[101] Kinzer stresses that "the two parties [genealogical Israel and the gentiles in the Messiah] remain distinct even in their unity."[102] Campbell argues that Jews and gentiles "continue as discrete and distinct entities but now without hostility and in a harmonious relation," since "it is hostility, . . . (rather than ethnic status) that is brought to an end by the reconciliation of both to God in one body in Christ."[103] Hardin points out that "oneness" is not the same as "ethnic collapse";[104] Fowl contends that "[p]eacemaking here is not homogenizing."[105]

This latter unity-in-distinction view fits better with various elements of the text of Eph 2:15–16. As we have seen, the thrust of this part of Ephesians is indeed on reconciliation and the eradication of hostility rather than on the eradication of difference. The term "both" (ἀμφότεροι, v. 16) is prominent in the context, occurring three times throughout Eph 2:14–18.[106] In v. 18, the term is the subject of a present-tense verb, implying that duality is not simply a feature of the past but continues as a pres-

100. Barth, *Israel and the Church*, 88–89; Barth, *Ephesians*, 310.

101. Yee, *Ethnic Reconciliation*, 133, 43, 76.

102. Kinzer, *Searching Her Own Mystery*, 77.

103. Campbell, "Unity and Diversity," 18.

104. Hardin, "Equality in the Church," 231.

105. Fowl, *Ephesians*, 90. See also Stott, *Ephesians*, 101–2.

106. The shift in gender from neuter (v. 14) to masculine (vv. 16, 18) reflects the movement from the general concept of reconciliation between two parties (v. 14) to the more specific concept of the "new humanity" (v. 15) (cf. Stuhlmacher, "He Is Our Peace," 185; Thielman, *Ephesians*, 172).

ent feature of life in Christ.[107] The word "one" (εἷς) in both the LXX and the New Testament often refers to a composite unity, rather than a simple or flat sameness. This is true in a number of passages that are describing similar concepts to those found in Ephesians, such as creation (e.g., Gen 1:5; cf. Eph 2:10, 15; 4:24), marriage (e.g., Gen 2:24; cf. Eph 5:31), and the church as a "body" (Rom 12:4–6; 1 Cor 12:12–30; cf. Eph 1:23; 2:16; 4:4, 12, 16; 5:23, 28, 30).[108] The reference to God "creat[ing]" a "new" humanity (κτίσῃ ... καινόν) does not necessarily imply the eradication of every feature of the old humanity;[109] the terminology implies eschatological renewal and transformation rather than destruction (cf. Pss 51:10 [LXX 50:12], 104:30 [LXX 103:30]).[110] Indeed, the scriptural witness to which Ephesians is strongly indebted assumes an ongoing distinction between Israel and the nations, even in passages that look to the eschatological consummation of God's purposes (e.g., Isa 19:24–25; Mic 4:1–4; cf. Gen 12:1–3).[111]

Hence the creation of the "one new humanity" in Christ does not necessarily imply the eradication of all distinctions between Israel and the nations. Rather, the focus is on reconciliation and the removal of hostility. The penultimate purpose of Christ's death is the reconciliation of Israel and the nations (v. 15b), while the ultimate purpose is the reconciliation of "both" of these entities to God (v. 16). As Stuhlmacher notes:

> The meaning of the atoning death of Jesus on the cross is the removal of the (double) hostility. The removal of the hostility is accomplished in that Christ atones for the guilt of Gentiles and Jews and thereby makes possible a new communion, free from guilt and judgment, between God and the creation. ... Reconciliation reaches its goal in the creation of the new humanity that overcomes the ancient separation of Gentiles and Jews through life together in the community.[112]

---

107. "We both have access in one Spirit" (ἔχομεν τὴν προσαγωγὴν οἱ ἀμφότεροι ἐν ἑνὶ πνεύματι).

108. Woods, "Jew-Gentile Distinction," 105–13. As Thielman maintains, the "one body" (2:16) refers to the "one humanity" in which Jews and gentiles are reconciled (cf. v. 15), rather than the physical crucified body of Christ (Ephesians, 172).

109. Pace Hoehner, Ephesians, 378.

110. Woods, "Jew-Gentile Distinction," 117.

111. Soulen, God of Israel, 120–33.

112. Stuhlmacher, "He Is Our Peace," 190.

While this double reconciliation implies a thorough, Christological transformation in Jewish and gentile identity, it does not imply an erasure of Jewish or gentile distinctiveness altogether.

The Peace-making Activity of Christ

Thus, Eph 2:14–16 describe how Christ has achieved "peace" through his sacrificial death on the cross. Does the "peace" that has been achieved refer to peace between God and human beings, or to peace between Israel and the gentiles? As several interpreters have pointed out, both of these must be in view.[113]

On the one hand, Ephesians often emphasizes a reconciliation involving the "vertical" relationship between God and humanity. In Eph 1, Christ's sacrificial death is described in terms of "redemption" and "forgiveness" (Eph 1:7). In Eph 2:1–10, the primary emphasis is on the transition human beings have undergone from being subject to God's "wrath" (v. 3) to having been "saved" as the objects of his "grace" and "kindness" (v. 7). Furthermore, the reconciliation that Christ achieves through the cross is described as a reconciliation "to God" (v. 16).

On the other hand, the key focus of vv. 14–18 is on the fact that this "peace" involves two previously hostile groups having been reconciled *together*. Christ is "our" peace (v. 14); he has made two groups "one" (vv. 14, 15), he has put an end to "hostility" (vv. 14, 16); he has reconciled "both" to God (v. 16); and he has preached to both far and near (v. 17) because "both" have access together in one Spirit to the Father (v. 18). Thus, as in the Isaianic texts that form part of the background to this passage (e.g., Isa 9:6, 57:19), "peace" is the "end of alienation," both from God and from other human beings. The word "salvation" could have been used for the former concept (cf. Eph 2:8–10), but this would not have had the same effect in highlighting in the latter concept, which is clearly central within this passage.[114]

---

113. E.g., Best, *Ephesians*, 251–52; Barth, *The Broken Wall*, 42–44; Fong, "Racial Reconciliation," 571.

114. Best, *Ephesians*, 251–52.

Christ Who Preached the Gospel of Peace (Eph 2:17–18)

While Christ's sacrificial death is foundational to his peace-making activity, there is a further, highly significant element. In v. 17, Christ's activity is described further in terms of *gospel mission*: "having come" (ἐλθών), he "preached the gospel of peace" (εὐηγγελίσατο εἰρήνην, v. 17). Starling rightly observes that this "suggests the continuation of a narrative sequence . . . rather than a summary, explanation or argument in support of what has been said in the preceding verses: the peace that has been 'made' on the cross is now 'proclaimed' (by Christ, through his agents the apostles)."[115] For Starling, the prominent place of v. 17 within vv. 11–22 demonstrates the centrality of "soteriological" rather than simply "ecclesiological" themes in this passage.[116] This is a valid insight, although perhaps it can be expressed in another way: central to the passage is a *missiological* theme which encompasses both the soteriological and the ecclesiological elements. In other words, the discourse is driven neither by a static conceptualization of the nature of "church" nor by a static conceptualization of the nature of "salvation." Rather, it is driven by a dynamic conceptualization of gospel-preaching, an activity that achieves both ecclesiological and soteriological purposes. In other words, gospel mission undertaken by "Christ" enacts the dual reconciliation achieved by Christ: a reconciliation of Israel and the nations, and a reconciliation of both Israel and the nations to God.

According to v. 17, Christ both "came" and "preached." The participle "having come" (ἐλθών) evokes a sense of movement. The verb translated "preached" is literally "evangelized" (εὐηγγελίσατο), and refers to the proclamation of good news or the "gospel" (cf. 1:13). Together, these two terms describe the dynamic gospel mission. The content of the missionary preaching is "peace" (εἰρήνην), i.e., the dual reconciliation achieved by Christ's death (cf. vv. 14–16). The recipients of the missionary preaching are named as two distinct groups: the gospel is preached "to you who were far off" (ὑμῖν τοῖς μακράν) and "to those who were near" (τοῖς ἐγγύς), denoting gentiles (including the readers of the letter) and Jews respectively (cf. v. 13).

As many have observed, v. 17 alludes to key passages in the LXX text of the prophetic vision of Isaiah.[117] In Isa 40:9, a herald appears, de-

115. Starling, *Not My People*, 174.

116. Ibid., 174–76.

117. Moritz, *A Profound Mystery*, 44–45; Starling, *Not My People*, 170–72.

scribed as "the one who evangelizes Zion" and "the one who evangelizes Jerusalem" (ὁ εὐαγγελιζόμενος Σιων/ὁ εὐαγγελιζόμενος Ιερουσαλημ). The "evangel"/"gospel" here concerns the "coming" (verb ἔρχομαι) of "the Lord" (κύριος) to bring reward and comfort to Israel (Isa 40:10; cf. "salvation," v. 5). In Isa 52:7, the figure of the herald reappears, literally "evangelizing a report of peace" (εὐαγγελιζομένου ἀκοὴν εἰρήνης).[118] This "peace" is achieved by the sacrificial death of the suffering Servant of the Lord (Isa 53:5, cf. the "report," ἀκοή, in 53:1). In Isa 57:14–21, the Lord himself appears and speaks. His appearance is described in language reminiscent of the "coming" of the Lord from Isa 40 (57:14, cf. 40:3–5; 57:18, cf. 40:1). When the Lord comes, he himself announces the message of "peace upon peace to those who are far and to who are near" (εἰρήνην ἐπ᾽ εἰρήνην τοῖς μακρὰν καὶ τοῖς ἐγγὺς οὖσιν, 57:19). Here in Eph 2, all these elements from Isaiah are present in a compressed form: the respective roles of suffering Servant, herald of peace, and Lord have all devolved onto Christ. In v. 17, Christ is identified as the one who "comes" and "evangelizes peace" to the "far" and the "near," i.e., to both Israel and the nations.[119]

When did this evangelistic mission of Christ take place? Some argue that v. 17 is referring to Christ's incarnation and earthly ministry.[120] However, as Sandnes points out, it is better to read Eph 2 from the perspective of the gentile readers of the letter, for whom Christ came "in the gospel-preaching of the apostles" (cf. 1:13).[121] "Christ," in other words, must be understood as operating through the agency of the apostolic mission. However, it is important to note that the apostles themselves are not at the forefront at this point in the letter. The key theme within this context is the united body of formerly hostile Jews and gentiles who

118. In the LXX, the evangelist is identified with the Lord himself (cf. vv. 3–6), anticipating 57:14–21 (Starling, Not My People, 172).

119. Stuhlmacher, "He Is Our Peace," 191. Starling identifies the apparent hermeneutical problem that arises from Ephesians' use of Isaiah: "Whereas, in the context of Isa. 57, the 'far' and 'near' appear to be the Jews of the diaspora and those living in the land, respectively, the same terms are used in Eph. 2 with reference to the Gentiles . . . and Jews" (Not My People, 177). He compellingly explains it thus: since Israel in exile shares the same plight as the nations under God's judgment (Eph 2:1–3), passages from Isaiah that originally spoke of the end of Israel's exile can be applied typologically to gentiles (ibid., 183–94). Thus, "Gentiles can find themselves addressed in a promise originally given to exiled Israelites because the predicament of exile which the promises addressed corresponded so precisely with their own predicament as Gentiles, spiritually dead and far off from God" (ibid., 193).

120. E.g., Moritz, A Profound Mystery, 44–45.

121. Sandnes, One of the Prophets?, 229.

have been reconciled together "in" Christ (v. 15, cf. vv. 13, 16), and who thus share Christ's identity (cf. "the fullness of him," 1:23). In some way, therefore, the entire "body" of Christ is caught up in this apostolic mission. In and through this united-yet-diverse body, Christ "comes" and "preaches" (v. 17). In other words, the nature of the church as a body called from both Israel and the nations is inextricable from the gospel-preaching mission. This is a mission that takes place to both "far" and "near." These two groups, the "far" and "near," are both distinct and united. They are distinct in that Christ is described as engaging in a distinct mission to each group: "he came and preached peace to you who were far off and peace to those who were near" (cf. the two forms of gospel mission in Gal 2:7–10).[122] Yet they are united by the fact that they receive the same message of "peace." Furthermore, as v. 18 shows, "both" groups share the same kind of access to God: "For through him we both have access in one Spirit to the Father."[123] This is later expanded upon in Eph 3:12, where the "access" (προσαγωγή) is explicitly said to be through "faith" (πίστις) in Christ. Thus, through the gospel-preaching mission and through the "faith" that arises from it (cf. 1:13), both Jewish and gentile identity is transformed. Nevertheless, even "in Christ," there remains a distinction between the two.[124]

Unity and Diversity in the Gospel-preaching Mission (Eph 2:19–22)

This theme of unity-in-diversity continues in vv. 19–22. The emphasis on unity is clear and undisputed. According to these verses, the negative elements of the gentile readers' former status with respect to Israel have been overcome "in Christ Jesus" (cf. vv. 11–13).[125] Although they were

122. In Eph 2:17, the distinction between the two gospel missions to "near" and "far" is emphasized by the rewording of the LXX "peace upon peace to those who are far and to those who are near" (Isa 57:19 LXX) to become "peace to you who [were] far, *and* peace to those who [were] near" (Eph 2:17). Lincoln comments on this rewording, although he draws different conclusions from it to those we are drawing here ("Church and Israel," 613).

123. Verse 18 begins with ὅτι, indicating that it is giving the reason for the previous verse. It may be explaining the reason for the mission to both Jews and gentiles; since both Jews and gentiles were subject to sin and God's wrath (cf. vv. 1–3).

124. *Pace* Lincoln, "Church and Israel," 616.

125. Ibid., 608.

once "alienated from the commonwealth (πολιτείας) of Israel" (v. 12), they are now "fellow-citizens (συμπολῖται) of the saints" (v. 19). Although they were once "foreigners" (ξένοι, vv. 12, 19) and "resident aliens" (πάροικοι, v. 19), they are now "members of the family (οἰκεῖοι) of God" (v. 19).[126] Although they were once "without God" (ἄθεοι) in the world (v. 12), they are now intimately related to God, since they are God's family (v. 19), and are being built together into God's dwelling (v. 22). Nevertheless, again, this radical change in status does not necessarily mean the erasure of all distinctions.[127] There are several elements of vv. 19–22 that indicate that Jews and gentiles, though united in Christ, still retain a distinct identity. Furthermore, there are several indications that the Jew-gentile relationship is intimately connected to the dynamics of the gospel mission, a mission that proceeded through the early Jewish apostolic community to the nations.

Jews and Gentiles "Together" (vv. 19, 21, 22)

As several interpreters have observed, the use of three *syn*-compounds[128] indicates a salvation-historical unity-in-diversity.[129] Gentile believers are "fellow-citizens (συμπολῖται) of the saints" (v. 19), every construction is "being joined together" (συναρμολογουμένη, v. 21), and the gentiles are being "built together" (συνοικοδομεῖσθε) into God's dwelling (v. 22). This emphasis on togetherness does not imply that the gentiles have *become* Israel; rather it is a claim that they have become equal sharers *with* Israel in God's blessings. There is a parallel here with vv. 5–6, in which three *syn*-compounds are used to describe believers' relationship to Christ. Believers have been "made alive together" (συνεζωοποίησεν) with Christ, "raised together" (συνήγειρεν) with Christ, and "seated together" (συνεκάθισεν) with Christ (vv. 5–6). While this claim that believers share in the status of the risen Christ is of course remarkable, it is not meant to imply that believers have *become* Christ. Similarly, vv. 19–22 asserts that the gentile believers share in the benefits of Israel. While this too is a

126. See below for the choice to translate οἰκεῖοι as "members of the family" rather than "members of the household."

127. *Pace* Lincoln, "Church and Israel," 614.

128. I.e., compounds beginning with the preposition σύν, "with."

129. Barth, *The Broken Wall*, 123; Hoch, "Syn-Compounds," 177; Campbell, "Unity and Diversity," 21–22; Kinzer, *Searching Her Own Mystery*, 78–79, cf. 73–74; cf. Vlach, *Has the Church Replaced Israel?* 153.

remarkable claim, it does not imply that the believers have *become* Israel. In the words of Paula Fredriksen, gentile Christ-believers can be understood as "ex-pagan pagans."[130] In one sense, they are no longer "gentiles," because they have been transformed into being God's people alongside Israel (cf. 4:17); yet in another sense they have a distinct "gentile" identity, albeit one that has been fully transformed in Christ (cf. 3:1, 6).[131]

Fellow-citizens of "The Saints" (v. 19)

The gentile Christ-believers are described as fellow-citizens "of the saints" (τῶν ἁγίων). As we noted in chapter 3, the meaning of the term "the saints" (literally "the holy ones") in Ephesians is contested. Some see "the saints" as a reference to Jewish believers,[132] while others see it as a reference to all believers.[133] However, a simple dichotomy like this does not do justice to the dynamics at work in this passage. Paul is not here claiming that one or other group is especially "holy"; he is claiming that gentile Christ-believers *share* in Israel's privileges, including in Israel's holy status (see v. 21; cf. 1:1, 4). Thus, even if "the holy ones" is taken to refer originally to Jewish believers, the burden of the passage is that gentile Christ-believers, as fellow-citizens with "the holy ones," are themselves also holy.[134] The key question in this passage, then, is not, "*Who* are the holy ones?" but rather, "*How* has Israel's holiness been shared with gentiles?" As Paul has already argued in vv. 14–18, the key is Christ's sacrificial death, proclaimed in Christ's apostolic mission. The apostolic preaching of Christ crucified has, in other words, brought the gentiles to share in Israel's blessings. This means they have come to share in the holiness that was once the prerogative of Israel alone.

This coheres well with certain passages in Romans, 1 Corinthians, and 2 Corinthians where "the saints" refers to the early apostolic

---

130. Fredriksen, "'Law-Free' Apostle?" 647; cf. Fredriksen, *Augustine and the Jews*, 34–35.

131. Tucker, "Continuation of Gentile Identity (SBL)."

132. E.g., Robinson, "The Saints," 50–53; Caird, *Letters from Prison*, 60; Dahl, "Gentiles, Christians, and Israelites," 35; Kinzer, *Searching Her Own Mystery*, 79.

133. E.g., Lincoln, "Church and Israel," 613–14; Best, *Ephesians*, 277–78; Thielman, *Ephesians*, 179. Other, slightly less common, interpretations of the term "the saints" include all Israel (Barth, *Ephesians*, 66–67) and angels (Schlier, *An Die Epheser*, 84, 140–41; cf. 1 Thess 3:13; 2 Thess 1:7, 10).

134. Yee, *Ethnic Reconciliation*, 195–98.

community in Jerusalem (Rom 15:25–26, 31; 1 Cor 16:1; 2 Cor 8:4; 9:1, 12).[135] It is through this apostolic community that the message of the gospel came to the world; thus, Paul can claim that the "saints" in Jerusalem have shared their "spiritual" blessings with gentiles (Rom 15:25–27).[136] These blessings apparently included their "holy" status itself. This can be seen from the fact that the gentile Christ-believers themselves can now also be addressed as those "called to be saints" (Rom 1:7; 1 Cor 1:2; cf. 2 Cor 1:1).[137] In other words, in Romans, 1 Corinthians and 2 Corinthians, "the saints" are firstly the Jewish apostolic community in Jerusalem, and subsequently—through the mission of the gospel—the gentile Christ-believers. This same dynamic appears to be at work in Ephesians also.

The Foundational Significance of the Apostolic Mission (v. 20)

The mission dynamic of these verses becomes explicit in v. 20. The gentile believers, as fellow-citizens of the saints and members of God's family, are "built on the foundation of the apostles and prophets" (ἐποικοδομηθέντες ἐπὶ τῷ θεμελίῳ τῶν ἀποστόλων καὶ προφητῶν, v. 20). Sandnes, referring back to the mission dynamic described in v. 17, argues persuasively that v. 20 is also referring to the apostolic mission.[138] His argument is confirmed by Eph 3:5–6, where the "apostles and prophets" are linked explicitly with the mission to the gentiles "through the gospel."[139] He concludes:

135. Kinzer, *Postmissionary Messianic Judaism*, 154; Dunn, *Theology*, 708.

136. Windsor, *Vocation of Israel*, 117–18.

137. Cf. the argument in Rom 11:16 concerning contagious holiness: "If the dough offered as firstfruits is holy, so is the whole lump, and if the root is holy, so are the branches."

138. Sandnes, *One of the Prophets?* 228–29. Many commentators understand the genitive to be appositional and so take the phrase to mean "built on the foundation which consists of the apostles and prophets" (Barth, *Ephesians*, 271; Caird, *Letters from Prison*, 61; Lincoln, *Ephesians*, 152–53; Best, *Ephesians*, 280–81; Thielman, *Ephesians*, 180; cf. Wardle, *Jerusalem Temple*, 215). They argue that the phrase cannot mean "the foundation laid by the apostles and prophets" since, in their view, this would mean that the foundation is "Christ" or, as Hoehner puts it, the "doctrine of Christ" (*Ephesians*, 398), and so this would create confusion in the passage because Christ is also the "cornerstone." However, Sandnes' interpretation resolves this problem. The cornerstone is Christ (or the gospel of Christ); while the foundation is the apostolic *preaching* of the gospel of Christ (or the gospel of Christ). Cf. 1 Cor 3:11 in light of 1 Cor 1:17.

139. Sandnes, *One of the Prophets?* 229.

> The foundation of "the apostles and prophets" upon which the
> status of the Gentile is built is, then, the preaching of the gospel.
> ... The "apostles and prophets" are, then, a reference to those
> who laid this foundation.[140]

This mission dynamic is caught up directly in the corresponding
Jew-gentile dynamic. As we saw in v. 17, so also in v. 20 there is a close
relationship between Christ and the apostolic mission:[141] the "cornerstone" is Christ,[142] while the "foundation" is the apostolic preaching of
Christ.[143] In other words, the apostolic mission is accorded a foundational
significance in Christ's work. In the context of this passage, Christ's work
is presented in terms of sharing Israel's blessings with the nations (cf.
v. 19). Conversely, we may say that the sharing of Israel's blessings with
the nations is presented as the *raison d'être* of the apostolic mission.[144] The
distinction between Israel and the nations is not thereby erased; rather it
is transformed so that it serves a positive, mission-related purpose.

"Every Construction" (v. 21)

The use of the phrase "every construction" (πᾶσα οἰκοδομή, v. 21) also
suggests that Paul has in mind an underlying diversity of missions and
communities, even as he is describing an overarching unity in Christ.[145]
Despite most English translations which render the phrase as "the whole
building," there is good reason to render it as "every construction." This
can be seen when we consider the context of the phrase, the grammar of
the phrase, and the meaning of the term οἰκοδομή ("construction").

Turning firstly to the context, we see that there is no reason to
assume that a single building is in view at this point in the passage.
In verse 19, the word "family members" (οἰκεῖοι) is used. Despite the

140. Ibid.

141. Ibid.

142. Or "capstone"; both understandings are possible and carry a similar significance (Thielman, *Ephesians*, 181–83).

143. Cf. 1 Cor 3:10–11, where Paul identifies the "foundation" which he laid as
"Christ"; yet Paul's actual activity involved preaching the gospel of Christ (1 Cor 1:17).

144. Robinson, "Jew and Greek," 108; Kinzer speaks of "*the inextricable connection
between the apostolic office and the people of Israel*" (*Searching Her Own Mystery*, 79,
emphasis original).

145. I am grateful to Benjamin Hudson for pointing out to me the potential
significance of this phrase.

common English translation of this term as "members of *the* household," the term does not necessarily imply that a single "household" or building is being envisaged at this point.[146] The word is not being used here to assert the presence of a single building, but to highlight the status of the gentiles. It is being used as a contrast to "resident aliens" (πάροικοι, v. 19).[147] Gentiles no longer have "alien" status, but have the rights of naturally born citizens. This is because they are "kin" or "members of the family" (οἰκεῖοι). The term certainly denotes close familial connections and kinship; however, it does not necessarily imply a single roof under which all the family members are living.

In v. 20 too, there is no reason to assume that a single "household" or building is being envisaged. Admittedly, there is a single "foundation" (the apostolic gospel-preaching mission) and a single "cornerstone" (Christ). However, the metaphor is not straightforward. What is "built" on this foundation and cornerstone is *not* a single building, but plural individuals—i.e. the plural "family members" (v. 19). The most we can say at this point is that there is a complex metaphor involving both unity and diversity.

In v. 21, the focus of the complex metaphor moves on to the concept of "construction" (οἰκοδομή) itself. The grammatical formulation used, πᾶσα οἰκοδομή, would normally mean that the phrase should be translated as "every building" or "every [act of] construction" (cf. πᾶσα πατριά, "every family," Eph 3:15).[148] Many interpreters, however, argue that this meaning cannot be accepted, because (they claim) a single building is in view throughout the passage. Thus, they claim that the formulation must be treated as an anomaly, and (despite the clear grammatical indications

146. This assumption is shared by many interpreters, even e.g., Barth, *Ephesians*, 269–70.

147. Caird, *Letters from Prison*, 60.

148. Here, the word πᾶς is being used adjectivally, with a noun but without the article, in the singular. When used in this particular construction, the word is either "emphasizing the individual members of the class denoted by the noun *every, each, any*" (BDAG, "πᾶς," 1.a.α), or it is denoting "any entity out of a totality, *any and every, every*" (ibid., 2.a), or it is denoting "everything belonging, in kind, to the class designated by the noun, *every kind of, all sorts of*" (ibid., 5). The construction can also be used as a "marker of the highest degree of someth." (ibid., 3.a), but the concept of "highest degree" does not apply to a building and so is not relevant in this case. The article ἡ is inserted in ℵ¹ A C P 6 81 326 1739c 1881 etc. However, as Best notes, "support is not strong" for this insertion, and it is easy to see how it would have come about to create an easier reading (*Ephesians*, 286; see also Thielman, *Ephesians*, 186).

to the contrary) the phrase must mean "the entire building."[149] However, we have seen above that there is no reason to suppose that a single building is being envisaged. Hence there is no reason to reject the regular understanding of this grammatical formulation. The phrase πᾶσα οἰκοδομή in v. 21, therefore, means "every construction."

The English term "construction" is useful as a translation here because it has the same kind of ambiguity as the Greek word on which it is based (οἰκοδομή). That is, it can refer to a *process* of construction, or it can refer to the *result* of the construction process. Given that the term refers to a process of construction elsewhere in Ephesians (4:12, 16, 29), it is best to understand it the same way here in 2:21. That is, Paul is referring in v. 21 to "every [act of] construction." This would also fit with the fact that an ongoing building process is described in v. 22 through the present tense "you are being built together" (συνοικοδομεῖσθε).[150]

What are the various acts of "construction" Paul is envisaging here? As we will see when we examine Eph 4,[151] the term can be used to describe both the gospel-preaching mission of the early apostolic community (Eph 4:12), and the resulting edifying speech and action occurring within "the whole body" (Eph 4:16, cf. v. 29). On this basis, we might conclude that the phrase "every [act of] construction" in Eph 2:21 is intended to encompass any kind of missionary or edifying activity based on the gospel of Christ. However, it is important to note that at this point in the letter the focus is not on the activity of the body (cf. "the construction of itself" in 4:16), but rather on the activity of Christ for the sake of the body (see 2:14–18, and the passive "built" in 2:20, 22). Hence the gospel

---

149. See e.g., Barth, *Ephesians*, 271–72; Best, *Ephesians*, 286; Hoehner, *Ephesians*, 407–9; Thielman, *Ephesians*, 183. Some of these commentators list possible precedents for this anomaly, but on closer inspection the posited precedents turn out to be spurious. Best, for example, lists Matt 28:18; Acts 1:21; 2:36; 7:22; 23:1; Col 1:15, 23; 4:12; 1 Pet 1:15 (*Ephesians*, 286). However, each use of πᾶς in these verses fits better into the categories listed in the previous footnote (BDAG, "πᾶς," 1.a.α, 2.a, 5). It is also sometimes claimed that the translation "the whole building" has precedents in the phrase "all Israel" (πᾶς Ἰσραήλ; LXX 3 Kgdms 8:65; 11:16; 1 Esd 1:19; 5:45, 58; Jdt 15:14; Rom 11:26) and the phrase "the whole house of Israel" (πᾶς οἶκος Ἰσραήλ; 1 Kgdms 7:2, 3; Acts 2:36). However, in these cases a proper (geographic) noun is being used, which enables the construction without the article to mean "pert. to a high degree of completeness or wholeness, *whole* . . . before proper names, mostly geographic" (ibid., 4.a). This does not apply in the case of πᾶσα οἰκοδομή in Eph 2:21, since there is no proper name. Hence none of the suggested expressions provide a true precedent.

150. Hoehner, *Ephesians*, 408–9; Fowl, *Ephesians*, 99.

151. See chapter 6.

mission—which has been presented as an activity undertaken by Christ (2:17)—seems to be primarily in view here. For this reason, it is best to understand the verb "grows" (αὔξει, v. 21) in a transitive sense.[152] That is, v. 21 is stating that in Christ Jesus, every instance of gospel-preaching mission ("every act of construction"), since it forms part of a complex but harmonious unity of missionary activity to both far and near ("being joined together," συναρμολογουμένη), is "causing growth" (αὔξει), with a goal in view ("into," εἰς), i.e. "a holy temple in the Lord" (ναὸν ἅγιον ἐν κυρίῳ). The introduction of the temple motif may reflect the eschatological expectations concerning the inclusion of gentiles in temple worship.[153] However, the emphasis in v. 21 is not on the newness of the temple in contrast to the physical temple,[154] nor is it on the *singularity* of the "holy temple"; rather, the emphasis is on the *harmony* that exists among the various gospel-preaching missionary endeavors. These missions, though they are taking place among different groups—both Jews and gentiles (cf. v. 17)—are united. This unity consists in having the same "foundation" (the apostolic preaching, cf. v. 20), the same "cornerstone" (Christ), and the same goal (growth into a holy temple).

152. The verb αὔξω/αὐξάνω can be transitive or intransitive (BDAG, "αὐξάνω"). When Paul uses the verb in the active voice in his undisputed letters, he does so with the transitive meaning (1 Cor 3:6, 7; 2 Cor 9:10; 10:15). Furthermore, the object may be implied rather than explicitly stated (as in 1 Cor 3:6, 7). So here in Eph 2:21, the transitive meaning with an implied object is possible and even likely.

153. Cf. Rom 15:16–19, 25–27, where Paul describes his apostolic ministry in priestly and Jerusalem-centric terms, particularly drawing from the expectations in Isa 60–61 (Windsor, *Vocation of Israel*, 114–19). Cf. also Thielman, *Ephesians*, 184.

154. Yet again, the Epistle of Barnabas provides a strong contrast with Eph 2. Barnabas, like Ephesians, describes the Christian community in terms of a spiritual temple, in the sense of being a dwelling for God. Barnabas, however, unlike Ephesians emphasizes this temple in "us" (Christians) as a *contrast* to the physical Jewish temple hoped for by "them" (Jews): "I will also speak to you about the Temple, since those wretches were misguided in hoping in the building rather than in their God who made them, as if the Temple were actually the house of God. . . . Now pay attention, so that the temple of the Lord may be gloriously built. And learn how: we have become new, created again from the beginning, because we have received the forgiveness of sins and have hoped in the name. Therefore God truly resides within our place of dwelling—within us" (Barn. 16.1, 8 [Ehrman], cf. 16.10). This supersessionist viewpoint, so clearly present in Barnabas, is entirely absent from Eph 2:21–22.

The Gentile Focus: "Also You" (v. 22)

In verse 22, Paul once again focuses his attention on his gentile read-ers. He uses the same emphatic formulation, "in whom also you" (ἐν ᾧ καὶ ὑμεῖς), that he had used in Eph 1:13 to focus his readers' attention on the results of the gospel-preaching mission through Israel to the nations.[155] Here in 2:22, having asserted that "every construction" (πᾶσα οἰκοδομή)—i.e., every instance of gospel-preaching mission—causes growth into a holy temple in the Lord (v. 21), Paul now presses this truth home to the experience of his gentile readers. Through the preaching of the gospel to them, *they too* are being "built together" (συνοικοδομεῖσθε) into a dwelling for God in (or by) the Spirit (v. 22). This verb—a *syn*-compound (see above)—continues to evoke the complex diversity-in-unity in which Paul's gentile readers are being caught up through their response to the preaching of the gospel. Together with Israel, they are being built into a dwelling-place for God by his Spirit.[156] Their privileges are indeed great; they have God's presence with them. However, this has not occurred apart from Israel, but together with Israel.

Summary of Ephesians 2

In this chapter, we have seen how the apostolic mission plays a climactic role in Christ's work of reconciliation for Israel and the nations in Eph 2. Paul's insistence that both "you" and "we" have been raised from death to life (Eph 2:1–10) places Israel's distinctiveness within a larger divine perspective that coheres with the prophetic witness and emphasizes God's gracious saving activity. Paul's emphasis on the fact that his gentile readers have been "brought near" to Israel (Eph 2:11–13) reminds them that while their gentile past is still relevant to their present identity, it has been thoroughly transformed in Christ: they were once gentiles *contra* Israel; now they are gentiles *blessed alongside* Israel. Paul's description of Christ's sacrificial death (Eph 2:14–16) draws out a key achievement of the cross: the reconciliation of Israel and the nations together to God. Paul's description of the gospel-preaching activity of Christ to both "near" and "far" (Eph 2:17–18) depicts Christ's missionary work—through the

155. See chapter 3.

156. *Pace* Lincoln, who claims that at this point "Israel's privileges in proximity to God, historically associated with the Jerusalem temple, have completely faded from view" ("Church and Israel," 615).

agency of the apostolic mission—as the culmination of his reconciling activity. Paul's description of gentiles being built together with the "saints" on the same apostolic foundation (Eph 2:19–22) indicates that the Jew-gentile relationship is intimately connected to the dynamics of the gospel mission, a mission that proceeded through the early Jewish apostolic community to the nations.

Thus, we have seen that supersessionist readings of certain texts in Eph 2 are, in fact, over-readings that do not account adequately for the context in which the texts appear. The purpose of the discussion of circumcision in v. 11 is not to cancel entirely the value of physical circumcision for Jews. Rather, the discussion is intended to remind the readers of the way in which Jewish circumcision had been used in the context of Jew-gentile hostility, and also to remind them that Jewish circumcision, as a human activity, could not achieve the divine purposes of overcoming such hostility. The reference to the "law of the commandments in decrees" having been "abolished" by Christ (v. 15) is not a claim that the law of Moses has been rendered invalid in all respects. Rather, it is a claim that Christ's death renders unnecessary some of the key functions of the law's commandments as interpreted by Jewish authorities in the first century—particularly those functions that involved protecting Israel from impure and hostile gentiles. The creation of the "one new humanity" in Christ (vv. 15–16) does not imply the eradication of all distinctions between Israel and the nations. Rather, the focus is on reconciliation and the removal of hostility between Israel and the nations.

In Eph 2, there is a strong focus on Christ as the primary agent of God's purposes. Christ is the subject of all the reconciling activity, including the gospel-preaching missionary activity (v. 17). However, as we have seen, there are indications that Christ's missionary activity occurs through the agency of others. In v. 20, while Christ is the "cornerstone," the "foundation" is the gospel-preaching activity of the early Jewish apostolic community (the "apostles and prophets"). This devolution of agency anticipates the argument of the following chapters of Ephesians, where a more active role is envisaged for "his holy apostles and prophets" (Eph 3:5), the "saints" (Eph 4:12), and Paul himself (Eph 3:1–13; 4:1; 6:19–20). It is to these chapters we now turn.

5

Christ's Riches through Paul's Ministry to the Nations (Ephesians 3)

The Place of Paul's Apostolic Ministry in Ephesians (Eph 3:1)

EPH 3:1 BEGINS WITH the phrase "for this reason" (τούτου χάριν). This implies that there is a logical connection between Christ's acts of salvation, reconciliation, and gospel-proclamation as portrayed in Eph 2, and Paul's self-identification as "the prisoner of Christ [Jesus] on behalf of you gentiles" (3:1). What is the nature of this connection? Several commentators have pointed to the prayer for knowledge (3:14–21), which resumes the clause that began in v. 1. These commentators understand the logic as follows: since Christ has effected such a great salvation and reconciliation (Eph 2), "for this reason" Paul prays that his gentile readers would come to a fuller comprehension of the greatness of this salvation and reconciliation (3:14–21).[1] However, Eph 3:14–21 alone cannot fully explain the nature of the connection with Eph 2. We also need to account for Eph 3:1–13. That is, we need to explain why Paul introduces himself in these precise terms—as someone who is imprisoned for the sake of the

---

1. Fowl, *Ephesians*, 106. *Pace* Shkul, it is highly unlikely that Paul is here asserting that his "egalitarian" message was the cause of his imprisonment (*Reading Ephesians*, 155–56). If that were the case, the verb "I am" (εἰμί) would be present, and/or the article would be absent. Rather, this verse (like 1:1) contains a series of nominative terms in apposition ("I, Paul, the prisoner . . .") forming a subject whose main verb "I bow" (κάμπτω) is found at the resumption of the clause in v. 14.

gentile mission—and why Paul includes such a detailed statement about his own apostolic mission to the gentiles (vv. 2–13) before beginning his prayer. In other words, we need to ask: what do Paul's apostolic ministry and sufferings (Eph 3:1–13) have to do with the themes we have already explored in Eph 1–2, including the prominent Jew-gentile dynamic?

As we approach this question, it is worth noting that Eph 3:1 is the first time in the letter that Paul refers to his imprisonment. This seems a little strange, given that Paul wants his gentile readers not to be discouraged by the sufferings of "their" apostle (3:13). If this were Paul's purpose, one might expect that he would seek to explain this imprisonment close to the start of the letter before entering into his argument proper (cf. Phil 1:12–26; Col 1:24; 2 Tim 1:8; Phlm 1). Yet Paul has avoided mentioning his imprisonment until now. Prior to this point in the letter, he has simply introduced himself as "apostle of Christ Jesus by the will of God" (1:1), then gone on to detail God's far-reaching purposes for salvation and reconciliation: purposes that have been achieved through Christ's death, resurrection, and missionary preaching, and which have resulted in the reconciliation of Israel and the nations (Eph 1–2). What is the effect of this delay in mentioning the imprisonment? It appears that Paul is deliberately seeking to locate his apostolic ministry (and sufferings) within the far-reaching, divinely foreordained purposes described in Eph 1–2. In other words, Paul wishes to highlight the fact that Christ's triumph in achieving his international, and indeed cosmic, purposes through the gospel comes about through (not just despite) the weakness of the one who preaches this gospel.[2] The ordering of the material in this way seems intentional: designed to ensure that the readers will see Paul's apostolic sufferings as part of God's great purposes for Israel, the nations, and indeed the cosmos.[3]

2. Gombis, "Ephesians 3:2–13."

3. The purpose of Eph 3:1–13 is explained differently by various interpreters, depending on their construal of the occasion and purpose of Ephesians. Dunn, for example, sees it as an attempt to prevent a scenario where "in a post-70 situation, with churches more and more predominantly Gentile in composition, this central aspect of Paul's mission [i.e., the reconciliation of Jew and gentile] might be forgotten and downplayed" (*Beginning from Jerusalem*, 1113). Shkul sees it as an exercise in "social entrepreneurship," "shaping Paul's reputation" for a later generation and "setting him on a pedestal in the community as a servant as well as exemplar and model" (*Reading Ephesians*, 145). Alternatively, if we accept Paul as the historical author of Ephesians, we can take 3:13 at face value and conclude that the historical Paul was genuinely concerned that gentiles throughout Asia Minor would be discouraged by news of the (perhaps prolonged) imprisonment of the apostle to the gentiles.

Thus, the extended discussion of Paul's apostolic mission in vv. 2–13 serves to connect his own personal ministry with the broader apostolic Jew-gentile dynamic described in Eph 1–2. This can also be seen by the use of "I" and "you" in Eph 3. We have already observed the prominent "we-you" distinction that features in a number of places in Eph 1–2 (Eph 1:11–14; 2:1–3, 11–13, 22). As we have argued at length, when this distinction is clearly in view, "we" refers to the early Jewish apostolic community, while "you" denotes the gentile readers of the letter.[4] In Eph 3, however, this "we-you" distinction is replaced by an "I-you" distinction. "I" refers to Paul in his role as apostle to the gentiles (3:1–4, 7–8, 14). Paul, the "I" in Eph 3, has a role parallel to the "we" in Eph 1–2. The term "you" in Eph 3 continues to refer to the readers; yet these readers are now explicitly named as "the gentiles" (3:1), who are the recipients of Paul's apostolic ministry (3:6, 8).[5] In this way, Paul deliberately places his own apostolic ministry to the gentiles (from "I" to "you") within the horizon of the Jew-gentile dynamic (from "we" to "you") that has been underlying the argument of the letter so far.

Formally, Eph 3:2–13 constitute a "digression" from the prayer-report clause that begins in v. 1 and is resumed in v. 14.[6] The classification of these verses as a "digression," however, does not imply that they are subordinate in terms of their content or their significance for the argument of the letter.[7] On the contrary, the connecting word γέ ("indeed," v. 2) is used to "focus the attention upon a single idea, and place it, as it were, in the limelight."[8] What precisely is being placed in the limelight? Several interpreters explain the significance of vv. 2–13 as a justification of Paul's authority to write the letter. Best, for example, understands the significance in terms of Paul's epistolary authority, providing "the grounds for Paul's right to address the readers."[9] Fowl understands the

---

4. See chapters 3 and 4. Of course, at times "we" refers inclusively to both (e.g., Eph 2:18).

5. Fowl observes: "Recognition of the Ephesians' Gentile identity is not only essential for them to understand themselves properly before God; it is also the rationale for Paul's apostolic activity" (*Ephesians*, 106–7).

6. Lincoln, *Ephesians*, 167–68; Hoehner, *Ephesians*, 417. Cf. Caragounis, *Mysterion*, 55–56.

7. *Pace* Barth, *Ephesians*, 327.

8. BDAG, "γέ." Cf. the same construction (εἴ γε) in 2 Cor 5:3; Gal 3:4; Eph 4:21; Col 1:23.

9. Best, *Ephesians*, 292.

significance in terms of Paul's hermeneutical authority: "The bold interpretive moves Paul makes in chapter 2 call forth an equally bold account
of Paul's authority as an interpreter of God's gracious activity in chapter
3."[10] However, there are good reasons to see this description of Paul's
apostolic authority as being more organically related to the content of
Eph 1–2. Gombis, for example, points to the images of divine warfare
and triumph in Eph 1–2, such as Christ's "victory shout" in 2:17.[11] He
argues that Eph 3:2–13 "plays a strategic role in the unfolding argument of Ephesians, in that it explains for Paul's readers how his current
situation, which appears to contradict the triumph of God in Christ, is
actually an epitome—a concrete manifestation—of that triumph."[12] We
can add to this observation that the portrayal of Christ as "preaching the
gospel of peace" in 2:17 not only highlights his victory, but also describes
the central means by which this victory is achieved: gospel-preaching
mission. Yet this also highlights a tension that Paul needs to resolve:
since Paul, the well-known apostle and gospel preacher, is in prison,
Christ's victory seems to be threatened. Hence Paul needs to explain in
some detail how his apostolic ministry has, and still is, achieving God's
victorious purposes for Israel, the nations, and indeed the cosmos.

This passage, then, while syntactically a "digression," is highly significant in terms of its content. Paul here locates his own apostolic ministry
within God's greater international and cosmic purposes, especially those
purposes that involve the dynamic of blessing flowing through Israel to
the nations. Several features of the passage, which we will now examine,
contribute to this goal.

Paul's "Administration" (Eph 3:2)

In v. 2, Paul reminds his readers of the "administration of the grace of
God given to me for you." When we examined Eph 1:10, we saw that the
term "administration" ($o\dot{i}\varkappa o\nu o\mu\dot{i}\alpha$) refers to an active task, office, commission, or responsibility to manage the affairs of a master.[13] In Eph 1:10, the
term "administration" refers to the task of putting into effect God's eternal, cosmic purposes "in Christ." Here in Eph 3:2, the "administration" in

10. Fowl, *Ephesians*, 104.
11. Gombis, "Ephesians 3:2–13," 315.
12. Ibid., 323; cf. Sherwood, "Paul's Imprisonment."
13. See chapter 3.

view is that particular task given to Paul. Paul has been commissioned to put into effect "the grace of God," which refers to those blessings that God has graciously given "in Christ": redemption, forgiveness, resurrection, eternal life, and salvation (Eph 1:6–7; 2:5, 7–8). Paul's administration of this grace is directed especially to his gentile readers: it is "the administration (τὴν οἰκονομίαν) given to me for you (εἰς ὑμᾶς)." Paul is thus bringing the "grace" of God to the nations. As the following verses make clear, this sharing of God's grace is taking place through the preaching of the gospel, particularly (though not exclusively) through Paul's apostolic mission.

Paul's Insight into the Mystery of Christ (Eph 3:3–6)

In vv. 3–6, Paul focuses on his own insight as an apostle. His apostolic mission is based on the revelation of "the mystery." Earlier in the letter, this "mystery" was said to be revealed to a wider group: God "made known (γνωρίσας) to us (ἡμῖν) the mystery (τὸ μυστήριον) of his will" (Eph 1:9). As we have seen, given the priestly dynamic evident in Eph 1, we may read Eph 1:9 as a claim that God revealed his will to the Jewish apostolic community, through whom this blessing of revelation was shared with the gentiles (cf. 1:13–14).[14] In Eph 3:3, the revelation of the mystery is focused (at least initially) on the apostle Paul: "the mystery (τὸ μυστήριον) was made known (ἐγνωρίσθη) to me (μοι)." Paul notes that he has already written about this "briefly" (ἐν ὀλίγῳ). Up to this point in the letter, Paul has only made a few brief mentions of his own apostolic ministry (Eph 1:1, 15–16).[15] He has been concentrating on expounding God's greater purposes for Israel, the nations, and the cosmos "in Christ," which form the context of his apostleship. Now in Eph 3, however, he speaks directly about his apostleship, and explains how that apostleship fits into God's wider purposes.

Although Paul has only mentioned his apostleship briefly so far, all that he has written enables his gentile readers to appreciate his own personal "insight" (v. 4).[16] Lincoln claims that this self-commendation is

14. See chapter 3.

15. This explains the term "briefly" (ἐν ὀλίγῳ) better than other explanations that point to broader aspects of Eph 1–2, such as the theme of gentile inclusion, which Paul has discussed in some detail and at some length (see e.g., Lincoln, *Ephesians*, 175; Thielman, *Ephesians*, 195; Fowl, *Ephesians*, 108).

16. Taking πρὸς ὃ δύνασθε ἀναγινώσκοντες νοῆσαι τὴν σύνεσίν μου to mean "with

evidence for post-Pauline authorship of Ephesians. In Paul's undisputed letters, self-commendation occurs only in polemical settings (e.g., 2 Cor 12:1–10). Since the setting here in Ephesians is not polemical, Lincoln argues, the self-commendation must be an attempt by a post-Pauline author of Ephesians to gain apostolic authorization for his views.[17] However, while the setting of Ephesians is not directly polemical, Ephesians does speak of a clear crisis that may well have given rise to the need for such an affirmation: Paul is in prison (v. 1), and so the secular powers appear to have the upper hand. This may certainly have caused the readers of Ephesians to question the validity and efficacy of Paul's apostolic mission and so to "lose heart" (v. 13). Paul thus needs to demonstrate that things are not what they seem: God has revealed a "mystery" to him which shows the situation in a whole new light.[18]

In vv. 5–6, Paul spells out the nature of this mystery. The concept of "mystery" is drawn from Jewish writings, especially the book of Daniel. It refers to a "secret" that can be known only through divine revelation. In Daniel, as in Ephesians, the mystery "is God's purpose, it is eschatological, it has cosmic dimensions, and it is a unified plan."[19] As we have already seen, in Eph 1:9–10, the mystery is portrayed broadly in terms of the unification of "all things" in Christ.[20] The use of the phrase "the mystery of Christ" in Eph 3 is connected to the "mystery" in Eph 1, but the scope here is more specific: it is used with special reference to Christ's role in bringing the gentiles to share in Israel's blessings (v. 6, cf. 2:19–22).[21] The use of the term "now" (νῦν, vv. 5, 10) also links the revelation of the mystery to the salvation-historical change in gentile status that has come about through the blood of Christ (cf. νυνί, 2:13).[22]

---

reference to which [i.e., these brief mentions of my apostleship], as you read [what I have written so far] you can understand my insight . . . ."

17. Lincoln, *Ephesians*, 176–77.

18. The claim to "insight," then, is not so much designed to be a defense of Paul's personal authority in light of personal attacks, but rather to be a defense of Paul's apostolic *mission* in light of seemingly disastrous circumstances. While this does not by itself prove historical Pauline authorship of Ephesians, it does demonstrate that it is not necessary to posit post-Pauline authorship to explain the verse.

19. Caragounis, *Mysterion*, 134–35.

20. See chapter 3.

21. Thielman, *Ephesians*, 197.

22. Sandnes, *One of the Prophets?* 231.

The revelation of this "mystery" is described as something genuinely new in salvation history: it was "not made known to the sons of men in other generations as it has now been revealed to his holy apostles and prophets by the Spirit" (v. 5). What is the "new" element of revelation when it comes to gentiles? It cannot be referring simply to the fact that gentiles are now blessed through Israel, nor that gentiles are now included in temple worship. These things were already anticipated in the Scriptures (see e.g., Isa 2:1–2; 60–61; 66:19–23; cf. Tob 14:5–7), and so cannot be described as a "mystery."[23] Furthermore, Paul cannot be simply claiming that gentile inclusion is now understood or known to a greater extent than it was before the advent of Christ. The language of "revelation" and "hiddenness" implies that something genuinely new has been revealed, something that was not previously known at all (cf. 3:9–10).[24]

The new element of revelation can, in fact, be found in the following verse (v. 6): "This mystery is that the gentiles are fellow heirs (συγκληρονόμα), members of the same body (σύσσωμα), and partakers (συμμέτοχα) of the promise in Christ Jesus through the gospel." Firstly, the mystery that has been revealed involves the *equality of status* between Jews and gentiles in Christ. The connection between the three *syn*-compounds in Eph 3:6 and the three *syn*-compounds in Eph 2:19–22 suggests that Paul is pointing his readers back to this prior affirmation of the equality of status between Israel and the nations brought about through Christ's death.[25] This *full equality* of status was not clear in the prophetic Scriptures and other Jewish writings, which often portrayed the nations as politically subservient to Israel at the eschaton (e.g., Isa 45:14; 60–61; Pss. Sol. 17.30).[26] Thus, it is a genuinely new element of revelation. However, there is something else quite new that has been revealed: the fact that this equal status between Jew and gentile comes about "through the gospel." This phrase recalls earlier references to the preaching of the gospel (2:17), and the hearing of the gospel (1:13). In other words, Paul is asserting that the expansive gospel *mission* from Israel to the nations, which brings about an equal status before God between Jew and gentile,

---

23. Thielman, *Ephesians*, 184.

24. Ibid., 198.

25. See chapter 4.

26. Thielman, *Ephesians*, 198. Cf. Paul's Christological reconfiguration of the phrase "the obedience of the nations" in Rom 15:18 (Windsor, *Vocation of Israel*, 116, 136–37).

is central to God's purposes through Christ, and is a genuinely new element in the revelation of God's purposes.[27]

"His Holy Apostles and Prophets" (Eph 3:5)

Furthermore, the horizons of this expansive gospel mission are broader than Paul's own personal apostolic ministry. Having asserted that the "mystery" was "revealed to me" and spoken of as "my" insight into the mystery (vv. 3–4), Paul then uses the same language to refer to a broader group: the "mystery" has been "revealed to his [Christ's] holy apostles and prophets" (v. 5).[28] Who are this group, and why are they described in this way? As we will now see, the phrase should be understood as a reference to the early Jewish apostolic community, through whom the gospel was preached to the nations.

According to Lincoln, Ephesians contains two contradictory perspectives on the early Christian mission. The first perspective views the mission in a similar way to Paul in his undisputed letters, and sees Paul himself playing the key role. It regards Paul as the great "apostle" (1:1) and the primary recipient of God's revelation (3:2–4, 7–8). The second perspective views the mission as it is portrayed in the Gospels and Acts, in which the twelve apostles play a key role. It tends to regard the "apostles," along with the "prophets," as revered figures of a former generation, and so designates them as "holy," i.e., set apart from humanity in general (3:5, cf. 2:20).[29] However, as Thielman points out, this hypothesis involving contradictory yet interwoven traditions in Eph 3:2–7 is unnecessary. The complexity in this passage reflects "the complexity of the actual situation in the early days of the church's mission," as evident both in Acts (e.g., Acts 22:21; 26:17–18) and in Paul's undisputed letters (e.g., Gal 2:7–9; 1 Cor 1:12; 3:22; 9:5; 15:5).[30] In Eph 3:2–7, then, Paul both includes himself among the wider group of "apostles and prophets," and also focuses on his own key role in bringing the gospel to the gentiles.[31] This may be

---

27. Caragounis, *Mysterion*, 104.

28. Sandnes, *One of the Prophets?*, 231.

29. Cf. Lincoln, *Ephesians*, 179–80; cf. Käsemann, "Ephesians and Acts," 291; Kümmel, *Introduction*, 360; Best, *Ephesians*, 96–97.

30. Thielman, *Ephesians*, 202–3; cf. Fowl, *Ephesians*, 109.

31. Sandnes, *One of the Prophets?* 231.

a complex perspective, but it has many precedents in both Paul's letters and the book of Acts.

The description of the early apostolic community in the book of Acts does, however, help to explain the significance of the reference to the "apostles and prophets" in Eph 3:5. The "apostles" in Acts are the foundational witnesses to Christ's life, death, and resurrection (Acts 1:2, 21–26). Their ministry is both Israel-centric and expansive. They are commissioned to be Christ's witnesses "in Jerusalem and in all Judea and Samaria, and to the end of the earth" (Acts 1:8). Their teaching formed the foundation of the community in Jerusalem (e.g., Acts 2:42; 4:33; cf. Acts 15:2, 4, 6, 22–23). In the first great outbreak of persecution, they remained in Jerusalem (Acts 8:1). Nevertheless, soon thereafter some of their number continued to work at the forefront of the mission (e.g., Acts 8:14; 10). Paul, after his conversion, is also called an "apostle" (e.g., Acts 14:4, 14). According to Acts, then, the apostles and the Jewish apostolic community around them are those who formed the nucleus of the early Christian mission to the nations.

Certain "prophets" also appear at several points in Acts. These "prophets" are members of the apostolic community whose activity involved assisting and extending the Jerusalem-centered mission of the apostles in various ways (Acts 11:27–30; 13:1; 15:32; 21:10).[32] The description of the "apostles and prophets" in Ephesians corresponds to this picture from Acts. As we have seen, in Eph 2:20 the apostles and prophets are associated with the "foundation" of Christ's mission.[33] The word-order of the phrase in Eph 3:6 (literally "the holy apostles of him, and prophets," τοῖς ἁγίοις ἀποστόλοις αὐτοῦ καὶ προφήταις) suggests that the prophets are closely linked to the apostles but have a subsidiary role.[34] In Eph 4:11, as we will see, the "apostles" and "prophets" are the first and second "gifts," respectively, associated with Christ's descent at Pentecost.[35] Thus, the role of the apostles and prophets portrayed in Ephesians corresponds to that portrayed in Acts.

---

32. Thielman, *Ephesians*, 180. Thielman's observations about Acts here are apposite; however, he (like many others) goes too far by extending the reference to cover any mention of "prophetic" speech (e.g., 1 Cor 14:24–25). Here in Eph 3:5 (and in 4:11) the reference is narrower: it is to those "prophets" of the apostolic community whose role was connected to the role of the apostles.

33. See chapter 4.

34. Thielman, *Ephesians*, 199.

35. See chapter 6.

These apostles (and also prophets) are described in Eph 3:5 as "holy." As we have seen, this adjective can be used substantivally by Paul in his undisputed letters to refer to the Jewish apostolic community in Jerusalem: "the saints" (Rom 15:25–26, 31; 1 Cor 16:1; 2 Cor 8:4; 9:1, 12; cf. Acts 9:13).[36] This usage fits well into Eph 3:5 also. The apostles and prophets can be described as "holy" because they are the core of the apostolic community in Jerusalem; they are thus Israelites with a central role to play in God's worldwide purposes (cf. Isa 52:1–10). This is not, of course, to claim that only the apostles and prophets can ever be called "holy." Indeed, as we have seen, Paul's use of the term "holy" in Ephesians is associated with an expansive *sharing* of holiness with the gentiles.[37] Nevertheless, the members of the apostolic community in Jerusalem have a certain priority when it comes to being called "holy." This is because their missionary endeavors are the foundation on which Christ builds all believers, both Jew and gentile, into a "holy temple" (Eph 2:20–22).[38]

The foundational apostolic mission is, therefore, at the same time a Jew-gentile dynamic. As Kinzer observes,

> the Jewish identity of the apostles is crucial. They represent the Messiah of Israel, and thus they also represent Israel itself. This connection to Israel is evident in the Gospel tradition concerning the Twelve, who are appointed and destined to rule over the twelve tribes of Israel (Matt 19:28; Luke 22:28–30). But Ephesians suggests that this connection applies equally to the entire company of apostles, including Paul.[39]

Paul's Role as a "Minister of the Gospel" (Eph 3:7)

Upon mentioning the word "gospel" (v. 6), Paul returns to his own apostolic gospel-preaching ministry. He describes himself as having become a "minister" (διάκονος) of this gospel (v. 7). Unfortunately, there is a pervasive assumption in scholarship on Ephesians that this term has a basic

36. See chapter 4.

37. See chapters 3 and 4; *pace* Lincoln, *Ephesians*, 179.

38. Fowl, *Ephesians*, 109. Cf. Paul's self-description in "priestly," Jerusalem-centered terms in Rom 1:1, 15:16 (Windsor, *Vocation of Israel*, 112–19). *Pace* Best, *Ephesians*, 308, who cannot envisage Paul ascribing such dignity to himself.

39. Kinzer, *Searching Her Own Mystery*, 81; cf. Barth, *Ephesians*, 337.

meaning of "servant."[40] However, this understanding of the term has been comprehensively refuted by the work of John N. Collins.[41] Collins has demonstrated that, despite earlier claims by the influential *TDNT*, the idea of "service" cannot be called the "basic meaning" of the "ministry" (διακον-) word-group. Rather, the underlying idea of the word-group is that of a "go-between." Many instances of the word-group involve the conveying of messages; in fact, the word-group is often used in contexts where a message is brought from gods to earth (cf. e.g., Josephus, *War* 3.354; 4.626). This usage seems to be the primary linguistic background for the use of the term in the Corinthian letters (1 Cor 3:5; 2 Cor 3:6; 6:4; 11:23), and also its use here in Eph 3:7. Paul is using the term to describe himself as a medium (or "bringer") of divine revelation and blessings to the world. Thus, Paul's role as "minister of the gospel" is here, as in other places, caught up with Paul's identity as an "Israelite" with a vocation to be the medium of God's blessings to the nations (cf. 2 Cor 11:22–23).[42]

Paul's gospel-preaching ministry is, therefore, intimately connected with God's gracious purposes for Israel and the nations as described in Eph 1–2. God, through his great grace (described in expansive and overflowing terms), has appointed Paul to the task of "administration" in order to achieve his gracious purposes (v. 2) and has made him a "minister" of his gospel (v. 7).

Paul as One of the "Saints" Preaching to "The Nations" (Eph 3:8–9)

In v. 8, Paul describes himself as the "very least of all the saints." There is a parallel here with 1 Cor 15:9, where Paul claims to be the "least of the apostles."[43] The fact that the expression "apostles" in 1 Corinthians has become "all the saints" in Ephesians is significant.[44] As we have seen above, the expression "the saints" can be used by Paul to refer to the

40. E.g., Hoehner, *Ephesians*, 550; Larkin, *Ephesians*, 79; Arnold, *Ephesians*, 262–63; Thielman, *Ephesians*, 206; Fowl, *Ephesians*, 142.

41. Collins, *Diakonia*. For a more thorough engagement with Collins, along with an overview of the history of the discussion and its significance for Ephesians, see Windsor, "Work of Ministry."

42. Windsor, *Vocation of Israel*, 75–76.

43. Thielman, *Ephesians*, 210–12.

44. *Pace* Best, who regards this as a reason why there is no link between 1 Cor 15:9 and Eph 3:8 (*Ephesians*, 316–17).

apostolic community in Jerusalem (Rom 15:25–26, 31; 1 Cor 16:1; 2 Cor 8:4; 9:1, 12; cf. Acts 9:13). As we have seen, this concept has already informed Paul's attribution of the adjective "holy" to the "apostles" (and "prophets") in v. 6. Here in v. 8, then, Paul's self-description as one "of all the saints" enables him to associate himself with the entire apostolic community centered in Jerusalem (cf. Rom 15:19). In this way, Paul is doing more than claiming that he is one of the apostles; he is in fact reminding his readers that he is associated with the *Jewish* apostolic community through whom God is bringing his blessing to the nations. The description of his ministry in terms of "enlightening" or "shining" (φωτίσαι, v. 9) may also be an allusion to the eschatological vision of Isa 60, in which "Jerusalem" is commanded to "shine" (φωτίζου, Isa 60:1 LXX) and so enlighten the nations with God's light (Isa 60:2–3, 19; cf. Eph 5:8–9, 13–14).

Of course, Paul's association with the apostolic community in Jerusalem is not a claim to personal greatness; he is after all the "very least" of all the saints.[45] This indicates that he is especially reliant on God's "grace" for his ministry (as well as his salvation cf. 2:5, 8–10). Nevertheless, Paul's association with the apostolic community in Jerusalem is significant. It demonstrates that Paul's own ministry is intimately associated with God's purposes through Israel for the nations. Thus, even Paul's seemingly demeaning state of imprisonment is no obstacle to God's working through Paul to achieve his purposes (Eph 3:1, 13).

The Cosmic Dimensions of the Apostolic Task
(Eph 3:9–12)

In v. 9, the focus shifts for a moment away from the apostolic Jew-gentile dynamic and onto the larger, cosmic divine purposes that form the goal and context of this dynamic. God is described as the one "who created all things" (v. 9); the mystery is described as "hidden for ages" (v. 9); the "manifold wisdom of God" is now "made known to the rulers and authorities in the heavenly realms" (v. 10); and this all occurs according to God's "eternal purpose" in Christ (v. 11, cf. 1:9–10). In other words, while God's eschatological plan is driving toward a unified goal "in Christ" (1:9–11), its outworking is diverse and intricate. The term "manifold"

---

45. The term "very least" (ἐλαχιστότερος) is a comparative of a superlative, which is technically redundant. It expresses the lowliness of Paul's status in an exaggerated manner.

(πολυποίκιλος, v. 10) is a compound of two adjectives: πολύς ("much" or "many") and ποίκιλος, referring to a richly embroidered or woven garment with many colors yet working together in a single pattern.[46] This is an appropriate description, given of the many strands in God's plan that have been laid out in Eph 1–3. The actors include Paul, the apostles and prophets, Israel, the nations, the church, and the rulers and authorities in the heavenly places. These all come together at this point.

Nevertheless, the apostolic "administration" (οἰκονομία, v. 9; cf. v. 2) remains pivotal to God's cosmic purposes. This is because the particular way in which God's manifold wisdom has been made known to the powers and authorities is "through the church" (v. 10)—that is, through Christ's united body consisting of Israel and the nations sharing together in God's blessings, which in turn is the result of Christ's apostolic mission (1:22–23; 2:16–17). Most commentators take the preposition "through" (διά) here as instrumental, and so understand v. 10 to be implying that "by its very existence as a unified body . . . the church makes known to the evil spiritual rulers and authorities the vastness of God's creative wisdom."[47] However, the preposition "through" can also have a sense of agency,[48] and even when used instrumentally the instrument is not entirely passive (see e.g., Eph 1:5; 2:18). Thus, there may be more to the church's role implied here than simply its existence, especially when a very active role for the church is envisioned in Eph 4:11–16, cf. 5:23. For Barth, the church has a "mediating" role, participating in the apostolic ministry and acting as an "agent of revelation." The fact that such revelation occurs to the heavenly powers does not limit the church's revelatory role; rather it demonstrates the cosmic scope of this revelatory role.[49]

Paul's Sufferings Achieving God's Purposes (Eph 3:13)

In v. 13, Paul provides the only explicit purpose statement in the letter: "So I ask you not to lose heart over what I am suffering for you, which is your glory."[50] If we accept Paul as the author, this statement may suggest

46. Hoehner, *Ephesians*, 461–62. Cf. Joseph's "variegated tunic" (χιτῶνα ποικίλον) in Gen 37:3 LXX.

47. Thielman, *Ephesians*, 216. Cf. Fowl, *Ephesians*, 111–12; Gombis, "Ephesians 3:2–13," 320.

48. BDAG, "διά."

49. Barth, *Ephesians*, 363–66.

50. There is an ambiguity in the phrase αἰτοῦμαι μὴ ἐγκακεῖν, which in the

the nature of the crisis that occasioned the letter itself: not a crisis within a particular congregation, but a more general "crisis of confidence" envisaged by Paul with respect to his worldwide apostolic mission, caused by his imprisonment and suffering. This may explain why Paul writes such a general letter intended for a range of gentile congregations in Asia Minor. He wishes to assure them that the great purposes of God have been and indeed are being worked out, even through Paul's own ministry and even through his imprisonment.[51] As Sherwood observes:

> Paul insists on the value of his role—both stewardship and imprisonment together—by identifying in v. 13 his sufferings with their glory. Paul's concern for the digression is that his audience would wrongly understand his apostleship in terms of his imprisonment, and so he takes pains instead to interpret his imprisonment in terms of his apostleship. Otherwise, his role in God's eschatological plan could have been subverted and viewed as shameful and, by extension, so could their own involvement in that plan detailed in ch. 2.[52]

Paul insists that even his sufferings are for their glory. This "glory" has a strongly eschatological element. It is a "glory" that is given by God to "the saints" (1:18) and has been shared, through the suffering apostle, with these gentile readers who now also share in Israel's glorious holy status and inheritance.[53] This, in turn, has cosmic repercussions, as Paul has just spelt out.

The Apostolic Prayer (Eph 3:14–21)

Paul's apostolic prayer in vv. 14–21 is a rich passage which cannot here be explored in detail. However, there are two elements of the prayer that further support our argument that the Jew-gentile dynamic is highly significant to the argument of Ephesians.

The first element is the mention of "every family (πᾶσα πατριά) in heaven and on earth" (v. 15). This seems to be a reference back to Eph

---

absence of an explicit subject for the infinitive could possibly be translated "I ask [God] that I might not be discouraged"; Thielman, however, argues persuasively for the ESV's rendering (*Ephesians*, 220).

51. Ibid., 221.

52. Sherwood, "Paul's Imprisonment," 108.

53. Thielman, *Ephesians*, 222.

2, which describes the diverse-yet-united results of Christ's missionary work to both near and far (Eph 2:17), bringing about access to God the "Father" (noun πατήρ) for all in Christ (Eph 2:18, cf. the various missionary endeavors in 2:19–22).[54] It may also contain hints of the eschatological fulfillment of the Abrahamic blessing (Gen 12:1–3), which we have argued is referred to in Eph 1:3.[55] In Gen 12:3, the promise is that "all the families/tribes of the earth" (MT "families," מִשְׁפְּחֹת; LXX "tribes," φυλαί) will be blessed (cf. Gen 28:14).

The second element involves the temple imagery that appears in vv. 18–19. Paul wants his gentile readers to "comprehend with all the saints what is the breadth and length and height and depth, and to know the love of Christ that surpasses knowledge, that you may be filled with all the fullness of God" (Eph 3:18–19). As Foster demonstrates, there is an important scriptural precedent to this expression in descriptions of God's glory filling the temple or the temple's sanctuary (Exod 40; 1 Kgs 8; Ezek 43). With this imagery in view, the "breadth and length and height and depth" (v. 18) may be understood as an allusion to the dimensions of the altar in Ezek 43:13–16. Furthermore, the idea of being "filled with all the fullness of God" (v. 19) may be an allusion to the fullness of God in that temple.[56] Ephesians 3:18–19 are, then, a Christological fulfillment of an Israel-centered eschatological vision. It is *this* scriptural vision that Paul wants his gentile readers to comprehend.

Furthermore, he wants them to comprehend this vision "together with all the saints" (σὺν πᾶσιν τοῖς ἁγίοις). Given what we have seen above about the use of *syn*-compounds to refer to the gentiles' status alongside Jews in Christ (v. 6), and the use of the phrase "all the saints" (v. 8) to denote the Jewish apostolic community, this is a further indication of unity-in-diversity between Christ-believing Jews and gentiles in Ephesians. Not only are the gentiles "together" with the Jews as fellow-heirs, members of the same body and partakers of the promise (v. 6), Paul prays they would also be "together" (σύν) with Israel in *comprehending* the full dimensions of the scriptural eschatological vision fulfilled in Christ. In other words, Paul prays that they would understand not only the *fact* of their salvation in Christ, but also the multidimensional and variegated implications of this salvation in Christ *as a fulfillment of the scriptural vision given to*

54. See chapter 4.
55. See chapter 3.
56. Foster, "Temple in the Lord."

Israel. This is, for Paul, is a key part of what it means "to be filled with all the fullness of God" (v. 19).

Summary of Ephesians 3

In this chapter, we have seen how in Eph 3 the apostolic mission is continuing through Paul, even in his suffering, so that Christ's riches are being poured out through Paul's ministry to the nations. Paul's turn toward a direct discussion of his own apostolic ministry (Eph 3:1) locates his ministry within God's greater international and cosmic purposes, especially those purposes that involve the dynamic flow of blessing through Israel to the nations. Paul's "administration" (Eph 3:2) is a reference to his apostolic mission to the gentiles. Paul's focus on his own insight as apostle (Eph 3:3–4) enables him to explain how his apostleship fits into God's greater purposes. Paul's understanding of the revealed "mystery of Christ" (Eph 3:4–6) is that Jews and gentiles have an equal status in Christ, and that this equal status comes about through the preaching of the gospel. Paul's reference to Christ's "holy apostles and prophets" (Eph 3:5) is intended as a reference to the early Jewish apostolic community, through whom the gospel was preached to the nations. Paul's self-description as a "minister of the gospel" (Eph 3:7) enables him to portray himself as a medium of divine revelation and blessing to the world, who is caught up in God's gracious purposes for Israel and the nations as described in Eph 1–2. Paul's humble self-identification as one of "the saints" (Eph 3:8–9) enables him to associate himself with the entire Jewish apostolic community. Paul's portrayal of the cosmic dimensions of the apostolic task (Eph 3:9–12) locates the Jew-gentile dynamic within the larger divine purposes, which form both the goal and context of this dynamic. Paul's appeal to his readers not to lose heart over his sufferings (Eph 3:13) may suggest that Ephesians was occasioned by a general "crisis of confidence" envisaged by Paul among gentile believers with respect to his worldwide apostolic mission. Finally, Paul's apostolic prayer (Eph 3:14–21) contains two elements that further support our argument that the Jew-gentile dynamic is highly significant to the argument of Ephesians: the mention of "every family" (v. 15, cf. Eph 2:17–22), and the allusion to the dimensions of the altar (vv. 18–19; cf. Ezek 43:13–16).

As we will now see, the theme of the apostolic mission through Israel to the nations continues to be significant in Eph 4–6.

6

Walking in Light of Christ's Mission through Israel to the Nations (Ephesians 4–6)

WE HAVE NOW SEEN many connections between the apostolic mission and the Jew-gentile dynamic in Eph 1–3. In chapter 3, we saw how in Eph 1 the apostolic mission is portrayed as the means by which Christ's blessings have come through Israel to the nations. In chapter 4, we saw how in Eph 2 the apostolic mission plays a climactic role in Christ's work of reconciliation for Israel and the nations. In chapter 5, we saw how in Eph 3 the apostolic mission is continuing through Paul, even in his suffering, so that Christ's riches are being poured out through Paul's ministry to the nations.

In Eph 4:1, there is a marked shift in tone, signaled by the phrase "Therefore I exhort" (Παρακαλῶ οὖν). In contrast to Eph 1–3, Eph 4–6 is more hortatory, with frequent use of imperatives.[1] Nevertheless, what Paul urges in Eph 4–6 is intimately connected with what he has already stated in Eph 1–3. Paul reminds them of his status as "prisoner" (δέσμιος, 4:1; cf. 3:1). Coming after the discussion in 3:1–14, this term is not simply a way of referring to Paul's humble status as an example for his readers (cf. v. 2); it now also connotes the place of Paul's gospel-preaching mission to the gentiles within God's greater purposes for Israel, the nations, and the cosmos.[2] Furthermore, in 4:1–6, there is an emphasis on the fact

---

1. In Eph 1–3 there is only one imperative (2:11) whereas in Eph 4–6 there are forty (Hoehner, *Ephesians*, 499).

2. See chapter 5.

that the readers have been "called" (verb καλέω, vv. 1, 4) with a "calling" (noun κλῆσις, vv. 1, 4). This recalls the prayer in Eph 1:18 that they would know "what is the hope of his calling" (τῆς κλήσεως αὐτοῦ). Paul also urges them to keep "the unity of the Spirit in the bond of peace" (τὴν ἑνότητα τοῦ πνεύματος ἐν τῷ συνδέσμῳ τῆς εἰρήνης, v. 3). This recalls the discussion in Eph 2:11–22, where the gentiles are said to have been made "one" (εἷς/ἕν, Eph 2:14, 15, 16, 18) "together" (σύν-, Eph 2:19, 21, 22) with Israel, having obtained access to God by the "Spirit" (πνεῦμα, Eph 2:18, 22), through Christ—who is, made, and preached "peace" (εἰρήνη, vv. 14, 15, 17). Further direct parallels between 4:1–6 and 2:11–22 include the mention of "one body" (v. 4; cf. 2:16), "one Spirit" (v. 4; cf. 2:18), and by implication "one God and Father" (v. 6, cf. 2:16, 18, 19, 22). Thus, in multiple ways, Eph 4:1–6 recalls the Jew-gentile dynamic that has been so prominent in the letter so far.

The connection between Eph 1–3 and 4–6 is often described in terms of an overarching Christian "theology" (Eph 1–3) informing the "ethics" or duty within the Christian community (Eph 4–6).[3] While this formulation is helpful as far as it goes,[4] it misses the key mission-related themes that, as we have seen, form a significant element of Eph 1–3. The exhortations in Eph 4–6 are issued on the basis of God's great purposes for his world as described in Eph 1–3—purposes in which the gospel-preaching mission through Israel to the nations plays a central role. Hence the centrality of the mission through Israel to the nations that has been established in Eph 1–3 is crucial to understanding Eph 4–6. Furthermore, the wide horizons of God's purposes spelled out in Eph 1–3 suggests that the "unity" in view in Eph 4:3 is not only a unity that is confined within the individual congregations of the readers. It also points to a wider unity between the congregations of the readers and the Jewish apostolic community.

In this chapter, I will argue that Eph 4–6 is setting out a generalized form of gentile *halakah* that confirms and conforms to the apostolic mission through Israel to the nations. This *halakhah* is appropriate to the situation of gentiles who have come to believe in Israel's Messiah and to receive his blessings through the preaching of the gospel. As such, this gentile *halakhah* becomes the key means by which these Christ-believing

3. Caird, *Letters from Prison*, 70–71; Lincoln, *Ephesians*, 234; Best, *Ephesians*, 353; Hoehner, *Ephesians*, 499.

4. However, Lincoln overemphasizes the shift from epideictic to deliberative rhetoric (Starling, *Not My People*, 169).

gentiles can express their unity with the foundational Jewish apostolic community from whom the gospel of Christ came. This, of course, raises the possibility that another appropriate form of *halakhah* might apply within the Jewish apostolic community itself, or indeed in other Christ-believing Jewish communities. While Paul in Ephesians would of course assume that any such Jewish *halakhah* would also be shaped primarily by the gospel of Christ (cf. Eph 2:17), the unity in Christ which is expressed here is not one that requires the erasure of all distinctions. Rather, it is a unity that involves gentiles conforming their speech and their lives to the gospel of Christ, as the fulfillment of God's purposes through Israel. Thus, the various distinctions spelled out in Eph 4–6, including the vocational distinctions associated with the early Christian mission (which, I will argue, are in view in Eph 4:11–12), are not a barrier to such unity. On the contrary, the distinctions are integral to the creation and expression of this unity in Christ.

The Foundations of Gentile *Halakhah* in Christ (Eph 4:1–6)

The key exhortation that governs vv. 1–6 is for Paul's gentile readers "to walk" (περιπατῆσαι, v. 1).[5] The term "walk" (περιπατέω) reappears in several key places throughout Eph 4–6 (4:17; 5:2, 8, 15). The term has, in fact, already been introduced in 2:1–10: firstly, by the negative statement that Paul's gentile readers once "walked" in trespasses and sins (2:1–2, cf. 4:17, 5:15); secondly, by the positive statement that those in Christ have been created in Christ Jesus to "walk" in good works (2:10; cf. 4:1; 5:2, 8, 15). Within the New Testament, the use of this verb to express Christ-believing conduct is a particularly Pauline usage. It derives from the LXX, where the word "walk" (περιπατέω) is used to translate the Hebrew *halakh* (הָלַךְ).[6] Indeed, Paul's various instructions to his gentile communities using the verb "walk" (περιπατέω) are in some ways akin to Pharisaic and Rabbinic *halakhah*, which may be described as "a way of giving increasingly definitive traditional shape to the practice of Judaism" by

---

5. Syntactically, this exhortation governs all that follows in vv. 1b–3. Furthermore, since vv. 4–6 appear to be an explanation of the "unity of the Spirit" (τὴν ἑνότητα τοῦ πνεύματος, v. 3; see Best, *Ephesians*, 366), the exhortation in v. 1a should be seen as governing all of vv. 1b–6.

6. Seesemann and Bertram, "πατέω, κτλ.," 942–44; cf. Hoehner, *Ephesians*, 309.

interpretation of the Torah for a new situation.[7] In certain places, the verb "walk" is used by Paul to introduce specific commands and traditions to regulate the conduct of believing communities (1 Cor 7:17; 1 Thess 2:12, 4:1, 12; 2 Thess 3:6, 11), often as a direct contrast with the conduct of the surrounding unbelieving "gentile" world (1 Thess 4:5). Many of these specific commands and traditions from Paul seem to involve applications of the Torah for the new, Christ-believing gentile situation.[8] Thus, the use of the verb "walk" in such situations appears to be indicating a form of Christ-believing gentile *halakah*.[9]

However, unlike the other Pauline letters referred to above, Ephesians contains no terms indicating specific "commanding" or "tradition-ing" processes.[10] This may be explained by the fact that Ephesians is most likely intended for a range of churches within the orbit of Paul's gentile ministry rather than for a specific congregation or set of congregations.[11] Because of this wide range of potential readers, Paul cannot presume that any specific traditions have been passed on them. However, he does use the more general educational terminology of "learning" and "teaching" in relation to Christ-believing conduct: "But that is not the way you learned Christ!—assuming that you have heard about him and were taught in him, as the truth is in Jesus . . ." (Eph 4:20–21).[12] Thus, while Paul cannot presume a specific tradition known to his gentile readers, he can assume that they have in some way "learned" to act in a way that is commensurate with Christ. To affirm, fill out, and supplement what they have

7. Bockmuehl, *Jewish Law in Gentile Churches*, 4. Bockmuehl outlines several parallels between Jesus' teaching and Pharisaic/Rabbinic *Halakhah* (ibid., 3–15).

8. See e.g., the connections between 1 Thess 4:3–8, which spells out the Thessalonians' "holiness" (vv. 3, 7) primarily in terms of sexual purity, and Lev 19–20, which exhorts Israel to be "holy" to the LORD by, among other things, avoiding sexual impurity (20:10–21). For further examples of *halakhic* patterns of teaching in the Pauline corpus, see Ciampa and Rosner, *First Corinthians*, 25–28.

9. See further Bockmuehl, *Jewish Law in Gentile Churches*, 167–72, who argues that Paul may be applying the Noachide commandments to his gentile converts.

10. Cf. e.g., Paul's reference to his "order" (verb διατάσσομαι) in all the churches (1 Cor 7:17), as well as his use of the verbs παραγγέλλω ("command," 1 Thess 4:11; 2 Thess 3:4, 6, 10, 12), and παραλαμβάνω ("receive [a tradition]," 1 Thess 4:1; 2 Thess 3:6). This last verb is also used in Col 2:6, which is also directed to a specific church.

11. See chapter 2.

12. The verbs here are μανθάνω ("learn") and διδάσκω ("teach"). For an exploration of the differences between the Pauline vocabulary of passing on traditions (e.g., "delivered"/"received") and the Pauline vocabulary of education (e.g., "teach"/"learn") see Smith, "Unchanged 'Teaching.'"

learned, he begins an extended exhortation with a command to "walk." Thus, we can say that Eph 4–6 is setting out a generalized form of *halakah* that applies to Christ-believing gentiles.

According to v. 1, this generalized *halakhah* must be conducted "worthily of the calling (noun κλῆσις) with which you were called (verb καλέω)." In Eph 1:18, the "calling" was said to be connected to a "hope," which was further described as "the riches of the glory of his inheritance among the saints." Here in Eph 4, the calling is also connected to a "hope," which is described as "one hope" (Eph 4:4). We can conclude from these explicit references that the "calling" of Paul's gentile readers has an eschatological dimension, and that it involves unity with others, including "the saints." Since these are key themes throughout Eph 1–3, it seems that the terms "called" and "calling" are here being used to refer, in summary form, to the participation of Paul's gentile readers in God's wider purposes—and in particular, to refer to the way Christ has brought them to share in Israel's blessings.

The gentiles' "calling" to unity with Israel in Christ does not imply that they are made the same as Israel in every respect. Their calling is a distinctly gentile calling. This may be implied by the precise wording of v. 1: they are urged to "walk worthily *of the calling to which you were called*" (τῆς κλήσεως ἧς ἐκλήθητε)" (v. 1, cf. v. 4). This double use of noun and verb is unlikely to be merely a stylistic redundancy. A similar use of both noun and verb occurs in 1 Cor 7:17–24. There are several further parallels between the use of "calling" language in 1 Cor 7:17–24 and Eph 4:1–6, which suggest that the former can shed light on the latter. In both passages, the verb "walk" (περιπατέω) is used to refer to the conduct of believers (1 Cor 7:17; Eph 4:1). Both passages occur in letters that affirm that all believers are "called" to receive eschatological blessings through Christ (1 Cor 1:9, cf. vv. 1–8; Eph 1:18, cf. 4:4). Yet 1 Cor 7:17, 20 refer to a distinct station in life, in which each believer is "called":

> Except, as the Lord assigned to each one, as God has called each one, in this manner let him or her walk and this is my teaching/ rule in all the churches (1 Cor 7:17 [Tucker]).[13]

As Tucker convincingly argues:

> This verse introduces four key components of Paul's formation of identity within the Christ-movement: (1) it is an inclusive

---

13. Tucker, *Remain in Your Calling*, 70.

approach that includes a continuing role for previous identities; (2) it appropriates and transforms existing cultural discourses; (3) it relies on Jewish halakhah and teaching discourse; and (4) it represents an empowering rule that Paul applies throughout his mission in the Roman Empire.[14]

In 1 Cor 7:20, Paul goes on to use the noun κλῆσις and the verb καλέω to refer to a distinct "calling" within which each believer is "called":

Each one should remain in the calling in which he/she was called (1 Cor 7:20 [my translation]).

Interestingly, although this passage is addressed to the issue of marital status (1 Cor 7:8, 10, 12), Paul uses Jewish and gentile identity ("circumcision" and "uncircumcision") as paradigms of distinct "callings" in which individuals should remain (1 Cor 7:17–20). This indicates that the Jew-gentile distinction is an archetype for Paul's identity-forming discourse in general, and his use of "calling" language in particular. Thus, the concept of distinct Jewish and gentile identity within an overarching unity "in Christ" can fruitfully inform our reading of the "calling" language in Eph 4:1–6.[15] Paul's gentile readers are urged "to walk worthily of the calling to which you were called" (v. 1). Within Ephesians, as we have seen, this means they must conduct themselves according to their status as gentiles who, through Christ, have been called to share in Israel's eschatological blessings. The gentile readers' *halakhah*, then, is to be conducted in solidarity with the renewed Israel with whom they have been united (v. 4).[16] There is a parallel here with the distinctively gentile *halakhah* formulated at the council of Jerusalem as described in Acts 15:13–21.[17]

14. Ibid., 70–75, quotation from 70; cf. Rudolph, "Paul's Rule."

15. This is true whether Ephesians is written by Paul or by someone deeply conversant with Paul's undisputed letters.

16. *Pace* Dahl, who claims that "the author of Ephesians . . . failed to show any concern for the relationship of his audience to contemporary Jews in or outside the church" ("Gentiles, Christians, and Israelites," 37).

17. Bauckham, "James and the Jerusalem Church," 452–62. The particular prohibitions given in Acts 15:20 are based on Lev 18–19. Bauckham here argues that these four prohibitions were not arbitrarily imposed; rather they were chosen because they are the laws that apply to "resident aliens" in Israel, on the basis that the eschatological temple of God has arrived (Acts 15:16–17; cf. Amos 9:11–12 LXX). The key to these prohibitions is the avoidance of idolatry, true worship of God (in the case of Leviticus through avoiding blood and strangled animals), and the avoidance of sexual immorality.

Furthermore, the mission dynamic that has been spelled out in Eph 1–3 lies behind the exhortation in Eph 4:1–6. Several terms used in the passage recall this dynamic to the minds of readers. Firstly, the phrase "in the bond of peace" (v. 3) recalls Christ's dual role in making "peace" through the cross (2:14–15) and in proclaiming "peace" through the gospel (2:17); furthermore, the term "bond" (σύνδεσμος, v. 3) may evoke Paul's status as one who is a "bound prisoner" (δέσμιος) for the sake of the gentile mission (3:1, 4:1).[18] Secondly, the references to the "unity of the Spirit" (v. 3) and "one Spirit" (v. 4) remind readers of the Spirit who "sealed" the gentiles after they had responded to the preaching of the gospel, guaranteeing the gentiles' shared inheritance with Israel (Eph 1:13–14, cf. 2:18, 22).[19] Thirdly, the reference to "one hope" (v. 4) reminds readers that although the Jewish apostolic community were the "first to hope" in Christ (1:12), through the apostolic mission (cf. 1:13–14), the gentiles have been brought to this same "hope" (1:18, cf. 2:12).[20] Thus, Paul's gentile readers are reminded of their indebtedness to the apostolic gospel mission through Israel to the nations, which binds them together with Israel in a common hope and future.

The Goal of Christ's Mission through Israel to the Nations (Eph 4:7–16)

This mission dynamic comes to the fore in Eph 4:7–16. Many interpreters approach this passage primarily in static terms, as a blueprint for the structuring, ordering, and unity of the "church."[21] Although some commentators note that the word "church" does not appear in this passage, and even the term "body" does not appear until v. 12, they do not regard these observations as undermining what they see as the fundamentally ecclesiological-structural nature of the discourse.[22] Several commentators, therefore, claim that the dynamic relationship between Israel and the nations, which features so prominently in 2:11–22, is in 4:7–16 only

18. Hoehner, *Ephesians*, 512.

19. See chapter 3.

20. See chapter 3.

21. See e.g., Barth, *Ephesians*, 451; Lincoln, *Ephesians*, 264; Best, *Ephesians*, 375; Hoehner, *Ephesians*, 521.

22. Barth, *Ephesians*, 451; Best, *Ephesians*, 375.

relevant as a "past event" that provides a paradigm of "unity" for a new ecclesiological situation.[23]

My contention, however, is that Eph 4:7–16 is more organically related to the concerns of Eph 1–3. It is not, therefore, primarily a blueprint for the structuring of the church; rather, it is describing *Christ's apostolic mission through Israel to the nations*: its past, its present, and its projected (pre-parousia) goal. The passage describes a nuanced interplay between diverse gifts and a united body. As we will see, the diverse "gifts" of v. 11 are best seen as the key figures in the early Jewish apostolic community, through which the gospel came to the nations (v. 12). The united body that appears at the end-point of this passage (vv. 14–16) is not an idealized, heavenly unity without diversity, but a future earthly goal of a greater unity-in-diversity within the body of Christ. This is not to deny that the ultimate unity to which Paul is looking forward is cosmic, heavenly, and eschatological (cf. 1:10). However, the horizon of unity in 4:7–16 is not ultimate; it is *pen*ultimate. It involves the earthly goal of the apostolic mission: that both Jewish and gentile believers would be so saturated with the "truth" of the gospel, and the "love" that flows from it, that the body might be able to engage in "building itself" (vv. 15–16). Thus, this passage is not assuming that Christ's mission through Israel to the nations is complete. Rather, it is depicting that mission as a work in progress, and eagerly anticipating its earthly goal.

As we saw above, most readings of the passage tend to see it as laying out a pattern for ecclesiastical ordering. A typical interpretation of the passage would be as follows: Verse 7 lays out a principle of the diversity of gifts Christ gives to the church; vv. 8–10 is a complex description of the work of the ascended Christ who has given gifts to the church; vv. 11–12 describe the relationship between the "officers" of the church (v. 11) and its members (v. 12); and vv. 13–16 show how the church is to guard against false teaching and come to a greater knowledge of the truth. However, there are two significant problems with this line of interpretation.

Firstly, as we have already seen, this typical line of interpretation tends to distinguish Eph 4–6 too sharply from Eph 1–3. As a result, the

---

23. Lincoln, "Church and Israel," 619. Even Percy, who regards the historical Paul as the author of Ephesians, argues on the basis of Eph 4:4, 16 that "for the author as well as for his addressees, the ethnic antagonism between Jews and Gentiles now evidently belongs once and for all entirely in the past" (my translation of *Die Probleme*, 284; original: "der völkische Gegensatz zwischen Juden und Heiden gehört offenbar für den Verfasser sowie für seine Adressaten nun ein für allemal ganz der Vergangenheit an").

issue of Jew-gentile reconciliation and mission, which was so intricately unpacked in Eph 1–3, plays a negligible or minor role in the interpretation of Eph 4–6. At most, the Jew-gentile unity-in-distinction described in Eph 2:11–22 is understood as an example from a former era that helps the present generation to understand the importance of church unity in Eph 4:1–16. However, as we have seen, the connections between Eph 1–3 and Eph 4–6 are much stronger than this. The view of the passage I will argue for here involves a much closer connection between this passage and the themes of Eph 1–3 than is normally allowed for.

Secondly, those who follow this typical line of interpretation are forced to read key phrases, which speak of a future goal, as if they are expressing a timeless ideal. In v. 13, the phrase "until we arrive at" (μέχρι καταντήσωμεν ... εἰς) implies a future goal: the word "until" (μέχρι) is a "marker of continuance in time up to a point,"[24] and the verb "arrive" (καταντάω) denotes a journey with a certain goal or end point.[25] This goal is spelled out explicitly in vv. 15–16 in terms of an earthly, pre-parousia situation in which the body continues to "grow" into Christ as the head. This creates great difficulty for interpreters who assume that the goal in this passage is a timeless ecclesiological ideal. Barth, for example, believes v. 13 must be a fragment, perhaps from a hymn, inserted by Paul or a later interpolator, perhaps based on the image of the church as the bride coming to meet Christ her "perfect man."[26] Best cannot explain the time references at all. He writes: "The goal, like all goals, would appear to be future, yet there is also a sense in which it has already been attained. . . . When the goal is given a future reference the question arises as to the time of its attainment (μέχρι implies the question exists). AE [i.e., the author of Ephesians] throws no light on the answer."[27] Hoehner claims that Paul "did not have a specific time frame in mind. Instead he emphasized the goal that could be attained at any time." Thus, paradoxically, "it is possible for this age but may not be completed until the future, possibly when the church meets her Lord."[28] Thielman says that the unity of the church "lies in the future," yet does not specify what future he is speaking

24. BDAG, "μέχρι."
25. Best, *Ephesians*, 399–400.
26. Barth, *Ephesians*, 484–89.
27. Best, *Ephesians*, 403.
28. Hoehner, *Ephesians*, 558.

of.[29] Many commentators describe it as a "goal" but do not specify the time any further.[30] Thus the assumptions of the typical line of interpretation tend to force interpreters to posit interpolations, speak in paradoxes, or claim that the passage contains unanswered questions. The view of Eph 4:7–16 I will argue for here, however, enables us to read the passage far more straightforwardly. It sees the passage, not as depicting a static ecclesiological ideal, but as looking forward to a pre-parousia goal for the apostolic mission.

Unity through Diversity (v. 7, cf. v. 16)

Verse 7 introduces a theme that informs the entirety of vv. 7–16: unity within diversity. While vv. 1–6 had emphasized the "unity" to which Paul's gentile readers had been called, v. 7 develops[31] this theme further to emphasize that God's "gift" was given "to each one of us" (ἐνὶ ... ἑκάστῳ ἡμῶν) according to a certain "measure" (μέτρον) of Christ's gift. In the final verse of the passage, the description of the body acting "in the measure of each individual part" (ἐν μέτρῳ ἑνὸς ἑκάστου μέρους, v. 16) completes the thought of unity-in-diversity from v. 7 and forms an inclusio around the entire unit. Paul is thus insistent that the unity described in vv. 1–6 does *not* cancel out all diversity; rather, there is a kind of diversity that enhances that unity. So far in Ephesians, the primary kind of unity-in-diversity has been that involving Israel and the nations (esp. 2:11–22).[32] We should expect the same theme to inform this passage, which also concerns unity in diversity.

The verb "was given" (ἐδόθη) is aorist, which suggests Paul is here describing a completed action. This completed action is most logically understood as those past "grace-giving" events already described in Ephesians: i.e., the "grace" by which the believers have received salvation (2:5, 8) and the "grace" that was "given" to Paul to preach the gospel to the nations (3:2, 7–8).[33] As we have seen, both of these events are intimately

29. Thielman, *Ephesians*, 282.

30. Caird, *Letters from Prison*, 76; Fowl, *Ephesians*, 142; Cohick, *Ephesians*, 113; Arnold, *Ephesians*, 264.

31. The conjunction δέ is a marker of development.

32. See chapter 4.

33. The confluence of the terms χάρις, δίδωμι and δωρεά links this verse strongly with 3:2, 7–8 (Thielman, *Ephesians*, 263).

connected to the apostolic mission, through which the gentiles have come to have a share in Israel's inheritance (cf. 1:13–14; 3:5–6). The apostolic mission, then, is still very much in the foreground here in 4:7–16.

Christ's Victorious Descent at Pentecost (vv. 8–10)

In vv. 8–10, Paul engages in a Christological interpretation of Ps 68:18:

> "Having ascended to the height, he led a host of captives; he gave gifts to people."
> 9 Now, what is the [significance of] "ascended,"
> if not [to imply] that he also descended into the lower, earthly regions?
> 10 The same one who descended is also the one who ascended far above all the heavens
> in order that he might fill all things. (Eph 4:8–10, my translation)

Verses 8–10 creates two related puzzles for interpreters. The first puzzle involves the relationship between this passage and the psalm to which it is referring. In Ps 68:18 (LXX 67:19), the Lord God, victorious in battle, receives gifts from people. However, in Eph 4:8, Christ *gives* gifts to people, which seems to reverse of the meaning of the psalm. The second interpretive puzzle involves the meaning of Christ's "descent." The meaning of the "ascent" is not difficult to discern; it refers to Christ's victorious ascension (cf. Eph 1:20–23).[34] However, interpreters differ about the meaning of the "descent." Some have taken it as a reference to Jesus' incarnation (often including his subsequent humiliation on the cross),[35] others to his victorious descent to Hades to secure or proclaim victory over the spiritual powers.[36] However, these interpretations do not adequately account for the fact that this passage is about Christ giving "gifts to people" (v. 8), which is also the main topic of the wider context (vv. 7, 11).

---

34. There are many parallels in concepts and terminology between Eph 4:8–10 and Eph 1:20–23. The fact that Christ has "ascended" (Eph 4:8–10) recalls the fact that God raised Christ and "seated him at his right hand in the heavenly places" (Eph 1:20). Christ is now "far above all the heavens" (Eph 4:10, cf. 1:21). The purpose is that he might "fill all things" (Eph 4:10), which recalls the description of "the church" (Eph 1:22) as "his body, the fullness of him who is filled with all things in every way" (Eph 1:23, cf. 4:10). The key difference between Eph 1 and Eph 4 is that God is the subject in the former whereas Christ becomes the subject in the latter.

35. E.g., Barth, *Ephesians*, 433–44; Best, *Ephesians*, 383–86.

36. E.g., Hoehner, *Ephesians*, 533–36; Thielman, *Ephesians*, 268–72.

Because of this, several interpreters have made a strong case that Paul is here referring to the giving of the Spirit at Pentecost.[37] Caird bases his argument on the use of Ps 68. He argues that this section reflects the kind of Jewish interpretation of the psalm found in the Targum, which also understands the psalm in terms of "giving"—i.e., it is about Moses' ascent to heaven to receive the law and then to distribute it to the people. Psalm 68 was a psalm appointed for Pentecost, and here in Ephesians the Psalm is interpreted in terms of the Christian Pentecost, i.e., the giving of the Spirit to believers. Paul here emphasizes two points: 1) that there is a *logical* connection between ascent and descent (v. 9), and 2) that the ascender and descender must be regarded as the same person (v. 10). The alternative theories—i.e., that the descent refers to the incarnation or the descent into Hades—cannot explain why these two points need to be emphasized. However, if this is about Pentecost, then it is understandable why both points are being emphasized:

> But it was worth saying that the visible Christ who ascended was identical with the unseen Lord who descended at Pentecost in the coming of the Holy Spirit.[38]

This understanding has been criticized on the grounds that Eph 4:9–10 refers to a one-off descent, whereas the giving of the Spirit would be relevant to believers in every generation.[39] However, this critique assumes that Eph 4:7–16 is providing a static model of church order for every generation. If, as we are arguing, Eph 4:7–16 is describing the progression of the early Christian mission through Israel to the nations, then a reference to the giving of the Spirit at Pentecost fits very well into the passage. As it is described in Acts 2, Pentecost is a critical stage in this mission. It was the time when the apostolic community in Jerusalem was equipped with "gifts" to proclaim the gospel to the world (cf. Acts 1:8). While this event is also relevant for future generations, it is first and foremost a significant one-off salvation-historical event.

Another objection may be raised: if vv. 8–10 are describing Pentecost, why is there no mention of the Spirit (as there is in, e.g., Acts 2:33)?

---

37. E.g., Caird, *Letters from Prison*, 73–75; Lincoln, *Ephesians*, 244–47; see also the summary of this position by Mouton, "Memory in Search of Dignity?" 141–43. The variant πρῶτον ("first") which appears after κατέβη ("he descended") in ℵ² B C* D² K L P Ψ 81, etc. is most likely not original. It is omitted in 𝔓⁴⁶ ℵ* A C* D F G, etc.

38. Caird, *Letters from Prison*, 74.

39. Best, *Ephesians*, 385.

This may be explained by noting that, for the purposes of Paul's argument at this point in Ephesians, Christ needs to be the focus of all the actions. Christ has ascended to the highest parts of heaven. However, Paul argues, this does not mean he is distant, passive, or unconcerned with things in the lower, earthly regions. On the contrary, his great ascent is a *victory*, and because of this victory he must also be active in bringing about his purposes on earth. Thus, Christ is described both as the subject of his own ascent (cf. Eph 1:20–23 where God is the subject) and as the subject of the descent and gift-giving activity. This ascription of all activity to Christ is not unique in this passage; it has a precedent in 2:17, where Christ is said to be the subject of the gospel-preaching apostolic mission, even though it was understood that his missionary activity took place through the agency of the apostles.[40]

Thus Eph 4:8–10 may be understood as follows: Verse 8, interpreting Ps 68:18, describes the victorious ascent of Christ to heaven. In interpreting the psalm, however, it must be understood that Christ's victorious ascent has ramifications for his people. Thus, he must be said not only to have "received" the spoils of victory, but also to have "given" gifts to his people (cf. the Targum on Ps 68). Verse 9 explains this further. Christ cannot be said merely to have "ascended" to the heavenly regions and so left his people behind in the lower, earthly regions. Rather, his victorious ascent implies a subsequent descent to share his victory with his people through the giving of gifts.[41] Verse 10 makes a further point about the identity of the ascender and descender. The one who was active in giving gifts to his people is indeed the same Christ who is victorious in the heavenly realms. This reminds the readers of the cosmic dimensions of Christ's earthly gift-giving activity (cf. 3:7–13).

---

40. See chapter 4.

41. The aorist verb κατέβη, "he descended," is rendered in the ESV with a pluperfect "he had . . . descended." This unhelpfully reverses the logical order of ascent and descent implied by the word-order of v. 9. The ESV's translation is possibly influenced by v. 10 which has the reverse order; however v. 10 is affirming the identity of the ascender and descender through the use of participles, not describing the order of ascent and descent through the use of indicative verbs, which is the case in v. 9.

The Speaking-gifts among the Jewish
Apostolic Community (v. 11)

Verse 11 begins, "And he himself gave . . ." (Καὶ αὐτὸς ἔδωκεν). That is, the victorious Christ who has just been described gave certain gifts. These "gifts" turn out to be people. As we have already noted above, it is common to understand the gifts as established church offices. Dunn, for example, sees v. 11 as a description of "established ministries" in an ecclesial setting that is quite different from the "occasional" ministries found in earlier church settings.[42] However, given that vv. 8–10 is best understood as a reference to Pentecost, it is far better to understand these "gifts" as particular roles found in the early apostolic community. This is confirmed by the syntax and vocabulary of the verse itself.

In this context, the verb "he gave" (ἔδωκεν) implies a completed action in Christ's past rather than an ongoing action in the church's present.[43] This is explicable on the understanding that vv. 8–10 are referring to the (past) pouring out of the Spirit on the Jerusalem apostolic community. Furthermore, the article ("the") is used repeatedly to identify particular groups of people: he gave "*the* apostles, *the* prophets, *the* evangelists, etc."[44] This may be understood as identifying those apostles, prophets, etc. who were instrumental in the early Jewish apostolic community. This view is confirmed by a comparison with Acts, which provides a detailed witness to early Christian understanding of this community and its mission.[45] As

42. Dunn, *Beginning from Jerusalem*, 1116.

43. The verb "he gave" (ἔδωκεν) in v. 11 is an aorist indicative verb describing an achievement (the giving of gifts). It recalls the same verbal form from the psalm citation (ἔδωκεν δόματα, "he gave gifts," v. 8), in which the aorist indicative verb is clearly used to indicate a past achievement. The citation is followed by further aorist indicative verbs indicating past actions (ἀνέβη, "he ascended"; κατέβη, "he descended," v. 9). This all implies that the aorist indicative verb in v. 11 is also describing a past action. While aorist indicative verbs can occasionally be used in such a way that the past temporal reference is subordinated to the perfective aspect and thereby loses some of its force, there are normally clear contextual and lexical indications when this is the case; e.g., the constructions in question often describe states rather than achievements (Matt 13:24; 23:2; Luke 3:22; see Fresch, "Nonpast Aorist Indicatives," 396–97). By contrast, in Eph 4:11, both the context and the lexical data strongly imply that the past temporal reference of the aorist indicative is significant and should not be downplayed.

44. The translation "*some* to be apostles . . ." (e.g., Caird, *Letters from Prison*, 76; Hoehner, *Ephesians*, 540), which is designed to render the force of the μὲν . . . δέ construction, also unfortunately obscures the force of the article.

45. The fact that the historicity of some of the details in Acts has been disputed is not directly relevant to the argument here.

we have already seen, Acts describes the "apostles" and certain "prophets" as having a foundational role in the early apostolic mission proceeding from Jerusalem (cf. Eph 2:20, 3:5).[46] As we will now see, "evangelists" and "teachers" also appear in Acts as key members of this apostolic community.

Philip is designated with the title "evangelist" in Acts 21:8. This designation is consistent with Philip's earlier ministry in Acts 8. There, the early Jewish apostolic community was scattered throughout Judea and Samaria, "except the apostles" (Acts 8:1). Those who were scattered began to "evangelize the word" (8:4), including Philip who preached to the Samaritans and displayed apostolic power (8:5–8). Philip also "evangelized" an Ethiopian Eunuch (8:35), and various towns between Azotus and Caesarea (8:40). The activity of "evangelism" does continue later through others (e.g., 11:20; 13:32; 14:7, 15). However, the only person with the title "evangelist" in Acts is Philip, whose role was centered on Judea and Samaria. There were also certain "teachers" alongside "prophets" at Antioch (Acts 13:1), including Barnabas and Saul. Through the commissioning of the Antioch church, two of these "prophets and teachers" became missionaries to the gentiles (Acts 13:2–3). "Pastors" are not mentioned in relation to the apostolic community in Acts, but we can presume they existed and perhaps were identical with or at least closely connected to the "teachers."[47]

None of this, of course, implies that prophetic, evangelistic, teaching or shepherding roles or offices were limited to the early Jewish apostolic community. However, at *this point* in Ephesians—i.e., following a description of the victorious Christ giving gifts at Pentecost—and with *this syntactical construction*—an aorist verb "he gave" followed by nouns marked by the article—those in view are best understood as *these* foundational apostles, prophets, evangelists, and shepherds and teachers of the early Jewish apostolic community.[48] If this is the case, then it has implications for how we understand v. 12.

46. See chapters 4 and 5; cf. Lincoln, *Ephesians*, 249.

47. The same article governs both terms. Cf. ibid., 250–51.

48. Cf. Kinzer, who argues that "the diverse 'gifts' that serve that unity in Ephesians 4 do not reside in each local congregation but are invested in translocal officials (apostles, prophets, etc; Ephesians 4:11), who in the early Yeshua-movement were (like Paul) usually Jewish! Thus the local Gentile ekklesia would be able to express its unity with the Jewish ekklesia by honoring the Jewish apostles and prophets who linked them to Israel" (*Postmissionary Messianic Judaism*, 171 n. 51).

The Jewish Apostolic Community Equipped for Mission (v. 12)

Verse 12 spells out the role of these foundational apostles, prophets, etc., within the apostolic community. Christ gave these ministries

> for the preparation of the saints for the work of ministry, for the construction of the body of Christ. (Eph 4:12, my translation)

The syntactical relationship between the three phrases in this verse is significant for understanding its place in the argument. Granados Rojas argues persuasively for the following construal of the relationship: the phrase "for the equipping [or preparation] of the saints" (πρὸς τὸν καταρτισμὸν τῶν ἁγίων) indicates an agreement with the main verb "he gave" (ἔδωκεν, v. 11); "for [the] work of ministry" (εἰς ἔργον διακονίας) further defines the equipping by indicating its purpose; and "for the building [or construction] of the body of Christ" (εἰς οἰκοδομὴν τοῦ σώματος τοῦ Χριστοῦ) indicates the result of the entire process.[49] The noun translated here as "preparation" (καταρτισμός) has a range of meanings. In this context, however, the idea of preparation (i.e., "arranging something to achieve a goal") is most likely.[50]

---

49. Granados Rojas, "Ephesians 4,12." Translations before the mid-twentieth century generally placed a comma after the word "saints" in v. 12. This punctuation implies that v. 12 consists of three coordinate prepositional phrases, all describing the activity of the officials listed in verse 11. A minority of modern scholars also argue for this view. Page, for example, argues that the phrases are "coordinate," and therefore that they are parallel phrases that all "describe the activities of the gifted persons mentioned in v. 11" ("Whose Ministry?" 46, following a grammatical argument by Lincoln, *Ephesians*, 253–54; cf. Davis, "Ephesians 4:12," 173–74; Barcellos, "Christian Ministry"). However, the syntactical concept of "coordination" is more complex than Page's analysis allows. Even if these phrases are syntactically "coordinate," this does not necessarily mean that they are strictly parallel nor that they all have the same relationship to the objects of the verb in the previous verse, especially when different prepositions are used (cf. Eph 4:14, which contains a similarly complex syntactical construction involving three prepositional phrases and two different prepositions). Granados Rojas' examination of the relationship between the prepositional phrases is far more precise and nuanced than Page's. Like Granados Rojas, most modern commentaries see the second phrase as extending the meaning of the first in some way (Caird, *Letters from Prison*, 76; Best, *Ephesians*, 397–99; Hoehner, *Ephesians*, 547–51; Arnold, *Ephesians*, 262–64; Thielman, *Ephesians*, 277–80).

50. Granados Rojas, "Ephesians 4,12," 88. Page seeks to refute the assumption that the verbal idea inherent in the noun καταρτισμός (the idea of "equipping" or "perfecting") requires a complement (i.e., equipping or perfecting *for* something) ("Whose Ministry?" 32–35). However, this is not the point at issue in the interpretation of these verses. It is not that the verbal idea *requires* a complement; the issue is whether the

Given the context of the verse for which we have argued, "the saints" at this point is best seen as a reference to the early Jewish apostolic community centered in Jerusalem. Paul has just spoken of Pentecost (vv. 8–10) and then noted that the "gifts" Christ gave at Pentecost were these foundational figures in the Jewish apostolic community (v. 11). Their task was directed initially toward this holy community in Jerusalem. As we have already seen, when the term "the saints" appears in Ephesians, a special reference to the Jewish apostolic community in Jerusalem is often in view (Eph 1:18; 2:19; 3:5, 8; cf. Rom 15:25–26, 31; 1 Cor 16:1; 2 Cor 8:4; 9:1, 12).[51] However, in each case, Christ-believing gentiles are said to share in this holy status (cf. e.g., 1:1; 5:27). As we have argued, the key to the gentiles sharing in Israel's privileges is the missionary preaching of the gospel. Indeed, it is this gospel-preaching missionary activity that enables us to understand the nature of the activity of "the saints," as spelled out in the following phrase.

Christ's gifts of apostles, etc., prepared the early Jewish apostolic community for "the work of ministry" (εἰς ἔργον διακονίας). In Eph 2:10, walking in "good works" was given as the goal of salvation. Here in Eph 4, there is a particular "work" in view: a particular response to salvation for particular people who have been saved by grace. This is the "work of ministry." What is this work of ministry? When we examined Paul's role as "minister" (διάκονος) in Eph 3:7, we noted that much Ephesians scholarship is still affected by the pervasive assumption that the "ministry" word-group has a basic meaning of "service." However, we saw that this assumption is unfounded. Rather, the word normally denotes acting as a "go-between," and often refers to a role to bring a divine message to humanity.[52] This is the meaning most germane to its use in Eph 3:7, where Paul identified himself as a "minister" of the "gospel" (cf. v. 6). In other words, Paul's role as "minister" was defined in terms of his role as a gospel-preaching missionary to the nations. Here in Eph 4:12, then, it is

prepositional phrase that follows ("for the work of ministry") is *best understood* as a complement to the verbal idea of equipping or perfecting. Given the context and the flow of the passage, it is indeed best understood this way.

51. See chapters 3, 4, and 5.

52. See chapter 5; for further discussion see Collins, *Diakonia*; Windsor, "Work of Ministry." In certain contexts (esp. in the Gospels), the word can refer to people who act as "go-betweens" between the kitchen and the table, i.e., table waiters. However, the fact that the word-group can be used to refer to table-waiters in some contexts does not mean that "serving at table" is the basic meaning of the word-group, nor that it should be translated as "service" in every instance when table waiters are not in view.

likely that the same understanding of "ministry" is in view. This is confirmed by the context of the verse, as we have outlined it above. At Pentecost (Eph 4:8–10), Christ gave certain apostles, prophets, evangelists, and pastors and teachers (Eph 4:11) to equip the early Jewish apostolic community for the work of "ministry," i.e., gospel-preaching mission to the nations. In Eph 3, this mission was conceived in terms of the activity of individuals, i.e., Paul (Eph 3:7), and Christ's "holy apostles and prophets" (Eph 3:5). In Eph 4, the gospel-preaching mission is conceived corporately: it is understood as a task for "the saints"; i.e., the early Jewish apostolic community collectively (although individuals may have played different roles within the mission, as we see described in Acts).

This gospel-preaching mission ("the work of ministry") of the early Jewish apostolic community ("the saints") was intended "for the construction of the body of Christ" (εἰς οἰκοδομὴν τοῦ σώματος τοῦ Χριστοῦ). This recalls the earlier passage in which these terms appear (Eph 2:11–22). There, Israel and the nations were said to be reconciled together to God "in one body" through Christ's death (Eph 2:16), which was put into effect through Christ's gospel-preaching mission (Eph 2:17). As a result, Christ-believing gentiles are now, together with Jews, "built on the foundation of the apostles and prophets" (Eph 2:20). In other words, the body of Christ is built on the gospel-preaching mission of the early Jewish apostolic community. In Eph 2:11–22, the body-building gospel-preaching activity was attributed primarily to Christ. In Eph 4:7–16, this same activity is spelled out, but with more detail given for the agents Christ used. The risen and ascended Christ has "descended" to give gifts at Pentecost. These "gifts" (i.e., the apostles, prophets, etc.) are instrumental in the preaching of the gospel. Through them, the Jewish apostolic community was collectively prepared to preach the gospel to the nations, which resulted in the construction of Christ's body.

The Vision: A Diverse, United Body (vv. 13–16)

In v. 13, Paul shifts from describing the past events that occurred among the Jewish apostolic community (vv. 8–12) to portraying his vision for the future effects of the apostolic mission among the entire body of Christ (vv. 13–16). This shift involves, firstly, a change to a future orientation, which can be seen in the use of the future-oriented formulations that govern the section.[53] Verse 13 begins with the words "until we all arrive at" (μέχρι καταντήσωμεν οἱ πάντες εἰς, v. 13), implying a future goal. Verses 14–16 involve two purpose clauses: "in order that we may no longer be infants ..." (ἵνα μηκέτι ὦμεν νήπιοι ..., v. 14), and "[in order that] we may grow into him ..." (αὐξήσωμεν εἰς αὐτὸν ..., v. 15). There is also a shift to a whole-body orientation, which can be seen in the emphatic use of the word "all" (πᾶς) throughout vv. 13–16. "All of us" (οἱ πάντες + first person plural verb) will arrive at a point of "unity" (ἑνότητα, v. 13, cf. v. 3). Terms such as "all" (πᾶς), "one" (εἷς), and first-person plural verbs (indicating an inclusive "we") dominate vv. 13–16. Thus, the section is marked out from vv. 8–12 both by its future orientation and by its focus on "all" members of the body, as opposed to the earlier focus on the particular "gifts" given in the past to the apostolic community.

Paul's future vision is characterized by a positive notion of gospel-based unity-in-diversity, which will replace the present dysfunctional plurality. Verse 13 emphasizes the "unity of the faith and the knowledge of the Son of God." This is a unity that is based on a common response to the gospel message of salvation ("of faith," πίστεως; cf. 1:13), and thus a common "knowledge of the Son of God." This means that the corporate "body" of Christ will (to extend the metaphor further) become a "fully-grown adult," having attained to the "measure of the stature of the fullness of Christ" (cf. 1:23).[54] Verse 14 depicts one of the key purposes of this gospel-based corporate unity: the end of dysfunctional plurality. At this point, many are now "infants" rather than fully grown (cf. v. 13). This is because there are various deceitful human teachings ("every wind of teaching") working against the common faith and knowledge of the Son of God (cf. v. 13, 20–21).

Verses 15–16, however, depicts the end-point of this dysfunctional plurality: a functional, gospel-based unity-in-diversity. The phrase "speaking the truth in love" (literally "truthing in love," ἀληθεύοντες ... ἐν ἀγάπῃ) refers to the working out of the effects of the gospel. Paul has previously identified "the word of truth" (τὸν λόγον τῆς ἀληθείας) with the "gospel of your salvation," which his gentile readers had heard and believed (Eph 1:13). This gospel of salvation had brought these gentiles into the sphere of God's "love" in Christ ("in love," ἐν ἀγάπῃ, Eph 1:4) and had brought about a response of "love for all the saints" (Eph 1:15).

53. The formulations are based on subjunctive verbs.
54. Son, "One New Man," 26.

Here in Eph 4:15–16, Paul's vision is that the mature body, working out the effects of the gospel in speech and action (cf. vv. 24–25), will "grow" into Christ as its "head" (v. 15). This will result in a dynamic unity-in-diversity, indicated by the description of a body "joined together and held together" (*syn*-compounds συναρμολογούμενον καὶ συμβιβαζόμενον, v. 16),[55] where "each part is working properly" (literally "according to the working in the measure of each individual part," κατ' ἐνέργειαν ἐν μέτρῳ ἑνὸς ἑκάστου μέρους). This mature unity-in-diversity entails a self-building body which literally "acts for the construction of itself" (ποιεῖται εἰς οἰκοδομὴν ἑαυτοῦ).[56] Previously, the early Jewish apostolic community ("the saints"), through the gospel-preaching mission ("the work of ministry") had been involved in "the construction of the body of Christ" (v. 12). In the vision of v. 16, however, the body of Christ will be able to grow and construct *itself* through the gospel. This is because they, together with "the saints," have attained to "the unity of faith and knowledge of the Son of God" (v. 13).

Thus, Paul is not here depicting a timeless ideal or a post-parousia state. Rather, he is looking forward to a future, pre-parousia, situation in which the "unity of the Spirit" (v. 3) will be realized in greater and more complete measure than it is at his own time. This will occur because the "truth" of the gospel, first believed and preached in the Jewish apostolic community (v. 11, cf. 1:11–12), then proclaimed to the nations (v. 12, cf. 1:13–14), will end up permeating all members of the body, whether Jewish or gentile, in equal measure (vv. 13–16).[57]

A Gospel-driven, Locally-manifested, Ecumenical Vision

We have argued that Eph 4:7–16 is not intended primarily as a blueprint for the ordering of the "church." Nevertheless, it does have ecclesiological implications. Indeed, our analysis of the passage provides a way forward in one of the recent debates surrounding the nature of the "church." Peter O'Brien has demonstrated that the kind of political or macro-structural vision of church unity arising from the ecumenical movement of the mid-twentieth century is not easily supported by the New Testament

---

55. For the significance of *syn*-compounds see chapters 4 and 5.

56. The emphasis on *self*-construction is seen both in the middle voice of the verb ποιεῖται and in the use of the reflexive pronoun ἑαυτοῦ.

57. See also Windsor, "Work of Ministry," 16–17.

use of the word "church" (ἐκκλησία).[58] In the Pauline corpus, the term normally refers to "*a local assembly or congregation of Christians*"[59] or to a "*house-church*."[60] Nevertheless, in Colossians and Ephesians as well as in Hebrews, there are instances of the term "church" with a "*wider reference*" than a local congregation.[61] The reference in these instances is not to the "church universal" on earth, "scattered throughout the world," but rather to the church that exists in the "heavenly plane."[62] In Ephesians, the church is depicted as the "body" of Christ. Since Christ is in heaven, his body is also in heaven (see esp. Eph 1:20–23; 3:10; cf. Col 1:15–20).[63] O'Brien notes that "[t]he New Testament does not discuss the relationship between the local church and the heavenly gathering. The link is nowhere specifically spelled out."[64] He tentatively suggests, however, that the link may consist in the idea that "the local congregations or house-groups are earthly manifestations of that heavenly assembly gathered around God and Christ."[65] Our reading of Eph 4:7–16, however, suggests that there is, in fact, a textual link between the heavenly "church" and the earthly congregation. This textual link consists primarily in the gospel-preaching mission.

---

58. O'Brien, "The Church"; cf. Knox, "The Church and the Denominations"; Robinson, *Church of God*; Knox, "The Church, the Churches and the Denominations of the Churches." For a thorough theological engagement with these views, see Kuhn, *Ecclesiology*.

59. O'Brien, "The Church," 91–92, emphasis original.

60. Ibid., 92–93, emphasis original.

61. Ibid., 93, emphasis original.

62. Ibid.

63. Ibid., 93, 110. O'Brien concedes: "This is not to suggest that believers have no relationships with one another if they do not gather together in church. As members of the body of Christ or of God's people they are not only related to Christ himself but also to one another even when separated by time and distance. But the point being made here is that *ekklesia* is not the term used in the New Testament of those wider, universal links" (ibid., 93–94).

64. O'Brien, "The Church," 97.

65. Ibid.; cf. O'Brien, *Colossians, Philemon*, 61. This suggestion has been criticized by some as "platonic" (e.g., Son, "One New Man," 30–31); however, this is an imprecise and unfair accusation. The "manifestation" view of O'Brien and others cited above is better understood theologically in terms of the work of the Holy Spirit. Thus, the heavenly gathering is not merely eschatological; rather, the spiritual connection between the heavenly and earthly gathering impinges on the present (see Kuhn, *Ecclesiology*, 191–93).

Admittedly, Eph 4:7–16 does not use the term "church" (ἐκκλησία). However, as we have seen, it speaks of Christ's heavenly status (vv. 8–10), which recalls the heavenly location of the "church" from Eph 1 as Christ's "body" (Eph 1:20–23). It also, significantly, affirms that the heavenly, ascended Christ has "descended" to earth (vv. 9–10). We have argued that Christ's descent is a deliberate reference to Pentecost, and so vv. 11–12 are depicting Christ as being active in mission through the early Jewish apostolic community to the nations. Thus, Christ has both victoriously "ascended" into heaven *and* victoriously "descended" through the gospel-preaching mission. The purpose of this descent is to bring about a diverse-yet-united "body." In v. 12, this "body" is something that is said to be "constructed" through the mission of the apostolic community. In vv. 13–16, the goal of such construction is spelled out: a "mature" body that is "constructing itself" through relationships of truth and love. The church as the "body" here, then, is *both* a "heavenly entity" and an "earthly reality."[66] The connection between the heavenly and the earthly is Christological: it comes about through Christ's "descent" from heaven in the form of equipping gospel-preaching missionaries through Israel to the nations. It is the unity of this "body" that the readers of the letter are told to "maintain" (vv. 3–4) through their daily life and speech. This unity is not a structural or totalizing unity that insists on uniformity. Rather, it is a "unity of the Spirit" (v. 3) driven by Christ, the message of the gospel, and the mission of the gospel. The key means by which these gentile recipients of the gospel are to maintain that unity is by living according to the kind of gentile *halakhah* spelled out in the chapters that follow.

Thus, Eph 4:7–16 may be described as depicting a gospel-driven, locally-manifested, ecumenical vision. It is not a politically-driven ecumenical vision seeking large-scale structural uniformity, nor is it a radical congregationalism with no concern outside the local congregation. Rather, it is a vision in which the unity achieved by Christ comes about through the work of gospel-preaching missionary activity, and is maintained through speaking and living according to the gospel, within local congregations, but always with a view to God's greater purposes in Christ.

66. Using the terminology of O'Brien, "The Church," 111.

The Details of Gentile Halakhah in Christ
(Eph 4:17—6:9)

In Eph 4:1, Paul appealed to his gentile readers to "walk" in a way worthy of their calling. Having now established the broad Christological and ecumenical dimensions of this calling (vv. 7–16), he now solemnly urges them to "walk," no longer as "the gentiles" (v. 17), but according to the new way that they have been "taught" and have "learned" in Christ (vv. 20–21). This begins the detailed description of gentile *halakhah* in Christ (4:17—6:9). The key features of this *halakhah* are 1) a life that conforms to the humility, patience, and "love" demonstrated by Christ in his sacrificial death (e.g., 4:2; 4:30—5:2); 2) an avoidance of sexual immorality (e.g., 4:19; 5:3–5); 3) an avoidance of idolatrous lifestyles (e.g., 4:18) and of greed, which is also identified as idolatry (e.g., 5:5); and 4) a life lived in expectation of future redemption (e.g., 4:30; 5:15–17).[67] Although the limitations of this study preclude a detailed examination of every element of this gentile *halakhah*, three elements are worth noting.

Firstly, in line with the great significance attached to the preaching of the gospel in the rest of Ephesians, it is noteworthy that there is a strong emphasis on proper speech in Eph 4:17—6:9. Those who have believed the "word of truth, the gospel of your salvation" (Eph 1:13) are now urged both to live *and to speak* in line with this truth in their own situation (e.g., 4:25, 29–31; 5:3–4, 6, 12, 19–20).

Secondly, in line with the unity-in-diversity that we have noted in the rest of Ephesians, the *Haustafel* in Eph 5:22—6:9 reflects a view in which diversity of vocation among different kinds of people is not destructive of unity or equality in Christ, but rather is an integral part of it.[68] As several scholars have noted, there are numerous verbal and conceptual parallels between the earlier description of Jew-gentile unity in Christ (2:11–22) and the *Haustafel* (5:22—6:9).[69]

Thirdly, in many places this gentile *halakhah* involves a gospel-driven application of the law of Moses. While references to the law are often allusive,[70] at certain points there is a clear quotation and application

---

67. This is a pattern that appears in other Pauline epistles; see Ciampa and Rosner, *First Corinthians*, 25–28.

68. See also chapter 4.

69. Sampley, *And the Two Shall Become One Flesh*, 162; MacDonald, "Politics of Identity," 439–41.

70. E.g., the use of concepts from Gen 1:26–28 in Eph 4:24 (Best, *Ephesians*,

of the law (e.g., Eph 5:31, cf. Gen 2:24; Eph 6:2–3, cf. Exod 20:12). The latter quotation is significant, since here Paul explains his interpretative stance toward the law:

> Children, obey your parents in the Lord, for this is right. "Honor your father and mother" (this is the first commandment with a promise [lit. "in promise," ἐν ἐπαγγελίᾳ], "that it may go well with you and that you may live long in the land." (Eph 6:1–3, cf. Exod 20:12)

Commentators often understand the phrase "in promise" (ἐν ἐπαγγελίᾳ, v. 2) as an expression of accompaniment, and so render it "with a promise [attached]."[71] This causes a puzzle for such commentators, however, because v. 2 is quoting the fifth commandment (Exod 20:12), which is not in fact the first commandment with a promise attached (cf. the second commandment, Exod 20:6). It is better, therefore, to understand the phrase as an expression of *association*: "the first commandment associated with promise." Furthermore, the term "promise," in light of Eph 1:13–14 and 3:6, is best understood not as any promise, but as the specific promise of Israel's inheritance in which the gentiles also have a share. Hence, Paul is here emphasizing the fact that "Honor your father and mother" (Exod 20:12) is the first commandment associated with the eschatologically-oriented "promise" of Israel's inheritance. This is why it is particularly applicable to the gentile audience to whom Paul is writing. Furthermore, as we noted when we discussed Eph 2:15, this demonstrates that Paul regards the law as relevant and applicable to gentiles when understood rightly in relation to the gospel and God's eschatological promise.[72] Although the law understood in terms of "the commandments in decrees" has been abolished (Eph 2:15), the law understood in terms of "promise" plays a foundational role in Paul's gentile *halakhah*.

The Call to Arms (Eph 6:10–24)

Paul's call to spiritual battle in Eph 6:10–20 recalls many of the themes that have already appeared in the letter.[73] It thereby reminds the gentile read-

---

436–37).

71. E.g., Hoehner, *Ephesians*, 789.

72. See chapter 4.

73. Lincoln, *Ephesians*, 438–40; Arnold, *Ephesians*, 435–37.

ers that their own response to the gospel, including their local *halakhah*, is in fact part of God's greater, indeed cosmic, purposes in Christ. It is a call to the readers to take their own part in seeing these purposes fulfilled. This includes a concern with the ongoing gospel mission, which we have argued is a key feature of the letter. Some claim that Ephesians exhibits a preoccupation with local concerns and a concomitant lack of interest in outsiders.[74] Others, however, argue for a broad missionary imperative implied in places in Eph 6:10–20, especially v. 15 (cf. 5:11).[75] This latter view is strengthened by our own findings about the significance of the gospel-preaching mission through Israel to the nations in Ephesians.

In v. 15, Paul speaks of the importance of "putting on, as shoes for the feet, the readiness of the gospel of peace" (ὑποδησάμενοι τοὺς πόδας ἐν ἑτοιμασίᾳ τοῦ εὐαγγελίου τῆς εἰρήνης). This alludes to the evangelistic herald portrayed in Isa 52:7, which reads (literally): "the feet of one evangelizing a report of peace" (πόδες εὐαγγελιζομένου ἀκοὴν εἰρήνης [LXX]). Several interpreters argue on this basis that Eph 6:15 is describing an active role for Paul's gentile readers in proclaiming that gospel of Christ (cf. the use of the same text from Isaiah in Eph 2:17 to refer to the gospel-preaching mission).[76] Others reject this conclusion, in large measure because they do not see a mission thrust overall in Ephesians and so deem it unlikely to be appearing at this point. Instead, they claim that this verse is stating that the gospel provides the "firm footing" by which the Christians may fight the spiritual battle in a defensive mode.[77] However, if the argument of this book is correct, and the gospel-preaching mission through Israel to the nations is a key feature of Ephesians, we have no reason to reject the view that Eph 6:15 is encouraging the readers to be ready to proclaim the gospel itself. Dahl's comments are apposite here:

> Ephesians no doubt presupposes that the mission to the Gentiles continues, probably carried on by special "evangelists" (cf. 4:11), but not exclusively by them. All Christians are to put on

74. E.g., Best, *Ephesians*, 34–35. For Best, this is a piece of evidence against historical Pauline authorship.

75. E.g., Arnold, *Ephesians*, 453–55; Dahl, "Gentiles, Christians, and Israelites," 34–35.

76. Schlier, *An Die Epheser*, 296; Arnold, *Ephesians*, 454–55.

77. E.g., Barth, *Ephesians*, 770; Lincoln, *Ephesians*, 449; Best, *Ephesians*, 599–600; Thielman, *Ephesians*, 426; Hoehner, *Ephesians*, 843–44.

the whole armor of God and—as imitators of God—resist and fight the powers of evil, not only with defensive weapons but also equipped with the "gospel of peace" and using the "sword of the Spirit, which is the word of God" (Eph 6:11–17; cf. Isa 59:17–18; Wis 5:17–21, and Eph 4:24; 5:1).[78]

At the very least, the gentile readers of Ephesians are being urged to see themselves as intimately caught up in this mission dynamic, which in turn is a key part of God's larger, cosmic, purposes in Christ (cf. Eph 3:1–13).[79] Thus, Paul urges them to pray along these lines (Eph 6:18–20). Just as Paul had earlier prayed for them to grasp, along with "all the saints," the dimensions of God's purposes and love in Christ (Eph 3:14–21), so now he asks them to pray for "all the saints" (v. 18), and to pray for him especially as he proclaims the "mystery of the gospel" (v. 19). Since he has already spoken of his imprisonment in the context of this "mystery" and God's greater cosmic purposes (cf. Eph 3:1–13), Paul can now refer to himself fittingly yet paradoxically as an "ambassador in chains" for this gospel (v. 20). It is as such that he asks his gentile readers to pray for him, and so see themselves as part of these great divine purposes in Christ.

Summary of Ephesians 4–6

In this chapter, we have examined Eph 4–6 and seen how the gentile readers of the letter are urged to "walk" in a way that reflects and maintains what the apostolic mission through Israel to the nations has achieved in and through them.

In Eph 4:1–6, Paul introduces a generalized form of gentile *halakah*. This *halakah* is the key means by which the Christ-believing gentile readers of the letter can express their unity with the foundational Jewish apostolic community through whom the gospel of Christ came to them.

In Eph 4:7–16, Paul is not primarily giving a blueprint for church order, but rather is describing Christ's apostolic mission through Israel to the nations: its past, its present, and its projected (pre-parousia) goal. In v. 7, he introduces the theme of unity through diversity. In vv. 8–10, by engaging in a Christological interpretation of Ps 68:18, Paul describes the events of Pentecost, in which the victorious and ascended Christ "descended" to give gifts to the early Jewish apostolic community. In

78. Dahl, "Gentiles, Christians, and Israelites," 34.
79. See chapter 5.

v. 11, Paul describes these gifts as particular roles within the early Jewish apostolic community. In v. 12, Paul describes how these people prepared the Jewish apostolic community collectively to preach the gospel to the nations, which resulted in the construction of Christ's body. In vv. 13–16, Paul portrays his vision for the future effects of the apostolic mission among the entire body of Christ. This vision is characterized by a positive notion of gospel-based unity-in-diversity, which is set in opposition to dysfunctional plurality. Thus, Eph 4:7–16 may be described as depicting a gospel-driven, locally-manifested, ecumenical vision.

In Eph 4:17—6:9, Paul spells out the details of gentile *halakhah* in Christ. Some relevant features of this *halakhah* include: an emphasis on proper speech, a view of vocational diversity-in-unity (5:22—6:9), and a gospel-driven application of the law of Moses (e.g., Eph 6:2–4). In Eph 6:10–24, Paul reminds his readers of God's greater, cosmic, purposes in Christ and calls on his readers to take their own part in seeing these purposes fulfilled. This includes a concern with the ongoing gospel mission (e.g., Eph 6:15).

7

Jews, Gentiles, and the Apostolic Mission in Colossians

IN CHAPTER 2, I summarized common supersessionist over-readings of certain texts in Colossians. I also surveyed critical questions concerning the nature and purpose of Colossians, which yielded two guiding principles for a post-supersessionist reading of the letter. Firstly, since the threat to the Colossians is most likely a syncretistic religious pluralism incorporating certain Jewish elements, we cannot assume that statements in the letter are straightforwardly directed against markers of Jewish identity. Secondly, we should be alert to the possibility that a feature in the foreground of Ephesians may also be in the background of Colossians: i.e., that the apostolic mission is closely connected with a priestly ministry of Israel to the nations.

In chapters 3–6, I conducted a focused exegesis of Ephesians. I demonstrated how a post-supersessionist perspective enables us to discern the dynamic of divine blessing "in Christ" proceeding through Israel to the nations by way of the apostolic mission. In chapter 3 (Eph 1), we saw how the apostolic mission was the means by which Christ's blessings have come through Israel to the nations. In chapter 4 (Eph 2), we saw how the apostolic mission plays a climactic role in Christ's work of reconciliation for Israel and the nations. In chapter 5 (Eph 3), we saw how the apostolic mission is continuing through Paul, even in his suffering, so that Christ's riches are being poured out through Paul's ministry to the nations. In chapter 6 (Eph 4–6), we saw how the gentile readers of the letter are urged to "walk" in a way that reflects and maintains what the apostolic mission through Israel to the nations has achieved in and through them.

We saw that in Ephesians, there is no thought that Jewish distinctiveness has been entirely abolished. Rather, it has been thoroughly transformed so that it serves a positive purpose in relation to the apostolic mission. Thus, we saw that in Eph 2:11, the value of circumcision is not entirely nullified; rather, it is relativized as a human activity which could never by itself overcome hostility. In Eph 2:15, the law of Moses is not entirely "abolished"; rather, Christ's reconciling work has rendered invalid the law's role in protecting Israel from impure and hostile gentiles. Further, in Eph 2:15 the creation of the "one new humanity" in Christ does not imply the eradication of all distinctions between Israel and the nations. Rather, the focus is on reconciliation and the removal of hostility.

In this chapter, I will be using my findings from Ephesians to suggest interpretive possibilities for elements of the text of Colossians. I will not be conducting an exhaustive exegesis of each section of Colossians. The aims of this chapter are more modest, though I hope still valuable. Firstly, I aim to question the supersessionist readings of Colossians identified in chapter 2 by providing plausible alternative interpretations of the respective passages. Secondly, I aim to demonstrate that an awareness of Israel's key place in the apostolic mission to the nations provides a plausible conceptual background to several of the statements made in the letter.

As we have seen in chapter 2, there are many parallels between the themes and vocabulary in Ephesians and Colossians. Most fundamentally, both letters describe Christ's death, resurrection, and exaltation as foundational events with immense significance both for the cosmos and for individual believers (e.g., Eph 1:20–23; 2:5–7, 14–16; Col 1:15–23). Nevertheless, there are also key differences between the two letters. For example, in Ephesians, there is a prominent, and explicit, Jew-gentile dimension involved in Christ's work of reconciliation: Christ's sacrificial death was "to reconcile us both [i.e., Israel and the nations] to God in one body through the cross" (Eph 2:16). In Colossians, however, the relationship with Israel is not directly in view in the statements about reconciliation (Col 1:20–22). The differences between the two letters can be understood, in part, as arising from different intended audiences. As we have suggested in chapter 2, Ephesians is addressed broadly to gentile believing communities throughout a wide region. Its horizons are more ecumenical. It thereby emphasizes such things as the place of the Jewish apostolic community in the gospel-preaching mission dynamic. Colossians, on the other hand, is addressed to specific issues threatening a particular community. Thus, while Ephesians speaks in general terms about "*every* wind of teaching, by human cunning" (Eph 4:14, emphasis added), Colossians describes *particular* "human precepts and teachings" that give rise to specific regulations ("Do not handle, Do not taste, Do not touch," Col 2:21–22). Colossians thus has a more local focus, emphasizing the application of the gospel to the situation of believers in Colossae. This understanding of the more focused horizons of Colossians may explain why the letter never deals explicitly with the relationship between its gentile readers and Israel.

Nevertheless, issues relating to Jewish identity are not entirely absent from Colossians. When it comes to Jewish identity, the letter displays two significant, yet seemingly opposed, features. On the one hand, the gentile believers in Colossae, like the gentile readers of Ephesians, are described in Israel-centric terms as "gentiles" who are nevertheless sharing in an "inheritance" through the gospel (Col 1:12, 27; cf. Eph 1:11–14). Thus, distinctive Jewish identity appears to have some positive value (Col 4:11).[1] On the other hand, distinctive Jewish identity and "circumcision" are at points used in negative formulations (Col 3:11), and the Colossians are said to have been circumcised with a different kind of circumcision (Col 2:11). Does this imply that "the social positioning of the [Colossian] community includes some social distancing from Jewish networks"?[2] How can we make sense of these seemingly opposed features of the letter? Our conclusions from Ephesians will assist us in this endeavor.

A Local Instance of the Apostolic Mission to the Nations (Col 1:1—2:5)

In previous chapters, we saw how Ephesians locates gentile faith (Eph 1) and Paul's apostolic ministry (Eph 3) within God's greater international and cosmic purposes, especially those purposes which involve the dynamic of blessing flowing through Israel to the nations.[3] Many of the features of the description in Eph 1 and 3 also appear in Col 1:1—2:5. Admittedly, in Colossians, the descriptions of gentile faith and Paul's

1. Dunn, *Beginning from Jerusalem*, 1037.

2. Shkul, "New Identity," 385. Thus, Shkul claims, Colossians effectively (if not deliberately) labels key markers of Jewish identity as "deviant" and would have resulted in pushing any "faithful Jewish believer" away from the community to which it is written (ibid.).

3. See chapter 3 (Eph 1) and chapter 5 (Eph 3).

ministry are more focused on a local setting. Nevertheless, the worldwide gospel mission to the gentiles is significant as a backdrop to these local concerns. We can see this at various points in Col 1:1—2:5.

Holy and Believing Brothers and Sisters at Colossae (1:1–2)

The salutation of Colossians (Col 1:1–2) has several similarities to its equivalent in Ephesians (Eph 1:1–2). These similarities include: the same identified author (Paul), the same description of Paul's role as "an apostle of Christ Jesus by the will of God," a similar description of the readers as "holy" and "believers" "in Christ," and a similar formulation "grace to you and peace from God our Father." However, there are also several key ways in which the salutation in Colossians differs from that in Ephesians. In Colossians, Timothy is identified as co-author (v. 1). The descriptions of "Christ" are also less expansive (v. 2).[4] Most significantly for our purposes, the addressees of the two letters are described differently. As we have seen, Ephesians is addressed "to the holy ones, who are also believers in Christ Jesus" (τοῖς ἁγίοις [τοῖς] οὖσιν καὶ πιστοῖς ἐν Χριστῷ Ἰησοῦ; Eph 1:1, my translation).[5] This formulation stresses the remarkable fact that the gentile readers of the letter participate in "holiness" through "faith" in Christ. Colossians, on the other hand, is addressed more straightforwardly "to the holy and believing brothers in Christ at Colossae" (τοῖς ἐν Κολοσσαῖς ἁγίοις καὶ πιστοῖς ἀδελφοῖς ἐν Χριστῷ; Col 1:2, my translation).[6] Gentile participation in holiness through faith in Christ is not stressed in Colossians as it is in Ephesians; rather the connection between holiness and faith is simply assumed. The stress, if any, lies on the connection between authors and readers indicated by dual use of the term "brother[s]" (1:1, 2).[7] Nevertheless, as the letter continues, the "holy" status of gentile believers is seen to be significant for their identity and consequent behavior (1:12, 22; 3:12).

---

4. Cf. "in Christ Jesus" (Eph 1:1) with "in Christ" (Col 1:2); cf. "from God our Father and the Lord Jesus Christ" (Eph 1:2) with "from God our Father" (Col 1:2).

5. See chapter 3.

6. The adjective "holy" is used attributively in Col 1:2; this stands in contrast with the substantival use in Eph 1:1 and Phil 1:1 (Foster, *Colossians*, 130).

7. Dunn, *Colossians and Philemon*, 49.

The Colossians' Response to the Worldwide
Gospel Mission (1:5-7)

In Col 1:5–7, the Colossians' faith is described in relation to the world-wide gospel mission. There are several parallels to the terminology and concepts found in Eph 1:11–14. In Ephesians, the readers are described as "having heard the word of truth, the gospel of your salvation, and believed in him" (ἀκούσαντες τὸν λόγον τῆς ἀληθείας, τὸ εὐαγγέλιον τῆς σωτηρίας ὑμῶν, ἐν ᾧ καὶ πιστεύσαντες; Eph 1:13). In Colossians, the readers' "faith" (noun πίστις, Col 1:4) is similarly described as arising from what they had "heard before in the word of truth, the gospel" (προηκούσατε ἐν τῷ λόγῳ τῆς ἀληθείας τοῦ εὐαγγελίου; Col 1:5).[8] In both cases, faith in Christ is portrayed as a response to the worldwide gospel mission to the "gentiles" (cf. Col 1:27).

Nevertheless, there is a difference in emphasis between the two letters with regard to the dynamics of this worldwide gospel mission. In Eph 1:13, the expression "in whom also you" (ἐν ᾧ καὶ ὑμεῖς) emphasizes the fact that the gentiles, through responding to the gospel mission, had received the same blessings as *the Jewish apostolic community* ("we who have first hoped in Christ," v. 12). The gospel mission in Ephesians is presented as a dynamic of blessing through Israel to the nations.[9] In Col 1:6, on the other hand, the expression "as also among you" (καθὼς καὶ ἐν ὑμῖν) emphasizes the fact that the gentiles, through responding to the gospel mission, had participated in a gospel that was bearing fruit and growing *throughout the world* ("as indeed in the whole world," καθὼς καὶ ἐν παντὶ τῷ κόσμῳ, v. 6). Colossians thus focuses on one specific instance of this worldwide gospel-preaching phenomenon: in Colossae (v. 2), on a certain "day" (v. 6), through the individual "Ephaphras" (v. 7).[10] Nevertheless, the apostolic foundation of the gospel mission is still in view (cf. Eph 2:20). Epaphras has not acted on his own; rather, Paul describes him as an apostolic agent: "a faithful minister of Christ on our behalf" (πιστὸς ὑπὲρ ἡμῶν διάκονος τοῦ Χριστοῦ, v. 7).[11]

8. The response also involved "hope" (noun ἐλπίς; Col 1:5; Eph 1:18) and "love" (noun ἀγάπη; Col 1:4; Eph 1:15).

9. See chapter 3.

10. Foster, *Colossians*, 144–45.

11. While several manuscripts (א² C D¹ K L P Ψ 075 33 81 104. etc.) have "your" (ὑμῶν), there is strong attestation (𝔓⁴⁶ א* A B D* F G 1505) for "our" (ἡμῶν). It is possible that early scribes changed the pronoun because they saw less of a need to focus

The Colossians' Portion in the Inheritance of the Saints (1:12)

In 1:12, Paul gives thanks to the Father who has qualified the Colossians "for a portion in the inheritance of the saints in light" (εἰς τὴν μερίδα τοῦ κλήρου τῶν ἁγίων ἐν τῷ φωτί, v. 12, my translation). The terms "portion" (μέρις) and "inheritance" (κλῆρος) are used in the LXX to describe an inheritance in the land of Israel (e.g., Deut 10:9; 12:12).[12] We saw in Ephesians that the term "saints" often occurs in contexts where Israel's blessings—including Israel's "inheritance"—are understood in eschatological terms, and said to be shared with Christ-believing gentiles through the gospel (Eph 1:18; 2:19; 3:5–6; 4:12; cf. 1:13–14).[13] These observations about Ephesians provide a possible conceptual backdrop for Col 1:12, which would strengthen Dunn's view that the verse is referring to the sharing of Israel's privileges with the gentiles. Dunn argues that the combination of concepts in this verse ("inheritance," "saints," and "light") also occurs in the Dead Sea Scrolls (e.g., 1QS 11.7–8; 1QH 11.10–12), with a spiritual and eternal "inheritance" in view.[14] With this Jewish background in mind, Dunn argues that this verse is describing

> heaven as the shared inheritance of the (human) saints. . . . [T]here is a strong sense of an inestimable privilege, previously understood as Israel's alone, and of a hope for choice companionship and social identity that will extend beyond death and whose quality can be experienced already in this mortal life.[15]

Paul's Apostolic Ministry to the Nations (1:24–29)

There are numerous parallels between Paul's description of his apostolic ministry to the gentiles in Eph 3:1–13 and that in Col 1:24–29. Although Col 1:24–29 needs to be understood on its own terms within its own

---

on Paul's apostolic ministry and more of a need to focus on the recipients of the gospel (ibid., 149–50; *pace* Metzger, *Textual Commentary*, 619).

12. Dunn, *Colossians and Philemon*, 75–76.

13. See chapters 3–6.

14. Dunn, *Colossians and Philemon*, 75–78.

15. Ibid., 77. However, *pace* ibid., 33–35, this does not imply a synagogue-based opposition in Colossae. Foster disagrees with Dunn's assessment, but his primary argument is that Israel's inheritance is not in view at all in Colossians (*Colossians*, 164). If, as we have shown, such a view can be present in Ephesians, it may also be in view in Colossians.

context, our findings from Eph 3:1–13 may nevertheless shed light on interpretive possibilities for the passage.[16]

In both Ephesians and Colossians, Paul describes himself as suffering (Eph 3:1, 13; Col 1:24, 29; 2:1–5) for the sake of his mission to the "gentiles" (Eph 3:1, 6, 8; Col 1:27). When we examined Ephesians, we suggested that Eph 3:1–13 (and perhaps the entire letter) may have arisen from a concern that gentile believers might be troubled by the prolonged imprisonment of the apostle to the gentiles, and so needed to be educated and assured that the apostle's afflictions were part of God's greater purposes involving Israel, the nations, and indeed the cosmos. This, in turn, would enable gentile believers to understand their own location in relation to these purposes. A similar concern may be identified in Colossians. The mention of Paul's afflictions serves a greater purpose than simply rebutting traditionalist Jewish teaching;[17] it helps the Colossians to understand their place in God's greater purposes. Paul's afflictions are caught up with his gospel-preaching mission for the sake of Christ's "body, that is, the church" (Col 1:24). This is the same "body" and "church" that had previously been described in terms of Christ's cosmic preeminence (Col 1:18). Thus, in both Colossians and Ephesians, the "church" is described as a heavenly entity that is being made manifest on earth through the apostolic gospel-preaching mission (cf. Eph 4:7–16).[18] Thus, in Ephesians Paul is a "minister" of the "gospel" (Eph 3:6–7), and in Colossians he is a "minister" of the "gospel" (Col 1:23) and of the "church" (Col 1:24–25). Both descriptions essentially mean the same thing: Paul brings the gospel for the sake of building the church (cf. the "ministry" of the "saints" for "building" the "body" in Eph 4:12).

Paul's role as gospel minister is "according to the administration of God given to me for you" (Col 1:25, my translation). We have seen that in Eph 3:2, 9, the term "administration" (οἰκονομία) refers to Paul's task of putting into effect God's eternal, cosmic purposes "in Christ" through preaching the gospel to the gentiles.[19] Here in Colossians, a similar idea is in view. In Colossians, however, the metaphor is extended further. Lang points to the economic imagery in the phrase in the previous verse, "I complete what is lacking in Christ's afflictions" (ἀνταναπληρῶ

---

16. See chapter 5.

17. *Pace* Dunn, *Beginning from Jerusalem*, 1048.

18. See chapter 6.

19. See chapter 5.

τὰ ὑστερήματα τῶν θλίψεων τοῦ Χριστοῦ, Col 1:24, cf. Phil 4:15–19). He argues persuasively that Paul is presenting his ministry in v. 25 as a fiduciary duty: the "administration" (οἰκονομίαν) of "the account of God" (τὸν λόγον τοῦ θεοῦ) which he must "disburse" (πληρῶσαι, v. 25). Christ's afflictions have generated "wealth" for the "nations" (Col 1:27; cf. Eph 3:8) and Paul's labor and afflictions can be described metaphorically in terms of distributing this wealth among those nations (v. 27). This is reinforced by Col 2:14, which describes Christ's death as cancelling their debt in God's "account."[20] "Read this way, the entire verse further reinforces Paul's apostolic (and economic) responsibility to allocate the redemptive wealth that has been credited to humanity in God's account by Christ's afflictions."[21]

Paul also describes his ministry in terms of "the mystery hidden for ages and generations but now revealed to his saints" (Col 1:26). This is similar to the description of the "mystery" in Eph 3:3–6.[22] In Ephesians, the content of the mystery is that "the gentiles" have a share in the inheritance, body, and promise with Israel, through the gospel (Eph 3:6). In Colossians, the content of the mystery is similar: it involves great riches "among the gentiles," and is specified further as "Christ in you, the hope of glory" (Col 1:27). The parallel in Ephesians suggests that the mystery is not simply that Christ inhabits individual believers in Colossae, but rather that Christ is "in" (or "among") *the gentiles* who have received the gospel—including "you" believers in Colossae. In Colossians, this mystery was revealed "to his saints" or "to his holy ones" (τοῖς ἁγίοις αὐτοῦ, Col 1:26). In the parallel expression in Ephesians, the mystery is revealed "to his holy apostles and prophets" (ἀπεκαλύφθη τοῖς ἁγίοις ἀποστόλοις αὐτοῦ καὶ προφήταις, Eph 3:5). If we allow the two passages to mutually inform one another, it strengthens our argument that at certain points, the identity of "the saints" in Ephesians and Colossians is caught up with the revelation of the gospel to the early Jewish apostolic community, who in turn collectively brought the gospel to the nations.[23]

Thus, if we read parts of Col 1:1—2:5 in light of our findings from Ephesians, we can plausibly suggest that Paul is describing the Colossians' reception of the gospel as a localized instance of Paul's wider apostolic

20. Lang, "Disbursing the Account"; cf. Clark, *Completing Christ's Afflictions*.
21. Lang, "Disbursing the Account," 131.
22. See chapter 5.
23. See chapter 5.

ministry to the nations. This apostolic ministry is, in turn, caught up with God's worldwide purposes through Israel to the world.

Walking in Christ—in the Face of Local Threats (Col 2:6–23)

In Col 2:6, Paul begins a section of the letter aimed at strengthening the Colossians' identity and conduct "in Christ" in the face of perceived threats. As in Ephesians, the readers are urged to "walk" (verb περιπατέω) in light of the gospel they had formerly accepted and which Paul had just outlined (Col 2:6–7; cf. Eph 4:1). As we have seen, Ephesians envisages a general situation: the gentiles are described using educational terminology as having "learned Christ" (Eph 4:20) and having been "taught in him" (Eph 4:21), and the threats to their "walk" are described in general terms as "every wind of teaching" (Eph 4:14).[24] Colossians, on the other hand, envisages a more specific situation. In Colossians, the readers are not only described as having been "taught" (Col 2:7); they are also described—using "traditioning" terminology—as having "received (παραλάβετε) Christ Jesus [as] the Lord" (Col 2:6). Furthermore, the threats to their "walk" are described—again using "traditioning" terminology—as "according to human tradition" (κατὰ τὴν παράδοσιν τῶν ἀνθρώπων, Col 2:8).[25] This implies that Paul, through Epaphras (cf. Col 1:7–8), has been made aware of specific information, both about the traditions the Colossians have received, and also about the alternative traditions that are threatening their faith in Christ. These traditions appear to be related to an alternative "philosophy" associated with the "elements of the world" (v. 8).

The specificity of the Colossians' situation is important to bear in mind as we approach this section of the letter. The section contains many of the key texts we identified in chapter 2 as giving rise to supersessionist over-readings of the letter. These supersessionist over-readings involve extrapolating from the explicit statements found in the texts to make further conclusions about race, ethnicity, or Jewish practice—conclusions that are not necessary implications of the texts themselves. In the reading that follows, we aim to avoid and critique such over-readings. We will

24. See chapter 6.

25. For the distinction between educational language and teaching language see chapter 6.

firstly seek to determine what we can about the threats facing the Colossian community, then seek to understand how the statements in the texts answer those specific threats. As we proceed, at various points we will use our findings from Ephesians to provide us with non-supersessionist interpretative possibilities.

The Circumcision of Christ (vv. 6–12, esp. v. 11)

In vv. 9–10, Paul insists that the Colossians have been "filled" (v. 10) in Christ, in whom "the whole fullness of deity dwells bodily" (v. 9). They have thus received everything they need through virtue of their union with Christ, including the benefits of Christ's supremacy over "every power and authority" (v. 10). Given the warning of v. 8, it seems that the Colossians are being tempted to look elsewhere for such benefits. In this context, Paul adds a further statement: "In him also you were circumcised with a circumcision made without hands, . . . by the circumcision of Christ" (v. 11). The questions before us are: 1) What can we determine about the nature of the threat against the Colossian community that this statement is seeking to counter? and 2) In what way does this statement counter that threat?

As we have seen, this text is often understood to be claiming that Christ, by bringing a new spiritual reality, has rendered physical circumcision invalid for all. Most readings take as their starting point the premise that many Jews understood physical circumcision as a sign designed to point to a greater spiritual reality. However, some interpreters go a step further, understanding the text to be arguing that, now that the greater spiritual reality has arrived in Christ, the physical sign stands in direct *conflict* with the spiritual reality. Others understand the text to be implying that circumcision has been entirely replaced by Christian baptism as the sign of a deeper spiritual reality. Still others understand the text to be arguing that circumcision has been superseded because it is no longer a valid boundary-marking practice for the Christian community.[26]

However, none of these are necessary implications of Col 2:11. It is important to note that physical circumcision is not explicitly opposed in this text.[27] Any such opposition needs to be inferred from the use of

---

26. See chapter 2.

27. Appeal is sometimes made at this point to Rom 2:28–29 and Phil 3:3. However, as I have argued elsewhere, these texts are speaking about Jewish circumcision, not

the term "made without hands" (ἀχειροποιήτῳ). However, the use of the term does not necessarily mean that there is a contrast between physical circumcision and spiritual circumcision in view here. Rather, it is possible—and, we will argue, preferable—to understand the implied contrast between *two kinds of spiritual circumcision*: on the one hand, a spiritual circumcision promised by rival religious traditions, and on the other hand, the spiritual circumcision they have already received in Christ.

In this passage, Paul tells the Colossians that they already have three great benefits "in Christ." Firstly "in him" they have "been filled" (vv. 9–10), and so all other spiritual powers are "inconsequential and powerless in comparison to Christ" (v. 10).[28] Secondly, in Christ ("in whom also," ἐν ᾧ καί) they have undergone a non-physical circumcision (v. 11), which involves being "buried with him in baptism" (v. 12a). Thirdly, in Christ ("in whom also," ἐν ᾧ καί) they have been raised together with him (v. 12b). Each of these elements implies a corresponding alternative. That is, we can plausibly infer that the "philosophy" was offering the Colossians an alternative fullness, an alternative "circumcision made without hands," and an alternative means to be raised.

If this is true, then physical circumcision is not in view at all in Col 2:11. Rather, the threat to the Colossians involves the offer of an alternative non-physical circumcision. This possibility is rarely considered, but it is eminently plausible. It merely requires us to assume the existence of a mystical tradition, perhaps syncretistic, associated with or deriving in some way from Jewish thought. Such a mystical tradition would offer some kind of spiritual circumcision, probably as a means to "raise" its adherents from physical passions (cf. vv. 20–23) and provide them with spiritual power. There is a partial precedent for this way of thinking about circumcision in Philo, *Questions and Answers on Exodus* 2.2. While Philo of course is entirely Jewish in his view that physical circumcision is an important marker of Jewish identity (cf. *Migr.* 89–93), he also sees a deeper spiritual circumcision that may be possessed by a non-Jewish person, a "sojourner (προσήλυτος)," who is in some ways like Israel when they lived in an uncircumcised state in Egypt (Exod 22:21 [LXX 22:20]). This kind of gentile

---

circumcision in relation to gentiles (Windsor, *Vocation of Israel*, 53–55, 181–91). In any case, even if Rom 2:28–29 and Phil 3:3 were speaking about circumcision in relation to gentiles, they would not affect the argument about Col 2:11 mounted here.

28. Foster, *Colossians*, 261.

is not the person who is circumcised in his foreskin, but the person [who is circumcised in] his desires and sensual pleasures and
the other passions of his soul. (Philo, QE 2.2, my translation)[29]

Philo, being Jewish, does not countenance the idea that a *Jew* could
be physically uncircumcised. However, he does speak of the value of a
kind of non-physical circumcision for gentiles. It is unlikely that Philo
was alone in this way of thinking.

It is quite plausible, then, that the Colossian gentiles were being
attracted to a kind of spiritual circumcision, perhaps achieved through
ascetic practices or mystical experiences, which may have brought them
an experience of spiritual power, removal from earthly temptations, and
elevation to heavenly realms. Paul, however, argues that they *already*
have a spiritual circumcision "in Christ," which achieves all these things;
hence to seek this spiritual circumcision outside of Christ is in fact to be
taken captive to another philosophy.[30] Since we do not have all the details, we cannot prove the exact nature of such a threat. However, we have
demonstrated that it is not *necessary* to assume that the Colossians were
being attracted to physical Jewish circumcision. Thus, it is not necessary
to assume that Col 2:11 is denigrating physical Jewish circumcision.

Some interpreters, however, argue that the very use of the term
"made without hands" (ἀχειροποίητος) is designed to denigrate physical
circumcision, especially since the term "hand-made" (χειροποίητος) is
often associated with idols in the LXX.[31] However, we have already seen
from our examination of Eph 2:11 that this is an illegitimate argument.[32]
The most the concept of a circumcision done "without hands" does is to
underscore the priority of divine action over human action. It does not,
however, necessarily denigrate every kind of human action.[33] Indeed,
Paul later commends various kinds of human activity (verb ποιέω) per-

29. McEleney, "Circumcision"; Watson, *Paul, Judaism and the Gentiles*, 77; Windsor, *Vocation of Israel*, 177. *Pace* Nolland, "Proselytes."

30. Cf. Lohse, *Colossians and Philemon*, 130.

31. See chapters 2 and 4; see also Gupta, *Colossians*, 94.

32. See chapter 4.

33. So Philo, who at times uses the term χειροποίητος to refer to idols (e.g., *Moses*
1.303; 2.165, 168), also uses the term in other ways: to speak of a physical house in
contrast to the world as Abraham's house and city (*Creation* 142); to describe human-
made calamities in contrast to divine calamities (*Dreams* 2.125; cf. *Spec. Laws* 1.184;
3.203; *Flaccus* 62); and to describe the physical temple in contrast to the universe as
God's creation (*Moses* 2.88). In none of these latter instances does he imply that the
thing "made by hands" is necessarily idolatrous.

formed in the name of the Lord (Col 3:17, 23). Thus, we cannot conclude that the term "made without hands" is being used in Colossians to imply that physical Jewish circumcision is necessarily idolatrous.

There are various options for understanding the exact nature of the non-physical "circumcision of Christ" in Col 2:11. Since all of the options are compatible with the reading offered here, it is not necessary to cover them in detail. The two most popular options are: 1) The "circumcision of Christ" is Christ's crucifixion, in which his physical body was "stripped off" and he was given a new resurrection body; believers participate in this crucifixion, and it is put into effect through baptism.[34] 2) The "circumcision of Christ" is a spiritual circumcision that God performs on believers, which Christ possesses also; it involves "the transformation of the sinful nature into a Christ-like nature" by means of union with Christ, and is also put into effect through baptism (v. 12a).[35] In either case, as we have argued, the "circumcision of Christ" is not being contrasted with physical circumcision, but with another kind of "spiritual circumcision" offered by the "philosophy." Thus, physical circumcision for Jews is not being denigrated or replaced in Col 2:11. This is because physical circumcision is not in view at all.

The Cancellation of the Record of Debt (vv. 13–15, esp. v. 14)

In Col 2:14, Paul speaks of Christ's death on the cross in terms of the cancellation of the "record of debt in [the] decrees" (χειρόγραφον τοῖς δόγμασιν) which was "against us." This cancellation of the record of debt is associated directly with being "made alive with" Christ (v. 13), the "forgiveness" of "trespasses" (v. 13), and God's triumph over the "powers and authorities" (v. 15). It may also be linked with the financial terminology in Col 1:24–27, where Paul describes himself as distributing "riches" to the gentiles.[36] As we have seen, some interpreters take this passage to mean either that Christ has abolished the Jewish ritual elements of the law of Moses for all people (including for Jewish believers in Christ), or

34. O'Brien, *Colossians, Philemon*, 114–19; Dunn, *Colossians and Philemon*, 157–58; Pao, *Colossians & Philemon*, 165–66. This takes the genitive as an objective genitive.

35. Wright, *Colossians and Philemon*, 106; Salter, "Does Baptism Replace Circumcision?" 24. This takes the genitive as a possessive genitive. Salter also notes the possibility of a subjective genitive: "a circumcision that Christ effects" (ibid.).

36. See above; cf. Lang, "Disbursing the Account," 136.

that Christ has abolished the law of Moses in its entirety.[37] However, it is going too far to claim that this text is implying the wholesale abolition of the law of Moses.

The "record of debt" (χειρόγραφον) which is cancelled cannot be identified directly with the law of Moses. The term refers to a record of debt or sin, not to a law. Foster notes that "while in secular contexts the term designated a legal or business document recording debt to be repaid, in Jewish or Christian contexts it takes on the technical designation for a list of sins used at the heavenly assize."[38] Bevere, however, argues that "the best explanation for the identity of the χειρόγραφον in Colossians 2:14 is that it is *primarily* and most specifically a reference to the Law of Moses."[39] Yet Bevere's argument is dependent on his understanding of the parallel passage in Eph 2:15. As we have seen, Eph 2:15 is not claiming that the law of Moses has been abolished in its entirety. Rather, what has been abolished is the law understood primarily as a set of "commandments" as expressed and promulgated by certain authoritative "decrees" concerning the observance of these commandments.[40] Thus there is no reason to assume that the "cancellation of the record of debt" is a reference to the abolition of the law of Moses.

Furthermore, the fact that the record of debt is said to be "in [the] decrees" (τοῖς δόγμασιν) does not imply that the law of Moses has been abolished. The term "decrees" might be referring to the ascetic rules of v. 20,[41] or it might be referring to God's moral law which found expression in the law of Moses.[42] In either case, it is not the decrees themselves which are abolished, but the record of debt. At most, then, Col 2:14 is claiming that human "trespasses" against the law led to a record of debt that was erased through Christ's death.

37. See chapter 2.

38. Foster, *Colossians*, 273. Foster cites *Apoc. Zeph.* 3.7–8 and *Apoc. Paul.* 17 (ibid., 272–73; cf. Dunn, *Colossians and Philemon*, 164).

39. Bevere, "Cheirograph," 206.

40. See chapter 4.

41. Weiss, "The Law," 304. Note the cognate verb in v. 20, which describes the Colossians as potentially "being subject to decrees" (δογματίζεσθε).

42. Caird, *Letters from Prison*, 195; Dunn, *Colossians and Philemon*, 165.

The Shadow and the Substance (vv. 16–19, esp. vv. 16–17)

In vv. 16–17, Paul urges the Colossians:

> Therefore let no one pass judgment on you in questions of food and drink, or with regard to a festival or a new moon or a Sabbath. These are a shadow of the things to come, but the substance belongs to Christ. (Col 2:16–17)

As we have seen, several interpreters take this text to mean that Christ has abolished the Jewish ritual elements of the law of Moses for all people (including for Jewish believers in Christ).[43] However, this conclusion is unwarranted. The list of practices in v. 16 should not be understood as a comprehensive list of Jewish observances.[44] The most we can say is that the mention of the "Sabbath" indicates a Jewish origin for one of the elements in the list. However, issues concerning food and drink, festivals, and new moons were elements of various pagan religious systems. It is far more likely that this is a list of practices adopted by the syncretistic religious philosophy, which had incorporated Jewish elements among others, and which poses a threat to the Colossians' faith in Christ.[45] If that is the case, Paul is not here opposing Jewish observances, but rather warning the Colossians against being caught up in the spiritual concerns of the syncretistic religious philosophy and its associated practices (cf. vv. 18–19).

Some commentators argue that the contrast in v. 17 between "shadow" (σκιά) and "substance" (σῶμα) refers to a contrast between the Old Testament rituals and Christ. In this view, the "things to come" means the things that were future from the point of view of Old Testament believers. With the coming of Christ, these things have now arrived.[46] However, as Foster compellingly argues, a future eschatology, rather than a realized eschatology, is in view in this verse. The "things to come" are thus future from the point of view of the *readers*. Paul is not, therefore, referring to Jewish laws being superseded by Christ. Rather, he is claiming that the ascetic/religious practices that promise powerful spiritual experiences for the practitioners (v. 18) are only an insubstantial shadow of the substan-

---

43. See chapter 2.

44. *Pace* Dunn, *Colossians and Philemon*, 171–75.

45. Foster, *Colossians*, 278–82; cf. Lohse, *Colossians and Philemon*, 116.

46. O'Brien, *Colossians, Philemon*, 140–41; Dunn, *Colossians and Philemon*, 177; Gupta, *Colossians*, 99.

tial reality that will come when Christ appears and the believers appear with him "in glory" (3:4).[47] Indeed, since the Colossians have already been "filled" in Christ (v. 10), if they look to any of these festivals as a means of participation in the heavenly or eschatological realms, they are missing out on the true means of getting there. Thus, vv. 16–17 have no bearing on the question of the value of Sabbath observances or Jewish festivals as a marker of Jewish identity.

Death to the Elements of the World (vv. 20–23, esp. v. 20)

In v. 20, Paul asserts that the Colossians have "died with Christ to the elements of the world" (cf. v. 8). The "elements of the world" literally refers to "the basic elements from which everything in the natural world is composed, namely, earth, air, fire, water," which must be the starting point in any discussion of the term since it is "by far the most common meaning of the term στοιχεῖα and then especially when complemented by the genitive τοῦ κόσμου."[48] As we have seen in chapter 2, some interpreters argue that the "elements of the world" is a direct reference to the law of Moses. This argument is based on Gal 4:3, 9, where the "elements of the world" are associated with the law.[49] However, in Gal 4:3, 9, the association between the "elements of the world" and the "law" is only indirect. As de Boer notes, in Gal 4:3, 9, the phrase "elements of the world" is used as:

> *a summary designation* for a complex of Galatian religious beliefs and practices at the center of which were the four elements of the physical cosmos to which the phrase concretely refers. In Paul's usage, then, the phrase is an instance of *metonymy* whereby a trait or characteristic stands for a larger whole of which it is a part. In this case τὰ στοιχεῖα τοῦ κόσμου—the four elements of physical reality—stand for the religion of the Galatians prior to them becoming believers in Christ. Calendrical observances and the physical phenomena associated with such observances—the movements of the sun, moon, planets, and stars—were an integral part of these religious beliefs and practices.[50]

47. Foster, *Colossians*, 283–84.
48. de Boer, "Τὰ Στοιχεῖα Τοῦ Κόσμου," 207.
49. E.g., Dunn, *Colossians and Philemon*, 148–51.
50. de Boer, "Τὰ Στοιχεῖα Τοῦ Κόσμου," 220.

Within the argument of Galatians, then, the "*only* relevant point of contact" between the law of Moses and the "elements" is the calendrical observances. The phrase does not refer directly to the law, but has a single point of comparison with the law within the context of this argument in Galatians.[51] Here in Colossians, since there is no explicit reference to the law of Moses, there is no reason to infer such a reference. The "elements of the world" here seems to be a metynomy for those syncretistic religious views, expressed in ascetic principles and calendrical observances, which are being used as a means of achieving heavenly elevation.[52] Yet again, the abolition of the law of Moses is simply not in view in the text.

We have now examined several key texts in Colossians that tend to give rise to supersessionist over-readings. These texts include the references to: the "circumcision of Christ" (2:11), the cancellation of the "record of debt" (2:14), the statement about the "shadow" versus the "substance" in relation to certain observances (vv. 16–17), and the assertion that the Colossians have "died" to the "elements of the world" (v. 20). In each case, after determining what we could about the particular threat facing the Colossian community and drawing from our findings about Ephesians, we have suggested a plausible and even preferable interpretation. None of these interpretations need imply the eradication of distinctive Jewish identity.

The New Humanity in Christ (Col 3:1—4:6, esp. 3:11)

In Col 3:1—4:6, Paul provides his readers with guidance for living in line with their exalted status in union with Christ. Since they have been "raised with Christ," they are to "seek the things that are above" (3:1). The way they are to go about seeking these "things that are above," however, is not through the ascetic or mystical practices of the rival philosophy (cf. 2:16–23). Rather, the Colossians must "put away" certain immoral and divisive practices (3:5–8) and "put on" certain practices and speech that build and strengthen the community (3:12–17). In vv. 9–10 this is described in terms of having "taken off the old human[ity]" and "put on the new [humanity]." This "new humanity" is then defined further as a sphere where certain naturally inimical pairings do not exist:

51. Ibid., 222; cf. Barclay, *Paul and the Gift*, 409–10.

52. Foster notes the possible connection with the worship of heavenly beings (cf. v. 18) (*Colossians*, 252–54).

> Here there is not Greek and Jew, circumcised and uncircum-
> cised, barbarian, Scythian, slave, free; but Christ is all, and in
> all. (Col 3:11)

As we have seen, this text is often understood to be claiming that
Christ, by forming a new kind of humanity, has nullified all forms of
Jewish distinctiveness. According to these interpretations, it is not simply
that ethnicity and other social distinctives no longer constitute a barrier
to unity in the Christian community. Rather, they have been "abolished"
and thus have "lost their meaning." This understanding of Col 3:11 is
sometimes seen as standing in tension with the idea that social distinctions should continue in the household code (Col 3:18—4:1).[53] The pur-
ported abolition of Jew-gentile distinctiveness is also, on occasion, seen
as evidence that Colossians is directed against a form of teaching being
espoused by people who are identifiably Jewish.[54]

However, this idea that Col 3:11 entirely abolishes any possibility
of social distinctiveness, including Jewish distinctiveness, is an unwarranted over-reading of the text. It is certainly not implied by the context.
The verse appears in a section in which divisive community behavior is
being condemned (3:8–9), and unifying community behavior is being
encouraged (3:12–15). The Colossians are told to exhibit such virtues
as "kindness," "humility," and "patience" (Col 3:12), "bearing with one
another" and "forgiving one another" (Col 3:13). "Love," the overarching
virtue, is described as a "bond" (σύνδεσμος) of completeness (Col 3:14; cf.
Eph 4:3). Furthermore, the Colossians are called "in one body" to "peace"
(Col 3:15; cf. Eph 2:14–16). In this context, Paul is not advocating the
abolition of social difference; rather he is advocating a patient and long-
suffering "love." Such love could even be exercised—indeed, it would be
profoundly relevant—in situations involving social difference.[55]

Given this context, the most natural understanding of Col 3:11 is
that in the new sphere of existence brought about by Christ, the *divisive-
ness* that had been inherent in certain distinct social identities (including the identities of Jew and Greek) has effectively been removed. These
social identities no longer constitute a barrier to unity. This is not because

53. For a summary of these views see chapter 2.

54. Dunn, *Colossians and Philemon*, 225. Lightfoot refers to the "Judaism of the
Colossian heretics" (*Colossians and Philemon*, 214). Foster sees the possibility of "tensions between Jewish and Gentile sections of the early Jesus movement" being referred
to here (*Colossians*, 341).

55. Pao, *Colossians & Philemon*, 229.

the social identities have been eradicated in every respect, but because there is a more fundamental identity that transforms all of them: "Christ is all, and in all." This perspective continues in the letter, even informing the discussion of slaves and masters in Col 3:22–4:1. While slaves are not told to stay in their position at all costs, and presumably would be advised to avail themselves of any opportunities for freedom that might arise (cf. 1 Cor 7:21; Phlm 15–16), such earthly emancipation is not the highest priority for Paul's teaching. Rather, the priority is the transformation of existing identities in Christ. Thus, slaves are to consider their calling in life as an opportunity to serve the Lord (Col 3:22–25), and "free" masters are to live considering the Lord as their true master (4:1).

This understanding of Col 3:11 is supported by our understanding of the parallel concept in Eph 2:11–22. As we have seen, the creation of the "one new humanity" in Eph 2:16 does not imply the eradication of all distinctions between Israel and the nations. Rather, the focus is on the reconciliation and the removal of hostility that occurs in Christ. This perspective is just as relevant in our interpretation of Col 3:11.

Jewish Partners in the Apostolic Mission (Col 4:7–18, esp. 4:10–11)

In Col 4:7–18, Paul lists several people who are involved directly in his apostolic mission. The mention of three individuals—Mark the cousin of Barnabas, Aristarchus, and Jesus called Justus—is significant for our purposes, since these individuals are described in terms of Jewish identity as being "from [the] circumcision" (ἐκ περιτομῆς, vv. 10–11). This singling out and identifying of particular Jews among Paul's colleagues needs an adequate explanation.[56] We have already noted how Paul views his apostolic ministry as caught up with God's worldwide purposes through Israel to the world.[57] This theme may go some way toward explaining the reference in 4:11. Furthermore, it may help to explain the reason for the unusual Greek syntax in vv. 10–11. A literal rendering of the Greek text yields the following:

---

56. Dunn sees Paul here as seeking to model the vision of variegated social inclusiveness expressed in 3:11 (*Beginning from Jerusalem*, 1038; cf. Gupta, *Colossians*, 192). This explanation is possible, but inadequate.

57. See the discussion on Col 1:1—2:5.

Aristarchus my fellow prisoner greets you, and Mark ... and Jesus who is called Justus—those who are from the circumcision, these [being] the only co-workers for the kingdom of God, who have been a comfort to me. (Col 4:10–11, my translation)[58]

This shows that there are various ways to understand vv. 10–11. The more typical rendering (e.g., the ESV) understands Paul to be stating that the three named individuals are Paul's only *Jewish* co-workers for the kingdom of God, leaving open the possibility that there are also gentile co-workers with Paul.[59] However, it is also possible to understand Paul to be stating that the three named individuals are Jews, *and also* that these three Jewish individuals are Paul's only co-workers for the kingdom of God (or at least, the only co-workers for the kingdom of God who are with Paul at the time).[60] The problem with the former interpretation is that it renders the Greek syntax a little awkwardly. The problem with the latter interpretation is that it seems to contradict vv. 12–14, which indicates that there are other people present with Paul, including people who are active in the apostolic mission (e.g., Epaphras, cf. 1:7).[61]

A possible solution to this issue may arise from our observation that Paul sees the gospel as a Jew-gentile dynamic. It is possible, then, that here Paul wishes to single out his *Jewish* colleagues from among his other colleagues because their Jewish identity gives them a special place in relation to the apostolic mission.[62] Paul singles them out using the expression "co-workers for the kingdom of God." Admittedly, in other contexts, the term "co-workers" can be used as a designation for Paul's gentile colleagues (e.g., 2 Cor 8:23). However, it is worth noting that "co-workers" is not a "fixed title" for Paul; it can be used in various ways to designate individuals involved in ministry with others.[63] In this case, the three named individuals are not simply called "co-workers" but rather "co-workers for the kingdom of God." This contains echoes of the early

58. Greek: Ἀσπάζεται ὑμᾶς Ἀρίσταρχος ὁ συναιχμάλωτός μου καὶ Μᾶρκος ... καὶ Ἰησοῦς ὁ λεγόμενος Ἰοῦστος, οἱ ὄντες ἐκ περιτομῆς, οὗτοι μόνοι συνεργοὶ εἰς τὴν βασιλείαν τοῦ θεοῦ, οἵτινες ἐγενήθησάν μοι παρηγορία.

59. Dunn, *Colossians and Philemon*, 279.

60. Foster, *Colossians*, 427.

61. Ibid., 424–28.

62. Cf. the prominence given to the Jewish identity of apostolic colleagues (and rivals) in other passages (Rom 16:3–4, 7; 2 Cor 11:22–23; cf. Phil 3:3; Gal 6:16) (see further Windsor, *Vocation of Israel*, 17–18, 53–61, 75–76).

63. Foster, *Colossians*, 427.

preaching of Jesus and the Jewish disciples commissioned by Jesus as found in the Synoptic tradition (see e.g., Luke 4:43; 8:1; 9:2, 60; 16:16).[64] These have also proved a "comfort" to Paul. This idea may be related to the anguish Paul expresses in Romans over his non-Christ-believing kin, who were both soteriologically imperiled and also not fulfilling Israel's vocation in being the source of the proclamation of the gospel to the world (Rom 9:1–5; 10:1).[65]

Thus, the possibility that Israel's special place in the apostolic mission is in the background here may help to explain an otherwise puzzling reference to the Jewish identity of certain of Paul's "co-workers for the kingdom of God" in Col 4:10–11. However, since we do not have enough information to make a firm conclusion, the idea must remain a possibility.

Summary of Colossians

In this chapter, I have used my findings from Ephesians to suggest interpretive possibilities for elements of the text of Colossians. Our findings here are both positive and negative.

Positively, we have seen that an awareness of Israel's key place in the apostolic mission to the nations provides a plausible conceptual background to several of the statements made in the letter. These include: Paul's explicit locating of the Colossians' response to the gospel in the context of the worldwide apostolic mission (Col 1:5–7), the reference to the Colossians' "portion in the inheritance of the saints in light" (Col 1:12), Paul's description of his own apostolic ministry to the nations (Col 1:24–29), and the singling out of three Jewish individuals as Paul's "co-workers for the kingdom of God" (Col 4:10–11). At the same time, we saw that the themes relating to Jewish identity are far less prominent than they are in Ephesians. We suggested that Paul is describing the Colossians' reception of the gospel as a localized instance of his wider apostolic ministry to the nations. This apostolic ministry is, in turn, caught up with God's worldwide purposes through Israel to the world, although this latter theme is at most in the background rather than the foreground.

Negatively, we have examined several key texts in Colossians that tend to give rise to supersessionist over-readings. In each case, after

64. Dunn, *Colossians and Philemon*, 279–80.
65. Windsor, *Vocation of Israel*, 203–16.

determining what we could about the particular threat facing the Colossian community and drawing from our findings about Ephesians, we have suggested a plausible and even preferable interpretation of each of these references in Colossians. The reference to the "circumcision of Christ" (Col 2:11) is not a denigration of physical circumcision, but a response to an alternative non-physical circumcision offered by the syncretistic philosophy or philosophies. The reference to the cancellation of the "record of debt" (Col 2:14) is not a denigration of the law of Moses *per se*, but at most a claim that human "trespasses" against the law were erased through Christ's death. The identification of certain observances as a "shadow" (Col 2:16–17) is not a denigration of Jewish observances, but a warning against being caught up in the spiritual concerns of the syncretistic religious philosophy and its associated practices, given the "substance" of the future glorious state of believers in Christ. The reference to the "elements of the world" to which the Colossians have "died" (Col 2:20) is not a reference to the law of Moses, but a metynomy for those syncretistic religious views, expressed in ascetic principles and calendrical observances, which are being used as a means of achieving heavenly elevation.

8

Conclusions and Implications

Conclusions[1]

AGAINST A PREVAILING APPROACH to Ephesians and Colossians in which the letters are read as documents situated outside Paul's historical mission, I have presented an *evangelical post-supersessionist reading of Ephesians and Colossians*. The term *evangelical* was intended to indicate that the dynamic of gospel proclamation (i.e., "evangelism") would inform my reading of these New Testament letters. I sought to read Ephesians and Colossians as gospel-driven documents—that is, as documents at least ostensibly situated within and arising from the apostolic mission to proclaim the gospel of Christ to the nations. The term *post-supersessionist* referred to a hermeneutical stance that sees some significance in a special place or calling for Israel, even in relation to Christ and his people, within the texts, and refuses to concede that unity in Christ necessarily destroys the positive value of all distinctions between Jews and gentiles. My *evangelical post-supersessionist* stance sought to read Ephesians and Colossians in a way that was sensitive to the position and role of Israel in relation to the proclamation of the gospel of Christ to the nations, in this case primarily within the horizon of the apostolic mission. I was not advocating a total reconfiguration of our understanding of every theme in Ephesians and Colossians. Rather, I was seeking to demonstrate that a greater emphasis on the apostolic mission, and its associated Jew-gentile

1. In this section, I am gathering together the summaries found at the end of each chapter—hence the repetition of wording for the sake of clarity.

dynamic, will enable us fruitfully to reconceive some of the contours in which these theological themes are expressed.

In chapter 2, I summarized some prior readings of these letters that are particularly relevant to the question of supersessionism. Firstly, I provided an overview of the main supersessionist tendencies in prior readings of these letters. Secondly, I discussed some significant prior post-supersessionist readings of Ephesians. Thirdly, I summarized some of the relevant critical questions raised by scholarship in the letters. Finally, in light of these earlier readings and critical questions, I outlined the main features of my own evangelical post-supersessionist reading of Ephesians and Colossians.

In chapter 3, we saw how the apostolic mission is portrayed in Eph 1 as the means by which Christ's blessings have come through Israel to the nations. Paul's introduction of himself as "an apostle of Christ Jesus by the will of God" is rich with connotations of a dynamic mission (Eph 1:1). The apostle, the missionary of Christ, is enacting the purposes of God in the world. He is writing to Christ-believing gentiles who, indeed *as* Christ-believers, can be called "holy ones," and he implies through his phraseology that this fact is remarkable. At the beginning of the *berakhah* in Eph 1:3, Paul alludes to Gen 12:3, thereby implying that Christ fulfills the role of the "offspring" of Abraham "in" whom the nations are "blessed." In Christ, God's promises through Israel to the nations have reached their eschatological fulfillment, with far-reaching and even cosmic implications. In Eph 1:4–14, a dynamic movement of blessing from "us" to "you" through the preaching of the gospel is evident. This blessing "in Christ" (v. 3) has been divinely predetermined (vv. 4–6a), given (vv. 6b–7), communicated (vv. 8–10), inherited (vv. 11–12), and shared with "you also" through the preaching of the gospel (vv. 13–14). The fact that the blessing is couched in language of Abrahamic promises and Jewish *berakhoth* hints that a dynamic movement of blessing through Israel to the nations is being envisaged. In Eph 1:15–23, the apostle prays that those who have responded to the preaching of the gospel would understand the far-reaching significance of the message they have embraced. While these blessings were first given to the early Jewish apostolic community, they have now, through the preaching of the gospel, come to the nations.

In chapter 4, we saw how the apostolic mission plays a climactic role in Christ's work of reconciliation for Israel and the nations in Eph 2. Paul's insistence that both "you" and "we" have been raised from death to life (Eph 2:1–10) places Israel's distinctiveness within a larger divine perspective that coheres with the prophetic witness and emphasizes God's gracious saving activity. Paul's emphasis on the fact that his gentile readers have been "brought near" to Israel (Eph 2:11–13) reminds them that while their gentile past is still relevant to their present identity, it has been thoroughly transformed in Christ: they were once gentiles *contra* Israel; now they are gentiles *blessed alongside* Israel. Paul's description of Christ's sacrificial death (Eph 2:14–16) draws out a key achievement of the cross: the reconciliation of Israel and the nations together to God. Paul's description of the gospel-preaching activity of Christ to both "near" and "far" (Eph 2:17–18) depicts Christ's missionary work (through the agency of the apostolic mission) as the culmination of his reconciling activity. Paul's description of gentiles being built together with the "saints" on the same apostolic foundation (Eph 2:19–22) indicates that the Jew-gentile relationship is intimately connected to the dynamics of the gospel mission, a mission that proceeded through the early Jewish apostolic community to the nations.

Thus, we saw that supersessionist readings of certain texts in Eph 2 are, in fact, over-readings that do not account adequately for the context in which the texts appear. The purpose of the discussion of circumcision in v. 11 is not to cancel entirely the value of physical circumcision for Jews. Rather, the discussion is intended to remind readers of the way in which Jewish circumcision had been used in the context of Jew-gentile hostility, and to remind them that Jewish circumcision, as a human activity, could not achieve the divine purposes of overcoming such hostility. The reference to the "law of the commandments in decrees" having been "abolished" by Christ (v. 15) is not a claim that the law of Moses has been rendered invalid in all respects. Rather, it is a claim that Christ's death renders unnecessary some of the key functions of the law's commandments as interpreted by Jewish authorities in the first century—particularly those functions that involved protecting Israel from impure and hostile gentiles. The creation of the "one new humanity" in Christ (vv. 15–16) does not imply the eradication of all distinctions between Israel and the nations. Rather, the focus is on reconciliation and the removal of hostility between Israel and the nations.

In chapter 5, we saw how in Eph 3 the apostolic mission is continuing through Paul, even in his suffering, so that Christ's riches are being poured out through Paul's ministry to the nations. Paul's turn toward a direct discussion of his own apostolic mission (Eph 3:1) locates his own apostolic ministry within God's greater international and cosmic purposes, especially those purposes which involve the dynamic of blessing flowing through Israel to the nations. Paul's "administration" (Eph 3:2) is a reference to his apostolic mission to the gentiles. Paul's focus on his own insight as apostle (Eph 3:3–4) enables him to explain how his apostleship fits into God's greater purposes. Paul's understanding of the revealed "mystery of Christ" (Eph 3:4–6) is that Jews and gentiles have an equal status in Christ, and that this equal status comes about through the preaching of the gospel. Paul's reference to Christ's "holy apostles and prophets" (Eph 3:5) is intended as a reference to the early Jewish apostolic community, from whom the gospel was preached to the nations. Paul's self-description as a "minister of the gospel" (Eph 3:7) enables him to portray himself as a medium of divine revelation and blessings to the world, who is caught up in God's gracious purposes for Israel and the nations as described in Eph 1–2. Paul's humble self-identification as one "of the saints" (Eph 3:8–9) enables him to associate himself with the entire Jewish apostolic community. Paul's portrayal of the cosmic dimensions of the apostolic task (Eph 3:9–12) locates the Jew-gentile dynamic within the larger divine purposes which form both the goal and context of this dynamic. Paul's appeal to his readers not to lose heart over his sufferings (Eph 3:13) may suggest that Ephesians was occasioned by a general "crisis of confidence" envisaged by Paul among gentile believers with respect to his worldwide apostolic mission. Finally, Paul's apostolic prayer (Eph 3:14–21) contains two elements that further support our argument that the Jew-gentile dynamic is highly significant to the argument of Ephesians: the mention of "every family" (v. 15, cf. Eph 2:17–22), and the allusion to the dimensions of the altar in (vv. 18–19; cf. Ezek 43:13–16).

In chapter 6, we examined Eph 4–6 and saw how the gentile readers of the letter are urged to "walk" in a way that reflects and maintains what the apostolic mission through Israel to the nations has achieved in and through them. In Eph 4:1–6, Paul introduces a generalized form of gentile *halakah*. This is the key means by which the Christ-believing gentile readers of the letter can express their unity with the foundational Jewish apostolic community through whom the gospel of Christ came to them. In Eph 4:7–16, Paul is not primarily giving a blueprint for church order, but rather is describing Christ's apostolic mission through Israel to the nations: its past, its present, and its projected (pre-parousia) goal. In v. 7, he introduces the theme of unity through diversity. In vv. 8–10, by engaging in a Christological interpretation of Ps 68:18, Paul describes the events of Pentecost, in which the victorious and ascended Christ "descended" to give gifts to the early Jewish apostolic community. In v. 11, Paul describes these gifts as particular roles within the early Jewish apostolic community. In v. 12, Paul describes how these people prepared the Jewish apostolic community collectively to preach the gospel to the nations, which resulted in the construction of Christ's body. In vv. 13–16, Paul portrays his vision for the future effects of the apostolic mission among the entire body of Christ. This vision is characterized by a positive notion of gospel-based unity-in-diversity, which is set in opposition to dysfunctional plurality. Thus Eph 4:7–16 may be described as depicting a gospel-driven, locally-manifested, ecumenical vision. In Eph 4:17—6:9, Paul spells out the details of gentile *halakhah* in Christ. Some relevant features of this *halakhah* include: an emphasis on proper speech, a view of vocational diversity-in-unity (5:22—6:9), and a gospel-driven application of the law of Moses (e.g., Eph 6:2–4). In Eph 6:10–24, Paul reminds his readers of God's greater, cosmic, purposes in Christ and calls on his readers to take their own part in seeing these purposes fulfilled. This includes a concern with the ongoing gospel mission (e.g., Eph 6:15).

In chapter 7, I used my findings from Ephesians to suggest interpretive possibilities for elements of the text of Colossians. Positively, we saw that an awareness of Israel's key place in the apostolic mission to the nations provides a plausible conceptual background to several of the statements made in the letter. These include: Paul's explicit locating of the Colossians' response to the gospel in the context of the worldwide apostolic mission (Col 1:5–7), the reference to the Colossians' "portion in the inheritance of the saints in light" (Col 1:12), Paul's description of his own apostolic ministry to the nations (Col 1:24–29), and the singling out of three Jewish individuals as Paul's "co-workers for the kingdom of God" (Col 4:10–11). At the same time, we saw that the themes relating to Jewish identity are far less prominent than they are in Ephesians. We suggested that Paul is describing the Colossians' reception of the gospel as a localized instance of his wider apostolic ministry to the nations. This apostolic ministry is, in turn, caught up with God's worldwide purposes through Israel to the world, although this latter theme is at most in the background rather than the foreground.

Negatively, we examined several key texts in Colossians that tend to give rise to supersessionist over-readings. In each case, after determining what we could about the particular threat facing the Colossian community and drawing from our findings about Ephesians, we suggested a plausible and even preferable interpretation of each of these references in Colossians. The reference to the "circumcision of Christ" (Col 2:11) is not a denigration of physical circumcision, but a response to an alternative non-physical circumcision offered by the syncretistic philosophy or philosophies. The reference to the cancellation of the "record of debt" (Col 2:14) is not a denigration of the law of Moses *per se*, but at most a claim that human "trespasses" against the law were erased through Christ's death. The identification of certain observances as a "shadow" (Col 2:16–17) is not a denigration of Jewish observances, but a warning against being caught up in the spiritual concerns of the syncretistic religious philosophy and its associated practices, given the "substance" of the future glorious state of believers in Christ. The reference to the "elements of the world" to which the Colossians have "died" (Col 2:20) is not a reference to the law of Moses, but a metynomy for those syncretistic religious views, expressed in ascetic principles and calendrical observances, which are being used as a means of achieving heavenly elevation.

Implications

There are several implications that arise from this evangelical post-supersessionist reading of Ephesians and Colossians.

Firstly, there are *hermeneutical* implications. While this reading has not sought to undermine the central significance of key theological themes in the letters—e.g., God's eternal purposes, Christology, salvation by grace through faith, and ecclesiology—it has demonstrated how a greater emphasis on the apostolic mission, and its associated Jew-gentile dynamic, enables us fruitfully to reconceive some of the contours in which these theological themes are expressed. If modern readers were to read Ephesians and Colossians in a way that is more sensitive to such contours, they may appreciate the rich dimensions of these theological dimensions even more deeply.

Secondly, we have seen that the overall dynamic portrayed in both letters involves a strong connection between *gospel proclamation* and *social transformation*. According to the perspective in these letters, as the "word of truth" (i.e., the preached gospel of Christ) comes to different groups (Eph 1:13; Col 1:5), it not only unites them to Christ, but also forms them into new communities that are "built" and grow together "in love" (e.g., Eph 1:15; Col 1:8), with the expectation that they will continue to do so (e.g., Eph 4:15–16; Col 3:14–17). Paying attention to the dynamic of the apostolic mission in Ephesians and Colossians has highlighted this strong connection between the verbal proclamation of the gospel and the "building" of the church. Not only is this vital for understanding the nature of the relationship between Jews and gentiles within the apostolic mission, it is also fundamental to understanding all the other human relationships discussed in the letters. This has implications for theological reflection on the nature and effects of gospel proclamation today.

Thirdly, we have seen that there are also *missiological* implications. Ephesians and Colossians present us with an apostle who is proclaiming a message about the God and Messiah of Israel to many other "nations" who have their own gods and social worlds. As Palu has noted, the difference between Jews and gentiles that we observe at various places in the New Testament, along with the "distance" of the modern missionary from ancient Israel, should not be seen as a barrier, but rather as a driving force, for modern theological contextualization.[2] Furthermore, as Fowl points out, the vision of reconciliation presented to us in Eph 2:11–22, in which national, ethnic, and cultural identities are transformed rather than erased, is of great importance for reflection on modern missionary practices. Reading Ephesians (and Colossians) in this way may help those engaged in Christian mission to address "the necessary relationship between Christian identity relative to God's call of Israel and the variety of issues one confronts when the world's cultures are confronted with the stories and doctrines surrounding God's gracious call of Israel."[3]

Fourthly, and connected to this, there are *ecclesiological* implications. Ephesians, as we have seen, presents us with a picture of the church as Christ's "body" which values, rather than eliminates, human differences and distinctions, within a climate of mutual acceptance.[4] This has implications not only for the relationship between Jews and gentiles in Christ, but also for the relationship between individuals who are distinct from one another in other ways.[5] With regard to the specific question of Jewish and gentile believers, there have been many different views on how these differences and distinctions could or should be expressed structurally. Most disturbingly, some have used the picture presented

2. Palu, "Theological Contextualization."
3. Fowl, *Ephesians*, 102.
4. See e.g., Fong, "Racial Reconciliation."
5. Cf. Tucker, *Remain in Your Calling*.

in Eph 2 to enforce a separation between differing congregations along racial lines—e.g., segregationists in South Africa and supporters of the "Aryan paragraph" in Nazi Germany.[6] As we have seen, others (for entirely different reasons) have advocated a "bilateral" ecclesiology in which Messianic Jews and gentile Christians form separate church structures which together comprise a transnational community of believers.[7] Many others, however, have insisted that such structural separation is out of the question, and that the unity-in-distinction in the body of Christ must be expressed concretely *within* each local congregation.[8] These are complex questions, and we cannot here resolve them entirely. However, it is hoped that the reading of Ephesians and Colossians presented here will provide some assistance for and insights into this question.

There are also *anthropological* implications. As we have seen, the existence of differences and distinctions between human beings can sometimes be understood merely as a problem that needs to be solved in Christ. All distinctions and differences in role, in this view, imply a fundamental inequality. However, our evangelical post-supersessionist reading of Ephesians and Colossians has demonstrated that differences in calling or role among human beings do not necessarily imply inequality. As Markus Barth observes in relation to Eph 2, "[t]he great example, the test of unity in difference and of distinctiveness in unity, is the common life of Jews and Gentiles under the gospel. . . . Precisely when Jews and Gentiles are united their mutual but distinctive responsibility is awakened and becomes actual and urgent."[9] This has implications for many other kinds of difference and distinction between human beings. An example that arises from the letters themselves is the relationship between men and women. Johnson, for example, links the mutuality of Jew and gentile in Eph 2 with the mutuality of man and woman in Eph 5:22–33, describing it as a "pluralistic unity."[10]

Finally, this reading may contribute toward the discussion of the *authorship* of the letters. I have adopted a perspective on these letters that locates the implied author (Paul) within the historical apostolic mission,

6. Rader, *Racial Hostility*, 211–22.

7. Kinzer, *Postmissionary Messianic Judaism*, 151–79.

8. Barth, *Israel and the Church*, 99; Fong, "Racial Reconciliation," 575–77; Blomberg, "Non-Supersessionist Alternative," 53–55.

9. Barth, *Israel and the Church*, 90.

10. Johnson, *New Testament*, 370; cf. Kinzer, *Postmissionary Messianic Judaism*, 170.

i.e., within the timeframe in which the gospel of Christ is going out through Israel to the nations.[11] I have also argued that the implied author is looking forward to a future time when the situation would be different, when both Israel and the nations would have the truth of the gospel in more equal measure and would therefore be equipped together to speak the truth in love (Eph 4:13–16).[12] If my reading is judged to be coherent, this may provide one piece of evidence that the implied author and the real author are identical. Thus, while my reading does not ultimately depend on historical Pauline authorship, it may go a small way toward supporting it.

11. See Barth, *People of God*, 48 on the relationship between Rom 9–11 and Eph 2.

12. See chapter 6.

Bibliography

Aquinas, Thomas. *Commentary on Saint Paul's Epistle to the Ephesians.* Translated by Matthew L. Lamb. Aquinas Scripture Series 2. Albany, NY: Magi, 1966.

Arnal, William E. *The Symbolic Jesus: Historical Scholarship, Judaism, and the Construction of Contemporary Identity.* Religion in Culture. London: Equinox, 2005.

Arnold, Clinton E. *Ephesians.* Zondervan Exegetical Commentary on the New Testament 10. Grand Rapids: Zondervan, 2010.

Atkinson, Kenneth. "Solomon, Psalms of." In *The Eerdmans Dictionary of Early Judaism,* edited by John J. Collins and Daniel C. Harlow, 1238–40. Grand Rapids: Eerdmans, 2010.

Barcellos, Richard C. "The Christian Ministry in the Church: Its Reasons, Duration and Goal, and Practical Effects (Ephesians 4:11–16), with Special Emphasis on Verse 12." *The Confessional Presbyterian* 11 (2015) 54–68.

Barclay, John M. G. *Jews in the Mediterranean Diaspora from Alexander to Trajan (323 BCE–117 CE).* Edinburgh: T. & T. Clark, 1996.

———. *Paul and the Gift.* Grand Rapids: Eerdmans, 2015.

Barnett, Paul W. "Apostle." *Dictionary of Paul and His Letters,* edited by Gerald F. Hawthorne and Ralph P. Martin, 45–51. Downers Grove, IL: IVP, 1993.

Barth, Markus. *The Broken Wall: A Study of the Epistle to the Ephesians.* London: Collins, 1960.

———. *Ephesians.* 2 vols. The Anchor Bible 34, 34A. Garden City, NY: Doubleday, 1974.

———. *Israel and the Church: Contribution to a Dialogue Vital for Peace.* Research in Theology. Richmond, VA: John Knox, 1969.

———. *The People of God.* Journal for the Study of the New Testament Supplement Series 5. Sheffield, UK: JSOT, 1983.

———. "St Paul—A Good Jew." *Horizons in Biblical Theology* 1 (1979) 7–45.

Bauckham, Richard. "James and the Jerusalem Church." In *The Book of Acts in Its First Century Setting Vol. 4: Palestinian Setting,* edited by Richard Bauckham, 415–80. Grand Rapids: Eerdmans, 1995.

———. "James and the Jerusalem Council Decision." In *Introduction to Messianic Judaism: Its Ecclesial Context and Biblical Foundations,* edited by Joel Willitts and David Rudolph, 178–86. Grand Rapids: Zondervan, 2013.

Best, Ernest. *Ephesians.* The International Critical Commentary on the Holy Scriptures of the Old and New Testaments. London: T. &. T. Clark, 1998.

———. "Ephesians 1.1." In *Essays on Ephesians*, 1–16. Edinburgh: T. &. T. Clark, 1997.

———. "Ephesians 1.1 Again." In *Essays on Ephesians*, 17–24. Edinburgh: T. &. T. Clark, 1997.

———. "Ephesians 2.11–22: A Christian View of Judaism." In *Essays on Ephesians*, 87–101. Edinburgh: T. & T. Clark, 1997.

———. *One Body in Christ: A Study in the Relationship of the Church to Christ in the Epistles of the Apostle Paul.* London: SPCK, 1955.

———. "Paul's Apostolic Authority—?" In *Essays on Ephesians*, 25–49. Edinburgh: T. &. T. Clark, 1997.

———. "Who Used Whom? The Relationship of Ephesians and Colossians." *New Testament Studies* 43 (1997) 72–96.

Bevere, Allan R. "The Cheirograph in Colossians 2:14 and the Ephesian Connection." In *Jesus and Paul: Global Perspectives in Honor of James D. G. Dunn for His 70th Birthday*, edited by B. J. Oropeza, C. K. Robertson, and Douglas C. Mohrmann, 199–206. Library of New Testament Studies 414. London: T. &. T. Clark, 2009.

Bird, Michael F. *Colossians & Philemon: A New Covenant Commentary.* Eugene, OR: Cascade, 2011.

Blomberg, Craig L. "Freedom from the Law Only for Gentiles? A Non-Supersessionist Alternative to Mark Kinzer's 'Postmissionary Messianic Judaism.'" In *New Testament Theology in Light of the Church's Mission: Essays in Honor of I. Howard Marshall*, edited by Jon Laansma, Grant R. Osborne, and Ray Van Neste, 41–56. Eugene, OR: Cascade, 2011.

Bock, Darrell L., and Craig A. Blaising. *Progressive Dispensationalism.* Grand Rapids: Baker, 2000.

Bockmuehl, Markus. *Jewish Law in Gentile Churches: Halakhah and the Beginning of Christian Public Ethics.* Edinburgh: T. & T. Clark, 2000.

Boer, Martinus C. de. "The Meaning of the Phrase τὰ στοιχεῖα τοῦ κόσμου in Galatians." *New Testament Studies* 53.2 (2007) 204–24.

Boyarin, Daniel. *A Radical Jew: Paul and the Politics of Identity.* Contraversions: Critical Studies in Jewish Literature, Culture and Society 1. Berkeley: University of California Press, 1994.

Brand, Chad O., Robert L. Reymond, Robert L. Saucy, Robert L. Thomas, and Tom Pratt. *Perspectives on Israel and the Church: 4 Views.* Edited by Chad O. Brand. Nashville: B. & H. Academic, 2015.

Bruce, F. F. *The Epistles to the Colossians, to Philemon and to the Ephesians.* The New International Commentary on the New Testament. Grand Rapids: Eerdmans, 1984.

Caird, George B. *Paul's Letters from Prison: Ephesians, Philippians, Colossians, Philemon, in the Revised Standard Version.* The New Clarendon Bible. Oxford: Oxford University Press, 1976.

Calvin, Jean. *The Epistles of Paul the Apostle to the Galatians, Ephesians, Philippians and Colossians.* Edited by David W. Torrance and Thomas F. Torrance. Translated by Thomas H. L. Parker. Calvin's Commentaries. Edinburgh: Oliver and Boyd, 1965.

Campbell, William S. *Paul and the Creation of Christian Identity.* Library of New Testament Studies. London: T. & T. Clark, 2006.

———. "Unity and Diversity in the Church: Transformed Identities and the Peace of Christ in Ephesians." *Transformation* 25.1 (2008) 15–31.

Caragounis, Chrys C. *The Ephesian Mysterion: Meaning and Content*. Coniectanea Biblica: New Testament Series 8. Lund: Gleerup, 1977.

Chrysostom, John. *Commentary on the Epistle to the Galatians, and Homilies on the Epistle to the Ephesians*. Translated by William J. Copeland. Library of Fathers of the Holy Catholic Church 5. Oxford: Parker, 1840.

Ciampa, Roy E., and Brian S. Rosner. *The First Letter to the Corinthians*. The Pillar New Testament Commentary. Grand Rapids: Eerdmans, 2010.

Clark, Bruce T. *Completing Christ's Afflictions: Christ, Paul, and the Reconciliation of All Things*. Wissenschaftliche Untersuchungen zum Neuen Testament. Second series 383. Tübingen: Mohr Siebeck, 2015.

Cohick, Lynn H. *Ephesians: A New Covenant Commentary*. Eugene: Cascade, 2013.

Collins, John N. *Diakonia: Re-Interpreting the Ancient Sources*. Oxford: Oxford University Press, 1990.

Cranfield, C. E. B. *The Epistle to the Romans*. 2 vols. The International Critical Commentary on the Holy Scriptures of the Old and New Testaments. Edinburgh: T. & T. Clark, 1975.

Dahl, Nils A. "Gentiles, Christians, and Israelites in the Epistle to the Ephesians." *Harvard Theological Review* 79 (1986) 31–39.

Davis, John J. "Ephesians 4:12 Once More: 'Equipping the Saints for the Work of Ministry?'" *Evangelical Review of Theology* 24.2 (2000) 167–76.

Diprose, Ronald E. *Israel and the Church: The Origins and Effects of Replacement Theology*. Waynesboro, GA: Authentic Media, 2000.

Donaldson, Terence L. *Paul and the Gentiles: Remapping the Apostle's Convictional World*. Minneapolis: Fortress, 1997.

Dunn, James D. G. *Beginning from Jerusalem*. Christianity in the Making 2. Grand Rapids: Eerdmans, 2009.

———. *The Epistles to the Colossians and to Philemon: A Commentary on the Greek Text*. The New International Greek Testament Commentary. Grand Rapids: Eerdmans, 1996.

———. *The Theology of Paul the Apostle*. Grand Rapids: Eerdmans, 1998.

Dunning, Benjamin H. "Strangers and Aliens No Longer: Negotiating Identity and Difference in Ephesians 2." *Harvard Theological Review* 99 (2006) 1–16.

Ehrman, Bart D. *The Apostolic Fathers*. 2 vols. Loeb Classical Library 24–25. Cambridge: Harvard University Press, 2003.

Eisenbaum, Pamela. *Paul Was Not a Christian: The Original Message of a Misunderstood Apostle*. New York: HarperCollins, 2009.

Elliott, Neil. *Liberating Paul: The Justice of God and the Politics of the Apostle*. Minneapolis: Fortress, 2006.

Esler, Philip F. *Conflict and Identity in Romans: The Social Setting of Paul's Letter*. Minneapolis: Fortress, 2003.

———. "An Outline of Social Identity Theory." In *T. & T. Clark Handbook to Social Identity in the New Testament*, edited by J. Brian Tucker and Coleman A. Baker, 13–39. London: Bloomsbury, 2014.

———. "'Remember My Fetters': Memorialisation of Paul's Imprisonment." In *Explaining Christian Origins and Early Judaism: Contributions from Cognitive and Social Science*, edited by Risto Uro, Ilkka Pyysiäinen, and Petri Luomanen, 231–58. Biblical Interpretation. Leiden: Brill, 2007.

Evans, Craig A., ed. *The Pseudepigrapha (English).* Accordance. OakTree Software, 2009.

Fong, Bruce W. "Addressing the Issue of Racial Reconciliation according to the Principles of Eph 2:11–22." *Journal of the Evangelical Theological Society* 38.4 (1995) 565–80.

Foster, Paul. *Colossians.* Black's New Testament Commentaries. London: Bloomsbury T. & T. Clark, 2016.

Foster, Robert L. "'A Temple in the Lord Filled to the Fullness of God': Context and Intertextuality (Eph. 3:19)." *Novum Testamentum* 49 (2007) 85–96.

Fowl, Stephen E. *Ephesians: A Commentary.* The New Testament Library. Louisville, KY: Westminster John Knox, 2012.

Fredriksen, Paula. *Augustine and the Jews: A Christian Defense of Jews and Judaism.* Garden City, NY: Doubleday, 2008.

———. "How Later Contexts Affect Pauline Content, or: Retrospect Is the Mother of Anachronism." In *Jews and Christians in the First and Second Centuries: How to Write Their History,* edited by Peter J. Tomson, 17–51. Compendia Rerum Iudaicarum Ad Novum Testamentum 13. Leiden: Koninklijke Brill, 2014.

———. "Judaizing the Nations: The Ritual Demands of Paul's Gospel." *New Testament Studies* 56.2 (2010) 232–52.

———. "Why Should a 'Law-Free' Mission Mean a 'Law-Free' Apostle?" *Journal of Biblical Literature* 134.3 (2015) 637–50.

Fresch, Christopher J. "Typology, Polysemy, and Prototypes: Situating Nonpast Aorist Indicatives." In *The Greek Verb Revisited: A Fresh Approach for Biblical Exegesis,* edited by Steven E. Runge and Christopher J. Fresch, 379–415. Bellingham, WA: Lexham, 2016.

Frey, Jörg. "Paul's Jewish Identity." In *Jewish Identity in the Greco-Roman World (Jüdische Identität in Der Griechisch-Römischen Welt),* edited by Jörg Frey, Daniel R. Schwartz, and Stephanie Gripentrog, 285–321. Ancient Judaism and Early Christianity 71. Leiden: Brill, 2007.

Fritz, Antoine X. J. *To the Jew First or to the Jew at Last? Romans 1:16c and Jewish Missional Priority in Dialogue with Jews for Jesus.* Eugene, OR: Pickwick, 2013.

Gager, John G. *The Origins of Anti-Semitism: Attitudes toward Judaism in Pagan and Christian Antiquity.* Oxford: Oxford University Press, 1983.

———. *Reinventing Paul.* Oxford: Oxford University Press, 2000.

Gaston, Lloyd. *Paul and the Torah.* Vancouver: University of British Columbia Press, 1987.

Gibson, David. "Sacramental Supersessionism Revisited: A Response to Martin Salter on the Relationship between Circumcision and Baptism." *Themelios* 37.2 (2012) 191–208.

Given, Mark D. "Restoring the Inheritance in Romans 11:1." *Journal of Biblical Literature* 118.1 (1999) 89–96.

Gnilka, Joachim. *Der Epheserbrief.* 2nd ed. Herders Theologischer Kommentar Zum Neuen Testament, 10/2. Freiburg: Herder, 1977.

Goldsworthy, Graeme. *Christ-Centred Biblical Theology: Hermeneutical Foundations and Principles.* Nottingham, UK: Apollos, 2012.

———. *Gospel-Centered Hermeneutics: Biblical-Theological Foundations and Principles.* Nottingham, UK: Apollos, 2006.

Gombis, Timothy G. "Ephesians 3:2–13: Pointless Digression, or Epitome of the Triumph of God in Christ?" *Westminster Theological Journal* 66.2 (2004) 313–23.

Graham, Glenn H. *An Exegetical Summary of Ephesians.* Dallas: Summer Institute of Linguistics, 1997.

Granados Rojas, Juan Manuel. "Ephesians 4,12: A Revised Reading." *Biblica* 92.1 (2011) 81–96.

Gupta, Nijay K. *Colossians.* Smyth & Helwys Bible Commentary. Macon, GA: Smyth & Helwys, 2013.

Hardin, Justin K. "Equality in the Church." In *Introduction to Messianic Judaism: Its Ecclesial Context and Biblical Foundations,* edited by Joel Willitts and David Rudolph, 224–34. Grand Rapids: Zondervan, 2013.

Harlow, Daniel C. "Early Judaism and Early Christianity." In *The Eerdmans Dictionary of Early Judaism,* edited by John J. Collins and Daniel C. Harlow, 257–78. Grand Rapids: Eerdmans, 2010.

Harnack, Adolf von. *The Mission and Expansion of Christianity in the First Three Centuries.* Translated by James Moffatt from *Die Mission und Ausbreitung des Christentums in den ersten drei Jahrhunderten* (Leipzig, 1906). London: Williams & Norgate, 1908.

Harrill, J. Albert. "Ethnic Fluidity in Ephesians." *New Testament Studies* 60.3 (2014) 379–402.

Hastings, James, ed. *The Speaker's Bible: The Epistle to the Ephesians.* Aberdeen: The Speaker's Bible Offices, 1925.

Heil, John Paul. *Ephesians: Empowerment to Walk in Love for the Unity of All in Christ.* Studies in Biblical Literature 13. Atlanta: Society of Biblical Literature, 2007.

Heine, Ronald E., ed. *The Commentaries of Origen and Jerome on St Paul's Epistle to the Ephesians.* Translated by Ronald E. Heine. Oxford Early Christian Studies. Oxford: Oxford University Press, 2002.

Hoch, Carl B. "The Significance of the Syn-Compounds for Jew-Gentile Relationships in the Body of Christ." *Journal of the Evangelical Theological Society* 25.2 (1982) 175–83.

Hocken, Peter. *The Challenges of the Pentecostal, Charismatic and Messianic Jewish Movements: The Tensions of the Spirit.* Ashgate New Critical Thinking in Religion, Theology and Biblical Studies. Farnham, UK: Ashgate, 2009.

Hoehner, Harold W. *Ephesians: An Exegetical Commentary.* Grand Rapids: Baker Academic, 2002.

Horner, Barry E. *Future Israel: Why Christian Anti-Judaism Must Be Challenged.* Nashville: B. & H. Academic, 2004.

Horton, Michael S. *The Christian Faith: A Systematic Theology for Pilgrims On the Way.* Grand Rapids: Zondervan, 2011.

Hudson, Benjamin. "'One New Humanity out of the Two': Ephesians 2 and the Restoration of Israel." Paper presented at the Fellowship of Biblical Studies National Conference, 2016.

Hvalvik, Reidar. *The Struggle for Scripture and Covenant: The Purpose of the Epistle of Barnabas and Jewish-Christian Competition in the Second Century.* Wissenschaftliche Untersuchungen zum Neuen Testament. Second series 82. Tübingen: Mohr Siebeck, 1996.

Jenkins, Richard. *Social Identity.* 3rd ed. Key Ideas. London: Routledge, 2008.

Jeremias, Joachim. *Infant Baptism in the First Four Centuries*. Translated by David Cairns. The Library of History and Doctrine. London: SCM, 1960.

Johnson Hodge, Caroline E. *If Sons, Then Heirs: A Study of Kinship and Ethnicity in the Letters of Paul*. Oxford: Oxford University Press, 2007.

Johnson, Luke T. *The Writings of the New Testament*. 3rd ed. London: SCM, 2010.

Käsemann, Ernst. "Ephesians and Acts." In *Studies in Luke-Acts: Essays Presented in Honor of Paul Schubert*, edited by Leander E. Keck and J. Louis Martyn, 288–97. London: SPCK, 1968.

Kinbar, Carl. "Messianic Jews and Jewish Tradition." In *Introduction to Messianic Judaism: Its Ecclesial Context and Biblical Foundations*, edited by Joel Willitts and David Rudolph, 72–81. Grand Rapids: Zondervan, 2013.

Kinzer, Mark. *Postmissionary Messianic Judaism: Redefining Christian Engagement with the Jewish People*. Grand Rapids: Brazos, 2005.

———. *Searching Her Own Mystery: Nostra Aetate, the Jewish People, and the Identity of the Church*. Eugene, OR: Cascade, 2015.

Knox, D. Broughton. "The Church and the Denominations." *Reformed Theological Review* 23.2 (1964) 44–53.

———. "The Church, the Churches and the Denominations of the Churches." *Reformed Theological Review* 48.1 (1989) 15–25.

Kok, Michael. "The True Covenant People: Ethnic Reasoning in the Epistle of Barnabas." *Studies in Religion* 40.1 (2011) 81–97.

Kreitzer, Larry J. *The Epistle to the Ephesians*. Epworth Commentaries. Peterborough, UK: Epworth, 1997.

Kuhn, Chase R. *The Ecclesiology of Donald Robinson and D. Broughton Knox: Exposition, Analysis, and Theological Evaluation*. Eugene, OR: Wipf & Stock, 2017.

Kümmel, Werner Georg. *Introduction to the New Testament*. Translated by Howard C. Kee. 17th fully revised edition. New Testament Library. London: SCM, 1975.

Lang, T. J. "Disbursing the Account of God: Fiscal Terminology and the Economy of God in Colossians 1,24–25." *Zeitschrift Für Die Neutestamentliche Wissenschaft Und Kunde Der Älteren Kirche* 107.1 (2016) 116–36.

Larkin, William J. *Ephesians: A Handbook on the Greek Text*. Baylor Handbook on the Greek New Testament. Waco, TX: Baylor University Press, 2009.

Lawler, Steph. *Identity: Sociological Perspectives*. Cambridge: Polity, 2008.

Lee, Jae-won. *Paul and the Politics of Difference: A Contextual Study of the Jewish-Gentile Difference in Galatians and Romans*. Eugene, OR: Pickwick, 2014.

Lightfoot, J. B. *The Epistles of St Paul: Colossians and Philemon*. 3rd ed. London: Macmillan, 1879.

Lincoln, Andrew T. "The Church and Israel in Ephesians 2." *Catholic Biblical Quarterly* 49 (1987) 605–24.

———. *Ephesians*. Word Biblical Commentary 42. Dallas: Word, 1990.

Lohse, Eduard. *Colossians and Philemon: A Commentary on the Epistles to the Colossians and to Philemon*. Translated by William R. Poehlmann and Robert J. Karris. Hermeneia. Philadelphia: Fortress, 1971.

———. "χείρ, κτλ." In *TDNT* 10:424–37.

Longenecker, Bruce W. "On Israel's God and God's Israel: Assessing Supersessionism in Paul." *Journal of Theological Studies* 58.1 (2007) 26–44.

Lowy, S. "The Confutation of Judaism in the Epistle of Barnabas." *Journal of Jewish Studies* 11 (1960) 1–33.

MacDonald, Margaret Y. "The Politics of Identity in Ephesians." *Journal for the Study of the New Testament* 26.4 (2004) 419–44.

Marshall, I. H. "Salvation, Grace and Works in the Later Writings in the Pauline Corpus." *New Testament Studies* 42.3 (1996) 339–58.

Martin, Ralph P. *Ephesians, Colossians and Philemon*. Interpretation: A Bible Commentary for Teaching and Preaching. Louisville, KY: John Knox, 1991.

McEleney, N. J. "Conversion, Circumcision and the Law." *New Testament Studies* 20.3 (1974) 319–41.

Metzger, Bruce M. *A Textual Commentary on the Greek New Testament*. 2nd ed. Stuttgart: Deutsche Bibelgesellschaft, 1994.

Moritz, Thorsten. *A Profound Mystery: The Use of the Old Testament in Ephesians*. Supplements to Novum Testamentum 85. Leiden: Brill, 1996.

Mouton, Elna. "Memory in Search of Dignity? Construction of Early Christian Identity through Redescribed Traditional Material in the Letter to the Ephesians." *Annali Di Storia Dell'esegesi* 29.2 (2012) 133–53.

Mussner, Franz. *Tractate on the Jews: The Significance of Judaism for Christian Faith*. Translated by Leonard Swidler from the German *Traktat über die Juden* (München, 1979). London: SPCK, 1984.

Nanos, Mark D. "Introduction." In *Paul within Judaism: Restoring the First-Century Context to the Apostle*, edited by Mark D. Nanos and Magnus Zetterholm, 1–29. Philadelphia: Fortress, 2015.

Nanos, Mark D., and Magnus Zetterholm, eds. *Paul within Judaism: Restoring the First-Century Context to the Apostle*. Philadelphia: Fortress, 2015.

Nolland, John. "Uncircumcised Proselytes?" *Journal for the Study of Judaism* 12.2 (1981) 173–94.

O'Brien, Peter T. "The Church as a Heavenly and Eschatological Entity." In *The Church in the Bible and the World*, edited by D. A. Carson, 88–119. Exeter, UK: Paternoster, 1987.

———. *Colossians, Philemon*. Word Biblical Commentary 44. Dallas: Word, 1982.

———. "Ephesians I: An Unusual Introduction to a New Testament Letter." *New Testament Studies* 25.4 (1979) 504–16.

Page, Sydney H. T. "Whose Ministry? A Re-Appraisal of Ephesians 4:12." *Novum Testamentum* 47.1 (2005) 26–46.

Paget, James Carleton. *The Epistle of Barnabas: Outlook and Background*. Wissenschaftliche Untersuchungen zum Neuen Testament. Second series 64. Tübingen: Mohr Siebeck, 1994.

Palu, Ma'afu. "The Significance of the Jew-Gentile Distinction for Theological Contextualization." In *Donald Robinson Selected Works: Appreciation*, edited by Peter G. Bolt and Mark D. Thompson, 141–52. Camperdown, NSW, Australia: Australian Church Record, 2008.

Pao, David W. *Colossians & Philemon*. Zondervan Exegetical Commentary on the New Testament 12. Grand Rapids: Zondervan, 2012.

Percy, Ernst. *Die Probleme der Kolosser- und Epheserbriefe*. Lund: Gleerup, 1946.

Perkins, Pheme. "The Letter to the Ephesians." In *The New Interpreter's Bible: A Commentary in Twelve Volumes*, 11:349–466. Nashville: Abingdon, 2000.

The Psalms of Solomon: A Critical Edition of the Greek Text. Translated by Robert B. Wright. Jewish and Christian Texts in Contexts and Related Studies 1. London: T. & T. Clark, 2007.

Rader, William H. *The Church and Racial Hostility: A History of Interpretation of Ephesians 2:11–22*. Beitrage Zur Geschichte Der Biblischen Exegese 20. Tübingen: Mohr, 1978.

Reumann, J. "Oikonomia-Terms in Paul in Comparison with Lucan Heilsgeschichte." *New Testament Studies* 13.2 (1967) 147–67.

Ridderbos, Herman. *Paul: An Outline of His Theology*. Translated by John R. de Witt. Translated from Paulus: Ontwerp van zijn theologie, Kampen: Uitgeversmaatschappij J. H. Kok N. V., 1966. Grand Rapids: Eerdmans, 1975.

Robinson, Donald W. B. *The Church of God: Its Form and Unity*. Punchbowl, Australia: Jordan, 1965.

———. *Donald Robinson Selected Works Vol. 1: Assembling God's People*. Edited by Peter G. Bolt and Mark D. Thompson. Camperdown, Australia: Australian Church Record, 2008.

———. *Faith's Framework: The Structure of New Testament Theology*. Blackwood, Australia: New Creation, 1996.

———. "Israel and the Gentiles in the New Testament." In *Donald Robinson Selected Works Vol. 1: Assembling God's People*, edited by Peter G. Bolt and Mark D. Thompson, 7–27. Camperdown, Australia: Australian Church Record, 2008.

———. "Jew and Greek: Unity and Division in the Early Church." In *Donald Robinson Selected Works Vol. 1: Assembling God's People*, edited by Peter G. Bolt and Mark D. Thompson, 79–109. Camperdown, Australia: Australian Church Record, 2008.

———. "Who Were 'the Saints'?" *Reformed Theological Review* 22.2 (1963) 45–53.

Roels, Edwin D. *God's Mission: The Epistle to the Ephesians in Mission Perspective*. Franeker, Netherlands: Weaver, 1962.

Rosner, Brian S. *Paul and the Law: Keeping the Commandments of God*. New Studies in Biblical Theology 31. Downers Grove, IL: IVP, 2013.

Rudolph, David J. "Introduction." In *Introduction to Messianic Judaism: Its Ecclesial Context and Biblical Foundations*, edited by Joel Willitts and David Rudolph, 11–18. Grand Rapids: Zondervan, 2013.

———. *A Jew to the Jews: Jewish Contours of Pauline Flexibility in 1 Corinthians 9:19–23*. Wissenschaftliche Untersuchungen zum Neuen Testament. Second series 304. Tübingen: Mohr Siebeck, 2011.

———. "Messianic Judaism in Antiquity and in the Modern Era." In *Introduction to Messianic Judaism: Its Ecclesial Context and Biblical Foundations*, edited by Joel Willitts and David Rudolph, 21–36. Grand Rapids: Zondervan, 2013.

———. "Paul's 'Rule in All the Churches' (1 Cor 7:17–24) and Torah-Defined Ecclesiological Variegation." *Studies in Jewish-Christian Relations* 5.1 (2010) 1–24.

Ryrie, Charles Caldwell. *Dispensationalism*. Revised and expanded edition. Chicago: Moody, 2007.

Salter, Martin. "Does Baptism Replace Circumcision? An Examination of the Relationship between Circumcision and Baptism in Colossians 2:11–12." *Themelios* 35.1 (2010) 15–29.

Sampley, J. Paul. *"And the Two Shall Become One Flesh": A Study of Traditions in Ephesians 5:21–33*. Society for New Testament Studies Monograph Series 16. Cambridge: Cambridge University Press, 1971.

Sandnes, Karl Olav. *Paul—One of the Prophets? A Contribution to the Apostle's Self-Understanding*. Wissenschaftliche Untersuchungen zum Neuen Testament. Second series 43. Tübingen: Mohr Siebeck, 1991.

Schlier, Heinrich. *Der Brief an die Epheser: Ein Kommentar*. Düsseldorf: Patmos-Verlag, 1968.

Schnabel, Eckhard J. *Early Christian Mission*. 2 vols. Downers Grove, IL: IVP, 2004.

Seesemann, H., and G. Bertram. "πατέω, καταπατέω, περιπατέω, ἐμπεριπατέω." In *TDNT* 5:940–45.

Sherwood, Aaron. "Paul's Imprisonment as the Glory of the Ethnē: A Discourse Analysis of Ephesians 3:1–13." *Bulletin for Biblical Research* 22.1 (2012) 97–111.

Shiner, Rory. "Reading the New Testament from the Outside." In *"All That the Prophets Have Declared": The Appropriation of Scripture in the Emergence of Christianity*, 185–97. Milton Keynes, UK: Paternoster, 2015.

Shkul, Minna. "New Identity and Cultural Baggage: Identity and Otherness in Colossians." In *T. & T. Clark Handbook to Social Identity in the New Testament*, edited by J. Brian Tucker and Coleman A. Baker, 367–87. London: Bloomsbury, 2014.

———. *Reading Ephesians: Exploring Social Entrepreneurship in the Text*. Library of New Testament Studies 408. London: T. & T. Clark, 2009.

Smith, Claire S. "Unchanged 'Teaching': The Meaning of Didaskō in 1 Timothy 2:12." In *Women, Sermons and the Bible: Essays Interacting with John Dickson's Hearing Her Voice*, edited by Peter G. Bolt and Tony Payne, Kindle loc. 755–2303. Sydney: Matthias Media, 2014.

Smith, Ian K. *Heavenly Perspective: A Study of the Apostle Paul's Response to a Jewish Mystical Movement at Colossae*. Library of Biblical Studies 326. London: T. & T. Clark, 2006.

Son, Sang-Won. "The Church as 'One New Man': Ecclesiology and Anthropology in Ephesians." *Southwestern Journal of Theology* 52.1 (2009) 18–31.

Soulen, R. Kendall. *The God of Israel and Christian Theology*. Minneapolis: Fortress, 1996.

———. "Post-Supersessionism." *A Dictionary of Jewish-Christian Relations*, edited by Edward Kessler and Neil Wenborn, 350–51. Cambridge: Cambridge University Press, 2005.

Stark, Rodney. *The Rise of Christianity: How the Obscure, Marginal Jesus Movement Became the Dominant Religious Force in the Western World in a Few Centuries*. New York: HarperCollins, 1996.

Starling, David I. *Not My People: Gentiles as Exiles in Pauline Hermeneutics*. Beihefte zur Zeitschrift für die Neutestamentliche Wissenschaft 184. Berlin: De Gruyter, 2011.

Stendahl, Krister. *Paul Among Jews and Gentiles: And Other Essays*. Philadelphia: Fortress, 1976.

Stott, John R. W. *The Message of Ephesians: God's New Society*. The Bible Speaks Today. Leicester, UK: Inter-Varsity, 1991.

Stowers, Stanley K. *A Rereading of Romans: Justice, Jews and Gentiles*. New Haven: Yale University Press, 1994.

Stuhlmacher, Peter. "'He Is Our Peace' (Eph. 2:14): On the Exegesis and Significance of Eph. 2:14–18." In *Reconciliation, Law & Righteousness: Essays in Biblical Theology*, 182–200. Philadelphia: Fortress, 1986.

Talbert, Charles H. *Ephesians and Colossians*. Paideia: Commentaries on the New Testament. Grand Rapids: Baker Academic, 2007.

Taylor, Miriam S. *Anti-Judaism and Early Christian Identity: A Critique of the Scholarly Consensus*. Studia Post-Biblica 46. Leiden: Brill, 1995.

Thielman, Frank. *Ephesians*. Baker Exegetical Commentary on the New Testament. Grand Rapids: Baker, 2010.

Tucker, J. Brian. "The Continuation of Gentile Identity in Ephesians." Paper presented at the Society of Biblical Literature Annual Conference. San Francisco, 2011.

———. "The Continuation of Gentile Identity in Ephesians 2:14–15." Paper presented at the Moody Theological Seminary MI Faculty Forum. Plymouth, MI, 2011.

———. *Remain in Your Calling: Paul and the Continuation of Social Identities in 1 Corinthians*. Eugene, OR: Pickwick, 2011.

Vlach, Michael J. *Has the Church Replaced Israel? A Theological Evaluation*. Nashville: B. & H. Academic, 2010.

Wallace, Daniel B. *Greek Grammar Beyond the Basics: An Exegetical Syntax of the New Testament*. Grand Rapids: Zondervan, 1996.

Wardle, Timothy. *The Jerusalem Temple and Early Christian Identity*. Wissenschaftliche Untersuchungen zum Neuen Testament. Second series 291. Tübingen: Mohr Siebeck, 2010.

Watson, Francis. *Paul, Judaism and the Gentiles: Beyond the New Perspective*. Rev. ed. Grand Rapids: Eerdmans, 2007.

Weiss, Herold. "The Law in the Epistle to the Colossians." *Catholic Biblical Quarterly* 34.3 (1972) 294–314.

Williams, Jarvis J. "Violent Ethno-Racial Reconciliation: A Mystery in Ephesians and Its Jewish Martyrological Background." *Criswell Theological Review* 12.2 (2015) 119–34.

Williamson, Paul R. *Abraham, Israel and the Nations: The Patriarchal Promise and Its Covenantal Development in Genesis*. Journal for the Study of the Old Testament Supplement Series 315. Sheffield, UK: Sheffield Academic, 2000.

Windsor, Lionel J. *Paul and the Vocation of Israel: How Paul's Jewish Identity Informs His Apostolic Ministry, with Special Reference to Romans*. Beihefte zur Zeitschrift für die Neutestamentliche Wissenschaft 205. Berlin: De Gruyter, 2014.

———. "The Work of Ministry in Ephesians 4:12." In *"Tend My Sheep": The Word of God and Pastoral Ministry*, edited by Keith G. Condie, 1–25. London: Latimer Trust, 2016.

Woods, David B. "Jew-Gentile Distinction in the One New Man of Ephesians 2:15." *Conspectus* 18 (2014) 95–135.

Wright, N. T. *The Epistles of Paul to the Colossians and to Philemon: An Introduction and Commentary*. Tyndale New Testament Commentaries. Leicester, UK: IVP, 1986.

———. *Justification: God's Plan and Paul's Vision*. London: SPCK, 2009.

———. *Paul and the Faithfulness of God*. 2 vols. Minneapolis: Fortress, 2013.

———. "Romans 9–11 and the 'New Perspective.'" In *Pauline Perspectives: Essays on Paul, 1978–2013*, 392–406. London: SPCK, 2013.

Yaakov, Ariel. "A Different Kind of Dialogue? Messianic Judaism and Jewish-Christian Relations." *CrossCurrents* 62 (2012) 318–27.

Yee, Tet-Lim N. *Jews, Gentiles and Ethnic Reconciliation: Paul's Jewish Identity and Ephesians*. Society for New Testament Studies Monograph Series 130. Cambridge: Cambridge University Press, 2004.

Yoder Neufeld, Thomas R. *Ephesians*. Believers Church Bible Commentary. Waterloo, Ont: Herald, 2002.

Zoccali, Christopher. "What's the Problem with the Law? Jews, Gentiles, and Covenant Identity in Galatians 3:10–12." *Neotestamentica* 49.2 (2015) 377–415.

Index of Authors

Aquinas, Thomas, 35, 35n16, 101–2, 102n79

Arnal, William E., 128n53

Arndt, William F., xiii, 138n88, 154n148, 155n149, 156n152, 161n8, 171n48, 183n24

Arnold, Clinton E., 37n26, 69, 69n175, 79n2, 80n7, 82n11, 83n17, 87n28, 169n40, 184n30, 190n49, 198n73, 199n75, 199n76

Atkinson, Kenneth, 125n47

Barcellos, Richard C., 190n49

Barclay, John M. G., 3n4, 21n87, 66n159, 122n36, 218n51

Barnett, Paul W., 79n4

Barth, Karl, xiii, 10n25, 93n45

Barth, Markus, 11n31, 15n58, 46–52, 47n61, 47n62, 47n63, 47n64, 47n65, 47n66, 47n67, 48n68, 48n69, 48n70, 48n71, 49n72, 49n73, 49n74, 49n75, 49n76, 49n77, 50n78, 50n79, 50n80, 50n81, 51n82, 51n83, 51n84, 51n85, 51n86, 52n88, 58, 66n162, 69, 69n177, 69n178, 69n179, 81n9, 87n28, 88n30, 90, 90n36, 92n43, 97n58, 98n65, 98n66, 98n69, 102n82, 104n87, 105n88, 119n25, 124n43, 124n44, 135n79, 139n91,

144n100, 146n113, 150n129, 151n133, 152n138, 154n146, 155n149, 161n7, 168n39, 171n49, 181n21, 181n22, 183n26, 185n35, 199n77, 231n8, 231n9, 232n11

Bauckham, Richard, 104n86, 139n92, 142n97, 180n17

Bauer, Walter, xiii, 138n88, 154n148, 155n149, 156n152, 161n8, 171n48, 183n24

Bertram, G., 177n6

Best, Ernest, 80n7, 81n9, 82n11, 82n13, 82n14, 84n19, 85n21, 87n28, 91n41, 95n55, 96n56, 97n62, 98n67, 100n73, 101n75, 101n77, 102n83, 105n90, 106n91, 109n100, 115n12, 119n24, 120n27, 120n31, 121n34, 124n43, 124n44, 127n49, 128n50, 128n52, 132n63, 132n66, 133n69, 133n71, 133n72, 133n73, 138n87, 146n113, 146n114, 151n133, 152n138, 154n148, 155n149, 161n9, 166n29, 168n38, 169n44, 176n3, 177n5, 181n21, 181n22, 183n25, 183n27, 185n35, 186n39, 190n49, 197–98n70, 199n74, 199n77

Bevere, Allan R., 34n15, 38, 38n28, 215n39

Bird, Michael F., 63n141, 74, 74n210

INDEX OF AUTHORS

Index of Scripture
and Other Ancient Sources

249

1 Samuel (LXX 1 Kingdoms)
7:2 LXX	155n149
7:3 LXX	155n149
25:32	87

1 Kings (LXX 3 Kingdoms)
1:48	87
8	173
8:14–21	92
8:15	87
8:22–53	92
8:65 LXX	155n149
11:16 LXX	155n149

2 Kings (LXX 4 Kingdoms)
8:41–43	92
8:54–56	92

Ezra (LXX 1 Esdras)
1:19 LXX	155n149
4:12	132
4:16	132
5:45 LXX	155n149
5:58 LXX	155n149
7:27	87
9:9	132

Esther
8:17 LXX	30n3

1 Chronicles
16:36	87
29:10	87

2 Chronicles
2:12 (LXX/MT 2:11)	87
6:4	87

Psalms
2	125, 126
41:13 (LXX 40:14; MT 41:14)	87
51:10 (LXX 50:12)	145
68 (LXX 67)	186, 187
68:18 (LXX 67:19)	185, 187, 200, 227
68:35 (LXX 67:36; MT 68:36)	83, 87
72:18 (LXX 71:18)	87
104:30 (LXX 103:30)	145
106:48 (LXX 105:48)	87

Isaiah
	125, 126, 148n119
2:1–2	165
2:18	123
5:5	132
9:5–6	129n54
9:6	146
10:11	123
11:1–5	89
11:4	125
11:10	125, 126
16:12	123
19:1	123
19:24–25	145
21:9	123
31:7	123
40	148
40:1	148
40:3–5	148
40:5	148
40:9	147
40:10	148
44	96
44:1	96
44:2	96
44:3	96
45:14	165
46:6	123
49:6	96
51:2	88
52:1–10	168
52:3–6	148n118
52:7	129n54, 148, 199
53:1	148
53:5	96, 148
57	148n119

✦

PSEUDEPIGRAPHA